CRUISIN' ABOVE THE CLOUDS

I0559145

PAUL DOUGLAS CASTLE

CRUISIN' ABOVE THE CLOUDS

PAUL DOUGLAS CASTLE

CRUISIN' ABOVE THE CLOUDS

COPYRIGHT © 2024 PAUL DOUGLAS CASTLE.

ISBN: 979-8-9912266-4-6 (PAPERBACK)
ISBN: 979-8-9912266-5-3 (EBOOK)
ISBN: 979-8-9912266-9-1 (HARDCOVER)

ALL RIGHTS RESERVED. NO PART OF THIS BOOK MAY BE REPRODUCED, STORED IN A RETRIEVAL SYSTEM, OR TRANSMITTED IN ANY FORM OR BY ANY MEANS, ELECTRONIC, MECHANICAL, PHOTOCOPYING, RECORDING, OR OTHERWISE, WITHOUT EXPRESS WRITTEN PERMISSION OF THE AUTHOR.

PAUL DOUGLAS CASTLE

WWW.PAULDOUGLASCASTLE.COM

LIGHTHOUSE LITERARY

PUBLISHED BY LIGHTHOUSE LITERARY
100 NE 5TH ST, OKLAHOMA CITY,
OK 73104, USA
SUPPORT@LIGHTHOUSELITERARY.US
(405) 339-0577

ACKNOWLEDGMENTS

The following stories, wherever scriptures appear, are taken from the excellent King James Special Study Edition Bible. I have to say, everyone interested in knowing God should read the Bible and abide by its perfect commandments.

The unique Study Edition Bible, outstanding and incredible, was published by the Global Bible Society at P.O. Box 6068, Ashville, NC 28816. Because I love His gospel truth, I thank them for the beautiful Bible they've created to edify God, and I enjoy it incredibly much.

I want you to know that everything else in this book is my analogy. The things I write in this book are for developing understanding, and I base my writing on the perfect word of God. I sincerely hope you enjoy reading these stories as much as I enjoyed writing them.

God bless you.

Sincerely, Paul Douglas Castle
Bible story writer
Theologian
Creative story designer

DEDICATIONS

Even though everyone doesn't accept the word of God, it's still available to all who are interested in finding it, and it's our responsibility to find it. Thanks to the God of creation, He's ensured we all have a chance to understand the reward of immortality and the consequences of damnation.

Maybe He doesn't expect us seeking after Him to be as wise as theologians, but maybe He does, and we should try to be as bright as them. Anyway, no matter how it may be with God, it doesn't hurt to understand His gospel exceptionally well because it will improve our character.

I assure you that He's provided us with enough information to understand the beginning of things until the end. If we do not seek understanding and the beautiful prize of immortality, our failure to grow wings is our fault, and we may not cruise above the clouds.

I dedicate these Bible stories first to my Creator God, then to my earthly father and mother, Bryan Paul Castle, Paul and Jason, nephew David, and grandson Aden, Kathy Sue Hager. I have my deepest love for all of them, and I wish the best for you, too.

CONTENTS

CHAPTER ONE
MOUNTAIN CLIMBING

This is personal to everyone's story concerning our growth with God, I call *Mountain Climbing*, fulfills the definition of a metaphor story. As you read Mountain Climbing, I hope you realize literal mountains covered with trees, grass, and rocks are not the intended subject within this metaphorical story.

However, mountain climbing is a perfect analogy, and it fits the subject this meaningful story illustrates. Because of the order of things and the toughness of life, you and I are the subjects climbing this metaphorical mountain, and regardless of race, color, or gender, we've all had a tall hill or many mountains to overcome.

I guarantee you that because of personal experiences, we are all mountain climbers in one way or another. We started climbing mountains soon after learning to walk and talk. Furthermore, I firmly assure you we'll be climbing mountains until the day we die.

The mountains in this metaphor story represent various trials and tribulations, and as always with God, our character is tested between righteousness and unrighteousness. I want you to know that this metaphor story parallels all our literal endeavors.

I assure you that the character gauge used by our Creator God to test everyone on this Earth has two critical words written upon the indicator, and every person living on this Earth climbs up or slides down the mountain.

This truth positively means that many everyday decisions are connected or based on His gauge words that gauge our character. His profound, gauging words are righteousness and unrighteousness, and I am sure His gauging words are never wrong.

Indeed, because of their great importance, I want you to know that righteous works advance us up the mountain and move us close to the top. However, unrighteous works have the opposite effect: They slide us down the hill and stop us from achieving our goals.

Beyond the shadow of a doubt, we all start at the bottom of the mountain, and we'll have to climb to the top, which will take a lot of effort and determination. Truly, the metaphorical mountains we encounter as we proceed through life aren't much different from a literal mountain, except for the terrain type.

Honestly, I do not know of anyone God created from the dirt of this Earth who started their expedition in life on the top of the mountain. Indeed, equal fairness means we'll all start from the exact location, and the same place is at the bottom of the hill.

However, I want you to know that the challenge in this story is to stand on the top of the mountain and claim victory over the stumbling blocks in life. Truly, achieving this victory against rebellious acts means we've fought against the powers of darkness and resisted and defeated many temptations.

I want you to know that the many stumbling blocks in the path of our life we encounter on the trail are similar to rock slides in our way and washouts in the road we must go around before reaching the top of the metaphor mountain. Truly, keeping a smooth road every day requires the wiseness of scripture wisdom.

Indeed, I hope you realize that all different types of sin are our enemies, and sin stands between us and the top of the mountain. Indeed, our determination must be strong because we must defeat sin's terribleness before we can claim victory and stand on the top of the hill.

Positively, life is a challenge every day we live and breathe, similar to climbing to the top of a steep mountain. We become closer to the top of the hill whenever we conquer a terrible sin. The closer we are to the top of the mountain, our feelings about ourselves will become increasingly euphoric, and we'll be closer to God.

Indeed, getting to the top of the mountain in this personal-to-everyone story cannot be accomplished in one or two days, and climbing to the top isn't always easy. I want you to realize that some parts of the mountain will be more complex to climb than other parts of the hill, and on some days, the temptation to do wrong will be harder to resist.

Positively, I want you to realize that we humans are on a long journey, day after day, and tomorrow is an unknown puzzle to overcome. Truly, because of our inability to know the future, we do not know how many mountains we'll visit on our daily walk before our adventurous journey ends.

Therefore, because spirit power prodding us to do wrong is strong, I assure you that the metaphorical mountain in this adventurous story will take a lifetime to conquer. I want you to realize that we'll start climbing the metaphor mountain again after waking up in the morning, and we may as well prepare ourselves because we'll have to climb the metaphor mountain daily.

Because we have to build a road as we go up the mountain, we'll have to remove all the roadblocks and the washouts. However, we cannot be quitters or refuse to fight ungodly temptations, please our wonderful Creator God, or reach the top of the mountain.

However, all the hard work we put into climbing this metaphorical mountain will make our climb worthwhile, especially after we finally stood on the top and looked down at the symbolic mountain we'd climbed. Because we want to live with God forever, this euphoric moment reveals why we are determined to climb the metaphorical mountain.

From the top of the metaphor mountain, I want you to know we can see where we've come from and all the foreign obstacles we've had to remove on our journey uphill. We will consider it a joy to have an improved road as we stand at the top of the mountain.

Standing on the top of the mountain elevates us to a greater height, way above our old sinful life. Truly, nothing feels better than having a clear vision as we stand on top of the hill and know we've conquered the ground underneath our feet.

I assure you that climbing this metaphorical mountain will take a lot of willpower, and we cannot accomplish the climb on our own. We'll need a Ghost Instructor as a lead man; without a Lead Man, we'll not reach the top of the mountain.

The path going up this metaphor mountain illustrates our footsteps in life. Because we have heavenly supporters, special people will be waiting for us at the top of the hill. Even though the special people are beyond our sight, they see every footstep we take along the way and rejoice because we continue to climb to the top of the mountain.

The metaphor mountain in this story reaches into the clouds, and after making it to the top, we may not desire to come back down. Because Heaven is our dream place, we've been waiting a lifetime to find it, and when we reach the top of the mountain, we've found our dream place.

Indeed, I pray that you climb to the top of the mountain and build your house in a high place, especially since everyone in Heaven observes us from the highest of places. I am sure when we reach their beautiful home, it won't be a symbolic mountain anymore.

Indeed, going to the top of the mountain means we've connected the loop of life, made a full circle, and are back to the same place we began. Therefore, making a full circle should be our plan every day we live and breathe.

Positively, I assure you, this time, when we make it to the top of the mountain, located in the land of Utopia. We'll have learned many things and be better citizens than we were the first time we knew God from before.

Happy mountain climbing! Enjoy every step you take on the metaphor mountain trail. Be assured that there's a grand prize given to everyone who rises to the top of the mountain. Furthermore, I am glad to tell you that the first and the last will receive the same prize!

Chapter Two
CRUISIN' ABOVE THE CLOUDS

This declaration story, which I call *Cruisin' Above The Clouds*, expresses a wonderful utopian metaphor. The wonderful Utopian metaphor illustrates you and me reaching for the stars in the heavens above and us looking for a dreamland God has reserved exclusively for dreamers.

Cruisin' above the clouds hasn't anything to do with plane rides, mechanical aircraft, or winged creatures. However, we know our Creator God provides transportation to our dreamland, and specific individuals have found a way to cruise above the clouds.

Cruisin' above the clouds is another way of saying something or that someone is going beyond normal to achieve the extraordinary. Indeed, conversion after conversion to Christianity proves that we dreamers have the faith to believe that we will accomplish the extraordinary and cruise above the clouds.

Cruisin' above the clouds reveals another world beyond the imagination of men, and brilliant creations in love with His Ten

Commandments call it their home. I can easily say these brilliant creations dreamed a wonderful dream, and their goal to live forever in His kingdom came true.

Furthermore, I want you to know that these brilliant, compassionate, righteous creations have incredible power and supernatural strength beyond our understanding. Truly, because of their unique design, these heavenly residents see everything we do and hear every word we speak.

Cruisin' above the clouds is our Father, the Son of God, and the Holy Ghost, the watchers and the holy ones in Heaven, all the salvation winners that have gone before us, and whoever has won the grand prize of immortality.

I assure you that our Father, His Son, and the beautiful Holy Ghost have unlimited power, as we've found out through examples. Their ability is without boundaries; we are the monitored subjects seeking to live in their world, which is the dream dreamers dream of achieving.

Indeed, I want you to know that these wonderful heavenly creations are the role models for wise men and women, and the not-so-smart do not believe in them. Sadly, I must say, the not-so-wise do not have the same dream as wise men and women.

Beyond the shadow of a doubt, I firmly conclude that the not-so-wise have impaired vision. The not-so-wise do not believe there's a beautiful Utopian city in the sky, having streets of gold, twelve gates of pearl, and walls embedded with diamonds and jewels.

The not-so-wise do not believe as the dreamers believe, and they do not think this Utopian city in the sky has pure water, clear as crystal, and it constantly flows from the throne of God, and it's more refined than any water we've ever tasted upon this Earth.

The not-so-smart do not believe this city in the sky has an exceptional fruit tree growing in the middle of the streets. It's called the tree of life, and it yields twelve manners of fruit every month, and the leaves growing thereon are for healing the nations.

As for you and me, and all other Christians too, cruising in the clouds of our imagination and not having tangible proof of anything means we believe these things are true and accurate. Because our faith is strong in the Lord, and we believe in the power of His resurrection, we dream about transitioning to this Utopian city in the sky.

Cruisin' in the clouds means we believe bible stories are true, and there's a special place in the heavens above for you and me, and we dreamers think we shall see the King face to face. Indeed, because we have faith in Him, we believe His name will be written on our forehead.

Cruisin' in the Clouds is a metaphor story; true believers in the Father and the Son of God are the cruisers, and the clouds symbolize our hopes, dreams, and desires. After converting to Christianity, we live for the day our Utopian dream comes true.

However, this dangerous place called planet Earth shakes our tree of reality, and gravity holds us down; we are lucky if we jump three feet off the ground. However, I am sure that gravity will not be a problem forever, especially after we become a spirit and grow wings.

The matter is straightforward and clear, and we dreamers are stuck here until our spirit departs from the flesh. However, when this precious moment of our life is over, we dreamers will overcome gravity, and compliments of God, we'll go cruisin' above the clouds.

However, please be aware that life isn't a bed of roses or as sweet as chocolate-covered cherries while we live here in the flesh. I am sure you already know through experiences that we believers in Christ will be put through a rigorous test in this life, and our loyalty to God will excel or fail upon planet Earth.

For this reason, the Creator of Heaven and Earth purposely gave us a set of Judgment Scales, and the scales have three essential words written upon them. I want you to know these three judgment words will decide who receives wings and cannot fly above the clouds.

These three meaningful judgment words, written on the Judgment Scales, exceed the pinnacle of importance to everyone; they are essential words paralleling our love for God in this world. The definition of these Three-Judgment Scale words sends us up or down from the surface of the planet Earth.

I guarantee you that every person living on this Earth, regardless of race, gender, or color, fits the definition of one of these Three-Judgement Scale words. I am sure the Utopian dreamers living in the flesh know these words and their importance.

These Three Judgments Scale words are called hot, cold, and lukewarm, and you do need to know they are the barometer words our Creator God uses for evaluating us. This truth means these Three Judgment Scale words divide people into three groups.

The three essential barometer words God has written on the Judgment Scales coincide and entwine with the conclusion to the whole matter. Furthermore, these three profound Judgment Scale words will decide who receives permission to cruise above the clouds.

The righteous conclusion to the whole matter is summed up in six easy-to-understand words that aren't complicated. These six essential words are to reverence God and keep His commandments; if we do keep His commandments, we'll cruise above the clouds after the flesh dies.

Cruisin' above the clouds means we've found the conclusion to the whole matter, and we love it and believe in its words' validity. I want you to know the dreamers who dream about living in the land of Utopia think there's nothing written as great as the conclusion to the whole matter.

Positively, I want you to know if we receive the privilege to cruise to the city in the sky, we'll have to intertwine the definition of hot and on fire for the beautiful word of God. This truth means that hot and on fire for the word of God is part of the formula for growing wings.

Unfortunately, not everyone receives their wings because of failure to comply with requirements. For this reason, I firmly warn you: the cold and the lukewarm person will not grow wings. Sadly, I must say, they'll not be able to cruise above the clouds or fly to the beautiful Utopian city in the sky.

Therefore, our boldness, courage, and loyalty to God are tested in the fire, and all our decisions in this life, coinciding with right and wrong, reveal the definition of our temperature. For this reason, this test we are taking is the most critical test we'll ever take in this lifetime.

I want you to realize that Earth is a neutral zone between Heaven and Hell, and stepping off the neutral zone designates us to one place or another. This truth is the word of God and a good reason to be a commandment lover.

The perfect Son of God, glorious and righteous, is the Mediator between God and us, and if we are ashamed of Him,

He'll be ashamed of us on Judgment Day. For the benefit of our future and because we care about our soul's destiny, we better not be ashamed of Yeshua.

I assure you that we have God-given requirements in this life, and please do not forget laying up treasures in Heaven is a requirement. Positively, our sincere and helpful works to enhance His gospel truth will build up our treasures in Heaven, and the number of godly endeavors we lay up in Heaven depends on the degree of our helpful works.

Beyond the shadow of a doubt, the lukewarm and the cold are forgetful people, and sadly, I must say, they are too uncaring to lay up treasures in Heaven. This truth means on Judgment Day, they'll be too broke to pass through the guarded gates of Pearl.

Therefore, because they didn't put God's word first while living in the flesh, cruising above clouds is a privilege they'll not receive. Since God warns us, no mansions are prepared for the cold and the lukewarm person, and we are told in advance not to be lukewarm or cold.

This dream about Heaven story and our new home in the Utopian world called Cruising above the Clouds is a warning story, too. It's saying to everyone, be hot and on fire for the beautiful gospel of God, or do not expect to cruise above the clouds.

Therefore, because I care about your soul, I hope to see you, dreamers, in Utopia someday, wearing beautiful wings and cruising above the clouds in your new Christ-like body. I am sure it'll be a pleasure to roam around in the land of Utopia, free and happy as a bird.

Furthermore, I am sure that having a beautiful set of wings will be much better than having an automobile or a motorcycle.

Before this unique story ends, I have a personal comment: The gift of wings is a special, monumental gift to whoever loves Him and endeavors to keep His commandments.

CHAPTER THREE
FALLING IN LOVE WITH THE WORD OF GOD

This sincere short story entwines the perfect gospel of God and the emotion of love together in a needed unity, similar to the heart needing blood. I want you to realize this is a perfect analogy, portraying the connection we should have with our wonderful Creator God.

Within this explanation story, I'll gladly use myself as an illustration person, and I am sure that many believers in the Son of God can be illustrated the same as me. I know I am not alone when I say I am in love with the beautiful word of God, and I want to live by it forever.

I know that many people fall in love with many things, but I've taken a great fall and fallen in love with the excellent word of God. I assure you this does happen to believers in the Son of God after they realize the beautiful characteristics His perfect word represents.

Beyond the shadow of a doubt, ungodly people not in love with the word of God would say, I am far out there and might say, I am a Christian fanatic. However, I am glad to be deep into the word of God, and I do not mind being called a Christian fanatic.

Furthermore, I want you to know that I consider it a compliment when someone identifies me as a loyal Christian. I am delighted with His commandments and not ashamed to say the beautiful word of God has captured my heart, and my heart will not part from the great word of God.

I've lived the sinner's life and am glad to tell you it's a terrible lifestyle to live. I am ashamed of it and am so happy I've fallen away from the things God hates. The new and improved me is changed for the better, and I gladly study the word of God intensely. My heart is overjoyed whenever I discover something new about God, and I cherish every enlightenment from the Holy Ghost that's no longer unknown to me.

I am thankful that the Holy Ghost always reveals mysteries to me, and He does so because He knows I've fallen in love with the perfect word of God. Truly, when I stand before the throne of God someday, I'll be glad to tell Him I've fallen in love with the righteousness of His gospel.

Positively, there are many roads and crossroads on this Earth, and going north, east, south, and west reveals a lot of different directions. I believe life is the same way, and we humans are symbolic of the many roads and crossroads and the various moral and immoral principles available to us.

Therefore, I want you to know that because we are free men and women, we can choose our likes and dislikes and reject God for a life of sin if we aren't afraid to die without having a Savior.

Furthermore, I firmly assure you that our great God will not interfere with our gift of free will.

However, I am telling you and warning you that there's no true happiness found within people who put the word of God out of sight. Especially if their heart is wicked and leads them in the wrong direction, they pursue and love the pleasures of sin.

Indeed, happiness is the great pearl a man finds in the field, and after locating the pearl, a man will sell all he has for the right to keep the great pearl. I can truthfully say falling in love with the word of God illustrates the same thing as finding a great pearl and not wanting to part with it.

The great pearl in this confused world is the righteous word of God, and falling in love with the required gospel of God reveals a person intending to travel to the end of the rainbow until they make it back to the source of the great pearl.

Therefore, I am sure, and because of my many experiences in life, I believe we cannot find true happiness when godliness is missing, and the pearl cannot be so meaningful to us unless we refuse to sin and fall in love with the perfect word of God.

I assure you and sincerely believe that we all deserve a life of peace and happiness. Happy heavenly creations reside in the heavens above, where Yehovah rules. They stayed on the right path, traveled to the rainbow's end, and returned home to our Great Creator God.

The common denominator entwining living creations in Heaven to peace and happiness is falling hopelessly in love with the excellent gospel of God. I believe the only loyal love in this fickle world, utterly faithful to us, is the beautiful word of God expressed through His love for you and me.

15

The truth of gaining entrance into His kingdom is evident and important, and we better not forget the statement I will reveal to you. No man, woman, or angel is invited to live in the kingdom of Heaven that's not in love with the righteous word of God.

In all my studies, which are many, I've found out some things break the boundaries of clarity. For this reason, I want you to know that we'll not achieve permanent and total happiness unless we fall hopelessly in love with the beautiful word of God.

Indeed, some people look for happiness in all the wrong places, and sex, drugs, alcohol, and getting rich will not provide permanent satisfaction. However, falling in love with God's required word will give us the keys to the heart of God, and He is the source of true happiness.

Indeed, this personal short story needs to end with me hoping you'll fall in love with the word of God as I have and find true happiness. Indeed, I know that God wants you and me to fall in love with His word and be happy all our lives.

I assure you that true happiness is the excellent gift God desires to give you and me, and keeping the superb gospel opens the doors to joy. However, we must choose this wonderful gift from God, or we'll not receive it.

Positively, I want you to know true happiness awaits you and me on the other side of the rainbow, and it's pretty possible; whenever the good angels pick us up and carry us home, the rainbow may be the road they choose to travel.

Meanwhile, as we live daily, we can achieve happiness here on Earth, and achieving satisfaction is highly possible if we live by God's beautiful word and hopelessly fall in love with His dream for you and me.

CHAPTER FOUR
THE JUNGLE WORLD

This short observation story coincides with an out-of-control wilderness environment called the *Jungle World*. It entwines the hypothetical with reality, the insolvable with an unobtainable solution, and the unobtainable solution means that humankind doesn't know how to fix its undesirable problems.

The definition of the jungle world has a parallel, and it parallels the image of our troubled world, similar to wheat and tares growing in the same garden. Furthermore, it's pretty apparent that none of us are alike, and everyone isn't going to abide by the same rules.

The animal world, wild and untamed, is the parallel illustration we flesh and blood creations emulate to some degree. This analogy concludes that the animal world has vicious predators and peaceful creatures, and the metaphor part of this story reveals that the lamb cannot lay down with the wolf.

For example, the wolf is a predator who hunts and kills his prey, and the lamb is a peaceful creature unable to do violence.

Sadly, the predators, whoever they are, cruelly devour and feed off the gentle animals. This accurate analogy reveals that the Earth is a hostile jungle world and has been since the first Earth age before the flood.

Furthermore, do not be naïve and believe that the literal wolves will resist feeding off the literal lambs because the wolves don't eat grass. This truth means that nature takes its course, and the literal animal world illustrates a metaphor that somewhat parallels the human world.

This exposure story requires much consideration; the jungle world has wild and untamed male and female predators. It has gentle as lamb's men and gentle as lamb's women living upon it. However, I must say, we cannot look at their face and know whether they are lambs or wolves.

For this reason, I call this wild and untamed place in the universe the jungle world. Because the lions hunt the lambs, I conclude, how could we consider this partially civilized Earth anything else? For this reason, and because the world will get worse and worse in every generation, we better lock our doors at night and guard ourselves against the lions and the wolves.

I know our Supreme Creator God gave us an extraordinary planet and the building instructions for a peaceful world, and His plan is perfect. I agree with God, meaning we could have a peaceful world and not lock our doors at night if we follow His character-building instructions.

However, it's pretty evident to me, and eyesight proves that not all men and women will follow the peaceful Earth-building instructions of God. Surely, it's easy to conclude that humankind isn't strong enough, wise enough, or godly sufficient to accept God completely.

I guarantee you that the wild predators upon this troubled Earth aren't compassionate and civilized people. Furthermore, I want you to know that they have a guiding spirit, a vicious predator god, and the wicked Lucifer is the wild and untamed predator god.

The cruel predator god of this world is the wolf pack's leader, and Lucifer and his wicked wolf pack will not eat grass. Common sense and the corridors of time prove the wolves aren't satisfied with only food on their table and clothing on their back.

Positively, this is a jungle world for as long as my Supreme Creator God allows the wolves to hunt the lambs. God wants you and me to know this troubled jungle world will not improve until my powerful God removes the wild and untamed wolves.

The reality of this story, The Jungle World, has a simple analogy, but it's true and absolute, and I am saying we must be blind to believe this unstable world has the right balance. Truly, we would have to be naive to think the flesh and blood man can create world peace and fix our social problems.

I assure you that this unstable jungle world is way out of balance, and it'll take a powerful Supernatural King to restore balance. The mighty King is Yehovah, and He says, I Am, That I Am. However, until He returns to the Earth, He's letting us live in a jungle world, and I assure you, door locks are necessary in this jungle world.

This exposure story's hypothetical, insolvable, and unobtainable solution entwines humanity and ungodliness. Sadly, I must say, humankind's history since before the great flood proves that the wild and untamed man and woman cannot solve the unsolvable.

This truth means this unstable jungle world is full of predators and lambs and cannot be anything different until God returns and establishes righteousness. Peace on Earth is a pipe dream because the wicked Lucifer will not let us be a united people, united under the leadership of our wonderful Creator God.

However, I am sure we believers in Christ look forward to having a peaceful world and one righteous God. He's called the God of the lambs, and when He returns to this Earth, the untamed jungle world will cease to exist.

Furthermore, I want you to know that the unobtainable will finally be obtainable, and the insolvable will be solved whenever Yeshua returns. Indeed, I have the faith to believe He will solve the unsolvable, and peace will be established on Earth, and this place I call a jungle world will not be a jungle world again.

Positively, before this heartfelt world observation story ends, I have a clarification to declare: I proclaim the world itself isn't a jungle world. However, it's the demonic spirits of the air and the ungodly people living on this Earth, turning this world into a jungle world.

CHAPTER FIVE
A THORN IN THE DEVIL'S SIDE

We've all heard it said: the wicked devil is a thorn in my side, and he's personally been a thorn in my side nearly all of my life. Sadly, because of bible illiteracy in my youth, it's taken me many years to realize that I am at war with an evil thorn tree that hates the God of creation.

Furthermore, I am sure he's a thorn in nearly every Christian's side, and I know the wicked Lucifer loves being a painful thorn. As you walk through this life, please realize sin hurts like a thorn, and I am letting you know we accumulate a new thorn every time we rebel against God and sin.

However, after we've been hurt a few times by acts of sin, we will become wiser in God's word and bolder at tearing down his sin structure implementations, especially after we realize the hurt sin causes and that the devil purposely influences us to sin against God.

However, after that realization, a thorn reversal can be successful, and the thorn can be pulled out of our side and stuck deep into his side, and we can be the thorn bothering him. Thanks to the helpful word of God, prodding us to live godly, victory against the devil is achievable because we've become wise to his sin game.

I assure you that the thorn situation's reversal will give us much joy, and we'll be glad to be the thorn puncturing the devil's side. I am sure it will please our wonderful Creator God to see us become a resister of sin and a thorn in the wicked Lucifer's side.

I know the wicked devil takes advantage of Bible-illiterate people and has dragged most of us through the briers, mud, and thorns too many times. For this reason, it feels good to overcome his power, give him a black eye, and be an oak tree, wherein we were weak saplings in the past.

Beyond the shadow of a doubt, the wicked devil is usually a winner at provoking sin, and he's accustomed to getting the best of everyone, weak in the required word of God. I am sure he's confident in his ability to deceive and not used to being defeated or having his strategy figured out by flesh-and-blood earthlings. But we can learn his game, resist his influence, and be a thorn in his side.

As for myself, I am sure I make him as angry as a rattlesnake, and I believe he would love to bite me and send poison through my veins. Lucifer hates everyone who loves God, and he would like to erase me from among the living and stop my needed work immediately.

However, the wicked Lucifer and I have mutual feelings about each other because I do not like him or the sin games he plays. However, I want to keep him from everyone, prevent his thorn attacks on our character, and erase him like he wants to erase you and me.

I've written approximately fourteen hundred Bible-related stories within the latter part of my life because I love my Creator God. I write furiously against the rebellious Lucifer and purposely expose the wickedness he imposes on all humankind.

I know for sure that the wicked and murderous devil is my adversary. He hates me, and I hate him. I am not trying to appease him, nor do I fear him. This statement of truth is the firm stance of my choice; my God advises me to defend and not compromise my view.

Positively, I want you to know that the wicked Lucifer and I understand each other, and because of hate, there's open warfare between him and me. I assure you with all my heart that I will steadfastly support my great Creator, God, and His gospel truth.

I wear God's armor for protection, and Lucifer's poison arrows cannot penetrate the armor my wonderful God provides for me. Because of my understanding of Him and because I am Bible savvy, I have tremendous faith in my great God.

I am proud to be a willing warrior for God, full of faith and trust in Him, and I'll do anything to carry the gospel of God forth to the lost. Indeed, whenever the opportunity knocks, I will advocate for God and a thorn in Lucifer's side as much as possible.

I guarantee that the wicked and murderous devil hates everyone who is passionately courageous in the Lord, and you should know that the rebellious Lucifer would prefer all believers in Christ to be passive, indifferent, lazy, and afraid of him.

In conclusion, if I were to sum up, as a faithful warrior for God, the formula for being a thorn in the devil's side in our daily walk among other people. Then, I am one hundred percent sure; the beautiful conclusion to the whole matter illustrates the sum expected of a faithful warrior.

The remarkable conclusion to the whole matter is summed up in six words, and the six essential words are to reverence God and keep His commandments. This acknowledgment is humankind's most important message and significant challenge, and we cannot avoid it.

Positively, I want you to know that keeping God's required commandments will increase our strength in the Lord, and combining a clean dwelling place for the helpful Holy Ghost to live creates a mighty warrior against the devil.

I assure you the wicked devil hates commandment keepers, and he hates all Christians with a clean home for the Holy Ghost to live inside of forever. I am telling you, determined commandment keepers with a strong Holy Ghost living within them are a thorn in his side.

Furthermore, I am sure it gives my Great God much joy to find a red-hot Christian who is wise in His word and willing to be a thorn in the devil's side. Truly, the Bible assures us that if we resist Lucifer and his demonic army, evil spirits will flee from us.

This powerful and revealing story is meant to be an awareness and inner strength-building story. The awareness to learn from this story reveals that we can be a thorn in the devil's side instead of him being a thorn in our side, and knowing this truth will increase our determination to be a loyal commandment keeper.

Without a doubt, the wicked and murderous devil will kill me someday, and I can die a martyr for the excellent Son of God. That's okay with me; I cannot think of a better way to leave this Earth and enter through the gates of Pearl in the kingdom of God.

Brave men die once, and cowards die many times, and the Bible illustrates the courageous servants of God always have wicked enemies. However, God will protect His own if they aren't afraid to stand on the word of God and aren't afraid of the evil Lucifer.

I want you to understand that I know there are great rewards for being brave in the Lord, and I must say, my Great God in Heaven will not be proud of any Christian afraid of Lucifer. However, my all-knowing Lord will be proud of us because we bravely carry His cross.

CHAPTER SIX
JOHN 3:16

Thishis detailed explanation of our belief's deepness or shallowness in one scripture, John 3:16, is an expressive story. It illuminates a few opposing opinions, some Christians assume, and I assure you, the whole meaning of John 3:16 needs examining closely.

This in-depth story, revealing and coinciding with our future life, is an eye-opener. Because we must know the truth, it examines whether this scripture from the Book of John is the ultimate and final analysis of the excellent gift of salvation.

After all, I want you to realize that there are many other scriptures to consider when evaluating the requirements for salvation. For this reason, as we formulate our plan for salvation, we need to know if John 3:16 supersedes all the other scriptures in the Bible.

However, because of the importance of this subject, this informative story will start with the scripture in John 3:16. After reading John 3:16, you can decide if it's a final decree or whether or not more is required to win the grand prize of salvation, immortality with a Christ-like body.

The Son of God speaks this following declaration scripture, and He's the ultimate authority in our great Bible. I assure you many Christians put all their faith in the following scripture as if it's the only scripture needed to win the grand prize of salvation.

However, whether John 3:16 is the conclusion or more should be considered is hard to say unless we are willing to dig deep into other meaningful scriptures and discover the correct answer. We need to find the correct answer.

John 3:16 For <u>God</u> (the Father) so loved the world (means all people), that He gave His only begotten Son, that whosoever believeth in Him should not perish, but have everlasting life.

Beyond the shadow of a doubt, the above important scripture reveals why God sent His Son to the Earth. John 3:16 reveals that our Father has obligated His Son to save this misguided world, and we should all realize that a wonderful Savior is born to immortalize believers in God.

However, because God's written word contains many different scriptures and requirements, it will take a serious study to find the correct answer. Indeed, we know that other scriptures have significant meanings connected to John 3:16, so we should expand our understanding to include all the scriptures.

The question is whether or not believing in the Son of God is the extent of our obligation. Because it matters, we need to know what degree of devotion our belief in Him has to be before we receive the gift of salvation. Also, is John 3:16 the sum of everything, and is nothing else required?

I conclude that it would be easier to understand where we stand with God if John 3:16 established a degree of faith. After all, some people strongly believe in the beautiful Son of God, and some have weak faith in Him. Furthermore, the excellent words revealed in John 3:16 don't specify any specific degree of belief.

I ask you, does it matter whether or not our belief in the Son of God is strong or weak? Because believing in Him seems to fulfill the definition of believing in His divinity, regardless of whether it's a strong or a weak belief.

The above scripture tells us that whosoever believes in Him shall not perish; they shall receive everlasting life, which is a pretty simple statement. I want you to know that I wholeheartedly believe in the written word of our great Creator God, and I want to know the fullness of the subject of salvation.

I believe God's excellent word is accurate, and His wonderful word doesn't throw curveballs. However, I sincerely conclude that interpreting His word correctly and to its fullest extent can sometimes be challenging.

Especially since I know that all of us will stand on the Judgment Scales of God, and He'll judge everyone by the temperature of hot, cold, or lukewarm. My God of Heaven and Earth tells us so, as written in the book of Revelation, chapter three, verse sixteen.

Furthermore, I know that the conclusion to the whole matter is to reverence God and keep His commandments. Throughout the Bible, a great emphasis is put on commandment keeping. Because it matters to God, keeping the conclusion to the whole matter means commandment-keeping is highly important.

The question is whether or not believing in the Son of God cancels out commandment-keeping and reverence for Him.

Or otherwise, I ask you, are all these critical commanded things entwined with our belief in God?

After all, the critical scripture in John 3:16 didn't add stipulations other than those who believe in Him, and I want you to realize that the beautiful Son of God didn't come into this world to condemn but to save. However, the Ten Commandments judge our lifestyle, and they save souls.

I suppose a little puzzle is exposed; it's up to you and me to determine how strongly we desire to obligate ourselves to our supreme God. For this reason, I ask you, on our day of Judgment, will a weak belief in Him be as reasonable as a strong belief in Him?

This truth means we can base our Christianity on simply believing in the Son of God or on the whole word of God. I assure you, there's a division among Christians concerning how much reverence and servitude they must dedicate to God.

Positively, we are none good and fall short of fulfilling our devotion to God, and I am sure a holier-than-thou feeling in God's eyes illustrates an awful feeling. However, being a sincere Christian means we are trying to conform to the whole gospel of God.

However, I want you to know that we all wrestle against the serpent of old and the wicked demonic spirits of the air. Truly, I know that firm believers in the Son of God will lose battles and occasionally sin, and none of us living in the flesh is perfect.

Therefore, regardless of our inability to be perfect, we are expected to overcome acts of sin and learn to resist ungodly temptations. I assure you that this is an expectation God has for all of us, and He'll never change His expectations. If our mind is right and we love righteousness, we'll not desire to compromise any part of the word of God.

Indeed, we would be foolish people not to fight against sin. If we battle against acts of ungodliness, as He expects us to, it illustrates our strong desire to live by the whole word of God. Furthermore, fighting against acts of corruption shows our overwhelming joy in finding Him.

However, if we do not fight against acts of sin, it reveals a weak desire to put godliness first, and we will travel down the wrong roads. Sadly, not fighting against acts of sin allows sin to be an unstoppable runaway train, and this is a true statement, even if we believe in Him.

Indeed, John 3:16 reveals our Supreme Creator God and the beautiful Son of God as our only Saviors from the Judgment of damnation. It's for sure; John 3:16 overwhelmingly tells their heart's desire to save us from the grips of Lucifer and the probability of losing our souls.

However, because of different beliefs on the meaning of John 3:16, we'll have to decide how intense our faith needs to be in the God of Heaven and Hell before our faith can guide the thoughts of our hearts and the works we do with our hands.

The holy Apostle Paul's following scripture adds requirements to John 3:16. The following declaration scripture, as crucial as heat on a cold night, reveals some of the added requirements. I want you to know that the God who judges the world expects more from us than saying we believe in Him.

Hebrews 12:14 Follow peace with all men, and holiness, without which no man shall see the Lord.

Even though the beautiful scripture called John 3:16 didn't

elaborate on salvation requirements. I firmly believe that believing in Him adds many of His other essential words to our commands from God. I am sure that knowledge of the Scriptures strengthens our belief in Him.

Therefore, I believe for sure, and this is my personal opinion. However, I conclude *that peace and holiness entwined with believing in the beautiful Son of God fulfill the definition of believing* in Him. Also, I know the word holiness expands to include sincere commandment keeping, and He admires commandment keepers loyal to His word.

Mainly because it's logical to have a strong belief in the Son of God, which is the ingredient entwined with His words of wisdom, peace, and holiness, and being a new creature in Christ means we have a new heart and a strong desire to conform to Christ-like characteristics.

Furthermore, since all three entwine together, how can we separate love for Him and love for His word from our belief in Him? However, the expressive scripture in John 3:16 tells us that whosoever believes in the Son of God shall receive everlasting life.

Conclusively, the definition of the phrase believing in Him must mean the same as loving Him. However, loving Him more than the things of this word seems to oppose a weak belief in Him. Because we must adore Him immensely before we can believe in Him, and the beautiful Son speaks through these following two scriptures.

John 14:15 If you love <u>Me</u> (the beautiful Son of God), keep My commandments.

Beyond the shadow of a doubt, we owe God more than a simple belief, and maybe the definition of John 3:16 wasn't thoroughly explained, and because we need clarification, within the above scripture, the Son of God is finishing the meaning of His requirements to believe in Him.

John 14:21 He that <u>hath</u> (love for) My commandments, and keepeth them, loveth Me.

Indeed, the above two revealing scriptures expose other requirements and entwine with John 3:16, and when they are combined, I am sure that they'll help complete the definition of believing in the beautiful Son of God. However, not having the faith to believe in Yeshua means that requirements aren't necessary for those unwilling to carry His cross.

Therefore, because of their connection to judgment, our daily walk, and their importance to God. Because of bible revelations, I believe with all my heart that the excellent Ten Commandments of God are a part of the definition of trust and faith in the Son of God.

Many Christians believe the Ten Commandments were nailed to the cross, and they aren't a requirement anymore after the death of Christ. Sadly, this is a common belief among many Christians, convinced that the gift of grace had replaced commandment keeping.

However, in more than one place throughout the scriptures, the excellent Son of God purposely entwines love for Him with commandment-keeping. The words Yeshua speaks are infallible, and no believer in Christ should overlook the need to learn the gospel of our Savior.

Within the following explanation of scripture, God's wise and perfect Son reveals the mystery of uniting us to His Father. The following scripture is powerful, easy to comprehend, and significant to understanding our relationship with the Son of God.

John 14:23 If a man loves <u>Me</u> (Yeshua, the Son of God), he will keep My words, and My Father will love him.

John 14:23 and <u>We</u> (the Father, the Son, and the Holy Ghost) will love him, and We will come unto him, and <u>make our abode</u> (means live) with him.

This story's explanation concerns understanding the truth, and John 3:16 comes with a severe warning from the perfect Son of God. I assure you words of truth from the Son of God are the pinnacle of advice, and we'd be foolish not to take His warning seriously.

John 14:24 He that loveth <u>Me</u> (Yeshua) not, keepeth not My sayings, and the word which ye hear is not Mine, but the Father's which sent Me.

Within the above scripture, the perfect Son of God tells us that whoever doesn't take His word seriously isn't a believer in Him. This truth means John 3:16 entwines with the whole word of God, and gaining everlasting life hinges on us keeping His required word.

Indeed, in this story, we need to consider expressive and meaningful; John 3:16 reveals my analogy, especially since John 3:16 seems controversial among many Christians. However, you are welcome to form your analogy to increase your understanding, and I will respect your thoughts on this subject.

However, which way might you believe concerning the beautiful meaning of John 3:16? I assure you, it's an advantage to live by the whole word of God, and I do not know of any logical reason a believer in Christ would want to do less.

I assure you that some characteristics prove sincere love, and caring about the whole word of God illustrates a noble Christian trait. Furthermore, expanding on John 3:16 demonstrates a Christ-like character and much love for the beautiful Son of God.

Conclusively, all Christians have a different degree of understanding. After considering the expansion of John 3:16, I firmly conclude that carrying the cross of Yeshua and being hot and on-fire Christians is the best way to proceed through this life, day after day.

Furthermore, let's not be passive and indifferent Christians and not consider our Christianity a parallel cruise ship to Heaven. However, let's be genuine Christians determined to keep the whole word of God and walk through the pearl gates in love with His word.

CHAPTER SEVEN
SPLINTERED CHRISTIANITY

I want to start this story by saying that Christianity's godly characteristics are the most beautiful and meaningful treasures anywhere one of His creations lives. I am sure that because of righteousness and the characteristics that Christianity represents, Christianity is our template for a perfect society.

Indeed, true Christianity has more to offer us than anything else revealed in this world, and I am confident that nothing else compares to authentic Christianity. I want to advise you that it's illogical to oppose the doctrines of God and then go in a different direction that doesn't meet God's approval.

I love true Christianity whenever it's authentic and presented in the correct definition. It's not distorted by additives or subtractions but explained fully in simple terminology. I want you to know that the correctness of the definition of Bible stories illuminates the greatness of true Christianity.

I am proud to say the excellent Ten Commandments, righteous

and perfect, are my treasured covenant with God, and they are your covenant as long as you live. His Ten Commandments burn in my heart, and I love every word God decreed, and everyone else should love them as much as I do.

I want you to know because of my overwhelming feelings for the righteous word of God. I am proud to tell you that Christianity is a passionate part of my life, and I take every word of God exceptionally seriously. Truly, for the glory of God, I desire to blend my life into His word. I love every one of the proclamations He's declared, and so should everyone else.

Indeed, I fail to understand why so many people reject being committed to a life of Christianity. It's hard to know why they hate it and poke fun at it, water it down, and live their entire life bible illiterate. I am confident that the people doing these negative things have been deceived for too many years, and the wicked spirit of Lucifer has overtaken them and changed their hearts.

Therefore, because of my great love for His wonderful word, I've written over two million words into story examples that exceed over one thousand individual stories. However, it's taken me years to realize how much Christianity has splintered and the various reasons it's fractured.

Christianity has fierce opponents to the Bible's quoted doctrines of God's righteous and excellent word. For some illogical reason, the bible opponents will not believe, practice authentic Christianity, or believe in the great God of Christianity.

The unbelievers will not accept the word of God, and many nations worship many gods and goddesses. However, sadly, they do not worship the great God of Israel, and our God-inspired Bible makes it clear that believing in other gods puts our gift of salvation at risk.

Beyond the shadow of a doubt, it's easy to conclude the unbelievers and the false god worshippers outnumber Christians by a large margin. Sadly, according to Bible scriptures, at the end of their lives, they'll go through the broad gate to the pits of Hell.

However, I want you to realize that the unbelievers and the false god worshippers are just one part of the splinters harmful to Christianity. Truly, as hard as it is to accept misleading sermons, some preachers teach the traditions of men from the pulpit and will cause harm to authenticity.

This truth means that the other part of Christianity's splinters is a result of Bible illiteracy and is caused within the family of Christianity. This mistake happens after a Christian deviates from authenticity, and I want you to know that every deviation from authenticity results in a new splinter.

Christianity, built on the gospel truth and correct authenticity, is a joy inside my heart. Sadly, it's easy to understand the unbelievers and the counterfeit false god worshippers not being concerned about the authenticity of Christianity. However, on the opposite side of the truth, misrepresentations of the facts will cause splinters in Christianity.

Indeed, it's not so easy to understand a Christian guilty of not caring about the authenticity of Christianity, and I want you to know that it's a terrible shame not to care about the accuracy attached to every word of God preached from behind the pulpit.

Indeed, Christians should understand both the Old Covenant and the New Covenant, and for increased enlightenment, they should understand their connection to each other. We must understand them because both covenants are nearly identical, revealing our great God's expectations for every Christian.

Furthermore, picking up the cross of Yeshua means we've picked up His covenant and are applying it to our everyday decisions. Our Covenant with God is all about decision-making, and carrying the cross of Yeshua is all about decision-making. The excellent Ten Commandments are our guidance counselor from above, and it's an honor for Him to share His wisdom with us.

For the above reasons, observing authenticity and the truth is a primary responsibility God lays on the shoulders of every believer in Christ. I assure you, our Creator God expects daily commandment-related decision-making from every Christian.

I want you to know Christianity doesn't need splinters, and when Christians practice anything other than authenticity and truth, it splinters Christianity. The right way becomes cluttered with half-truths, and because this practice happens often, all sermons should be carefully analyzed and preached cautiously.

Imagine a tree imploding from within, revealing all the individual splinters the implosion causes and the weakness it does to the tree. Then, realize that men's traditions are similar to half-truths, and men's rules, contrary to the perfect word of God, are identical to a tree exploding into many splinters.

Conclusively, every sermon a preacher teaches the congregation that does not align with God's perfect word results in a new splinter. Sadly, erroneous preachers and teachers, not Bible-savvy, are the primary reason Christianity suffers from deviations and splinters into many fragments.

Good-hearted Christians do not want to blame preachers and teachers for splintering Christianity. However, the truth is the truth, and the fact shouldn't be hidden or denied because preachers and teachers are responsible for doing more harm to Christianity than the unbelievers and the false god worshippers.

False god worshippers and unbelievers cannot splinter a church from within the house of Christianity. However, I assure you, the unlearned preacher or the misguided Christian can. It's not a little thing whenever misguided sermons are taught to the believers in Christ, and whenever this happens, they add another splinter to Christianity.

I blame preachers, teachers, and Christians for splintering Christianity because some of them erroneously represent and express the definition of various Christian issues. The truth is true, and I want you to know that if the shoe fits, the analogy also fits.

Megachurches get on the airways and preach and teach to millions of people worldwide. However, if they interpret wrongly and deviate from authenticity, their deviations will have a domino-splintered effect on authentic Christianity.

Positively, many people will believe the erroneous sermons misguided preachers teach. Sadly, I must say, the people taught by them might pass the wrong teaching down the line and cause others to believe the wrong way, and if they do teach wrongly, splinters in Christianity are multiplied.

I suppose most Christians believe preachers and teachers will not misrepresent the commanded word of God and will not stray from authenticity. This naive belief coincides with thinking cats can grow wings and fly through the sky.

However, to increase your awareness, I warn you: it's naïve to believe all preachers and teachers understand the subject they teach to the congregation. It's also naïve to believe all preachers care about authenticity concerning the perfect word of God.

Many preachers and teachers in the house of God are usually splintering Christianity, and sadly, I must say, they are doing it without showing concern concerning what they are doing to the unchangeable word of God. It's a terrible injustice to bend and twist His gospel truth, but it always happens in every generation.

Furthermore, it's easy to see many preachers in the house of God are making themselves extremely rich from the congregation. They tell themselves God is blessing them when it's the wicked Lucifer blessing them for distorting the required word of our Creator God.

My great creator, the God of Heaven and Earth, doesn't bless preachers and teachers who misrepresent His precious words of truth. However, sadly, kind-hearted and unlearned people sitting in the congregation contribute to their prosperity.

However, I conclude that most Christians are too naïve to believe the wicked Lucifer will bless a preacher man with prosperity. The deceiving Lucifer will bless a preacher man with prosperity because of some circumstances meeting Lucifer's approval.

Indeed, if a preacher strays from authenticity and causes splintered Christianity, I believe Lucifer will bless the preacher for harming the perfect word of God. Mistakingly, the preacher will probably think God approves of his teaching and is blessing him, and the preacher will continue teaching contrary to the word of God.

The splintered world of Christianity, weakened by splinters, seems to be in a relaxed state of mind these days. This high-priority grace age, the centerpiece of some preachers' sermons, has many blind guides and, sadly, many blind followers.

This next need to realize teaching scripture reveals blind

guides, and blind guides lead men and women astray, and leading them away from authenticity is harmful. Truly, the Son of God assures you and me that blind guides lead bible illiterate people astray through erroneous teaching.

Indeed, blind guides are the primary reason for splintered Christianity, and misrepresenting the commanded word of God is more harmful than opposing it. Therefore, we should be wise enough to realize that blind guides harm Christians in the name of God.

Furthermore, whenever blind guides teach opposition to authentic Christianity and impose false teachings on their fellow Christians, the compromise they make amounts to more than an opposing opinion or something unimportant, and you need to know accepting an inaccurate alternative will have consequences.

Positively, I want you to know that opposing opinions to the required word of God have hurtful consequences, and I want you to know God doesn't like opposing views concerning His perfect word. Therefore, I warn you, the definition of a fool entwines with whosoever follows the blind guides.

Matthew 15:14 Let <u>them</u> (blind guides) alone; they are blind leaders of the blind, and if the blind lead the blind, both shall fall into the ditch.

I assure you that authentic Christianity is our caring Creator God's ultimate gift to us living in the flesh. However, uncaring blind guides preaching the imagination of their mind will keep us from receiving the fullness of our gift from God if we let them lead us away from authenticity and cause us to accept a false belief.

Therefore, opposition to the perfect word of God amounts to more than an opposing opinion because opposition to His infallible word has misleading abilities. I want you to know that deceptive teaching will cause some men to think opposition to authenticity doesn't matter, one way or the other.

Throughout the rest of this, a need-to-understand story illustrates splintered Christianity. I will gladly dig deep into God's original word and give examples of opposition to authenticity. I want you to know that resistance to His word is a compromise.

This declaration story's opposition to authenticity needs to be recognized and amended. If we do not acknowledge and amend mistakes, then we are too passive to the passionate word of our great Creator God, and passive Christians cannot please God.

Opposition to authenticity happens because preachers and teachers stray away from the perfect word of God and then teach the traditions of men for one illogical reason or another. I want you to understand that we may as well realize that men's rules aren't His infallible word.

Number one > Many Christians believe in unlimited grace, while others believe the gift of grace is limited. I assure you authenticity doesn't allow both beliefs in the gift of grace to be correct, and only one of the two mentioned beliefs illustrates the Bible-quoted truth.

Honestly, I want you to understand the wrong belief in the gift of grace is a hurtful doctrine to believe, and we shouldn't accept a misleading philosophy on grace as authenticity or consider the gift of grace will erase the price tag for sin every time we sin.

I assure you that pleasing God does matter, and choosing the wrong over the right doesn't please Him. I guarantee He'll not say, to each their own opinion, as if our opinion compares to His perfect word; it doesn't. Furthermore, we are Bible illiterate to believe an artificial idea will compare to His infallible Word.

Indeed, His perfect word is authenticity, absolute and unchangeable; it's our guiding light from above. I am sure our Creator God expects all preachers and teachers to learn and teach the truth and for all Christians to love and follow His authenticity.

Number two > Many Christians believe that we'll wait in the grave until the day Christ returns, and then we'll rise again, and other Christians believe that we'll go to Heaven or Hell after the death of the flesh. However, we can be sure that our spirit will disappear from this Earth after the end of the flesh and go up or down from where we live now.

I assure you preachers and teachers everywhere teach both analogies and because of a lack of understanding, we often hear both concepts being taught. However, because it's impossible to fulfill both beliefs, only one analogy among the two is correct.

Number three > Many Christians believe the Sabbath Day of the Lord is on the Bible's quoted the seventh day, and the seventh day is Saturday. However, many Christians believe the Sabbath Day of the Lord is on the first day of the week, and the first day of the week is Sun-day.

Furthermore, many Christians believe it doesn't matter what day we call our Sabbath Day; for some reason, they firmly believe we can pick and choose it. Nor do they believe that His authentic Sabbath Day is any more special than the other six days of the week or the counterfeit Sabbath Day.

Positively, some Christians say they worship our perfect Creator God every day as if the hallowed Sabbath Day of God is on every day of the week, and maybe this is wishful thinking, an illustration of bible ignorance, or a lack of concern; you decide.

Example three gives us three different beliefs multitudes of Christians assume concerning the Sabbath Day of our Lord. However, I want you to know that God's required word isn't optional, and only one of the above beliefs is correct.

This truth means that, according to the perfect word of God, the other two beliefs are misrepresentations imposed on Christians by blind guides. Sadly, I must say, some mistakes are being preached behind the pulpit and imposed on Christians quite regularly.

Number four > Many Christians believe it's okay to eat unclean foods, and the swine's flesh is forbidden meat to eat, and my Creator God says so, and He made the law, and we are foolish to eat an animal that eats its feces and roots up the ground it pisses on. If it were different, and there wasn't a good reason not to eat the swine, I am sure our Creator God would've told us so.

However, there are many other Christians in the church world today, and they believe otherwise. They think eating the swine's flesh or even touching its carcass is *not okay*. They believe in following the word of God and firmly believe imposing uncleanness on our hearts is not okay.

I assure you that only one of the above choices is correct, according to the infallible word of God, and the incorrect choice is a painful splinter. Yehovah is our All-Knowing God, and because He loves us, He puts absolute definition to cleanness and uncleanness.

Indeed, our body is the redefined living temple of God, and the perfect, clean-living Holy Ghost is choosy, and He'll not live in an unclean temple. If ours is unclean, it's regardless of how often we profess to love Him or attend a crowded church building.

Furthermore, many Christians will live their entire life unconcerned about eating the unclean and unconcerned about the dwelling place of the Holy Ghost. Sadly, I must say, whoever eats the unclean will go to their grave and never know how it feels to have a clean-living temple.

Example four illustrates two choices, but only one is correct: according to the accurate word of God. You, I, and everyone else can live by the infallible word of God, or we can do our own thing. However, I am asking you: Do we have the right to request the clean Holy Ghost to live within an unclean temple?

Number five > Many Christians believe salvation has come to the Gentiles, and it's through the teaching of the Apostle Paul. Paul is a great teacher, renowned for teaching us many beautiful things, and I must say, the Apostle Paul was a dedicated man to the Father and the Son of God.

However, many other Christians believe quite differently in teaching the gift of salvation to the Gentiles. They firmly believe the wonderful gift of salvation is offered to the Gentiles through the caring Son of God, and I must tell you He has the power to grant the gift of eternal life.

I guarantee you that only one of the above choices is correct, according to God's accurate and beautiful word, and I want you to realize that the other choice is a wrong analogy. Because the truth and the way we think matter, this is a severe subject worth pursuing and understanding.

Number six > the most significant event in the history of Christianity, is the death, burial, and resurrection of the outstanding Son of God. I assure you no other event in the history of Christianity compares to His willing blood sacrifice on the cross.

However, many Christians worldwide call the death, burial, and resurrection event the name of Easter, and others call it the

Second Passover. However, only one of these two choices is correct, according to the perfect word of God, and the other choice is a lie.

The truth is clear, and the fact needs to be wholly understood. Sadly, I must say, many preachers and teachers call the death, burial, and resurrection of the beautiful Son of God by the wrong name all the time.

Furthermore, the people they teach pick up their lies and spread them like pollen in the wind, and we Christians do not need to be pollinated by misrepresentations or inaccuracies from any source. It's for sure; all Christians shouldn't call His memorial event by a pagan name.

Honestly, I am sure the Father, the Son, and the Holy Ghost would like all Christians to call the most extraordinary event in the history of Christianity by the correct name. We are foolish to believe that anything other than correctness is acceptable to them. Truly, I am asking you why the right name shouldn't be used to illuminate his memorable event.

I assure you, and you should already know, that God's perfect and required word isn't a chopped salad, and we cannot slice, dice, and treat it any way we want. Furthermore, we are fools to try such a silly endeavor as our Creator, God, watches us from the heavens above.

Number seven > Many Christians believe in the much-taught rapture and the gift of a feather-weight body, not restricted by gravity during the tribulation event yet to come. Because of popular belief, this is a widely expected assumption, but it's still an assumption.

Some Christians believe in the fly-away doctrine, and I am sure they hope they'll float into the clouds to meet Christ and escape the violent and terrible tribulation event. The thought of such an escape plan sounds good, and it's easy to believe, but should we believe someone else's assumption?

However, I want you to know that the truth doesn't conform to assumptions. Not everyone who believes in God shares the same opinion about the rapture, and most Bible-savvy Christians do not believe in the mythical rapture. They believe they'll live through the great tribulation time and watch it unfold, and His seal protects them.

Beyond the shadow of a doubt, according to the written word of God, only one of the above two beliefs is correct, and the other is false. Sadly, I must say, a mistaken belief is preached throughout the world of Christianity all the time.

Number eight > Many Christians believe the righteous Ten Commandments of God were nailed to the cross with the beautiful Son of God during His cruel crucifixion. These same Christians will say that everything was fulfilled at His death without showing evidence to support their belief.

This truth means many Christians believe the Ten Commandments aren't valid anymore, as if God made a mistake when He wrote them. Or otherwise, they think without having proof, the wonderful gift of grace has replaced commandment keeping.

However, many devout Christians are well-studied and Bible-savvy, and correctness matters. They firmly believe the Ten Commandments are as valid today as before Christ, that all people need them after His cruel death, and that if we profess to love the Son of God, we will love His commandments.

I assure you that according to the excellent word of God, only one of the above beliefs is correct concerning the validity of the beautiful Ten Commandments of God. Truly, it's logical to assume misbelieving the gospel of God will cause us to make judgment mistakes.

However, both of the above beliefs are preached and taught regularly, but I assure you that only one of the two beliefs is true and correct. The other idea is false, a misrepresentation of authenticity, and the wrong belief will cause blind believers to fall into a ditch.

Number nine > Many Christians believe that God is one hundred percent unconditional love and will be merciful to all people and not send anyone to the pits of Hell. They believe He'll give automatic salvation to everyone, regardless of their spiritual condition. Sadly, I suppose these believers in the Son of God do not believe in Hell or the lake of fire.

However, many other Christians believe everyone isn't redeemable, and the God of Heaven and Earth will send unrepented violators to Hell and cast them into the lake of fire. Truly, according to the perfect word of God, only one of these two analogies is correct.

Number ten > Many Christians believe there's only one God, and all the other so-called gods are inferior to our Creator God. However, many other Christians believe this world is full of gods and goddesses and is the same as our supreme Creator God.

However, many other Christians wholeheartedly believe this world is full of counterfeit gods and goddesses and aren't all the same. Because of different analogies, it's easy to conclude that not all beliefs men conceive are from our God-inspired Bible.

Indeed, many Christians firmly believe there's only one Supreme Creator God, Yehovah, and He's the King of kings. They believe He's a miracle worker and the Creator of everything our eyes behold, and they look forward to living in His kingdom forever.

I want you to realize multiple assumptions do not add up to a truth, and only one of the above beliefs is correct. I want you to be Bible-savvy and know that the other belief is a lie, a myth greater than the tooth fairy, a tale more remarkable than the Earth is flat, or the myth that rabbits lay eggs.

Number eleven > Many Christians believe favors and blessings from above are a reward for giving seed money, and they believe that seed money multiplies our prosperity by many folds. They think It's regardless of the denomination that receives the cash or the church or temple that benefits from it.

However, many other Christians believe favors and rewards from above aren't for sale, and we cannot buy them like merchandise with seed money. So, for the sake of doing right, they are choosey, and the type of Christianity they support does matter to them.

I assure you that only one of the above beliefs is correct, and the other is a lie that preachers and teachers often tell. Sadly, I must say, naïve Christians are taken advantage of for the love of money, and I am sure being taken advantage of happens quite often in the name of God.

Number twelve > Many preachers and teachers in the house of God teach that the tribulation battle will be fought exclusively by flesh and blood men. However, many other Christians believe an angel from Heaven will open the gates of Hell; for some reason, his name isn't mentioned in the Bible.

Although we can be sure that the angry residents of Hell will come to the surface of this Earth, they'll war against Christ with all their strength. This truth means some Christians believe the prophesized tribulation battle will include Lucifer, and the demonic angels from the past will be here among us, including the spirit of everyone locked away in Hell.

Only one of the above beliefs is correct, and the other misrepresents the truth. I want you to realize that lies and misrepresentations will affect how we prepare ourselves for trials and tribulations and future events. It would help if you realized that lies do not set anyone free from the powers of darkness.

Number thirteen > Many Christians believe in total free will for everyone, and they think everything we do in this world is performed through the heart's free will. Indeed, they believe all our lifestyle choices, good or bad, are ours to choose.

However, other Christians believe some of us live under a supernatural God-imposed curse because of scripture evidence. I want you to know it's entirely possible, as hard as it is to accept, that all our lifestyle choices aren't wholly ours to choose.

I assure you, because of bible illiteracy, the wrong teaching, and a lack of interest, there's a difference of opinion between the Christians who believe in totally free will and those who believe in God-imposed curses. Please realize you can know the truth by studying the Bible and looking for answers.

Indeed, according to God's beautiful and perfect word, only one of the above analogies is correct, and the other is a lie. If I were you, I would consider example number thirteen, read the Bible and search hard to understand the truth.

Number fourteen > Many Christians believe the Holy Ghost lives within them and teaches them the right way because they believe in the Son of God. They feel this way regardless of the unclean things they eat, including the nasty swine's flesh.

This truth means many Christians aren't conforming to the will of God, and they are trying to force the beautiful Holy Ghost to live inside an unclean temple simply because they want to eat the unclean flesh of a forbidden animal and still keep the Holy Ghost.

However, other Christians firmly believe the supernatural Holy Ghost cannot teach from within every Christian, and it's because some of them have an unclean temple, and their eyes are closed to the truth. Truly, eyes with scales covering their spiritual understanding will not open until the Holy Ghost teaches from within our hearts.

I assure you that only one of the above analogies is correct, and the other is a false assumption. Believing in the mistaken belief can keep an unclean temple from cleaning up. Therefore, I conclude that the demonic spirits of the air love an unclean temple.

Number fifteen > Many Christians believe the Jewish people have a higher calling, and God commands them to keep the law and the commandments to secure the gift of salvation. This message is a fact, and our Supreme Creator God does require Christians to be commandment keepers.

Although, for some odd reason unknown to me, some Christians want to believe God is holding the Jewish people to a higher moral standard. They seem to think that because God has spent so much time with them, He's asking more from them than He does everyone else.

Positively, reaching the same agreement is hard for some Christians because there are other Christians who believe the Gentiles are exempt from keeping the laws and the commandments. They believe the gift of salvation is given to them because they claim to believe in God.

For some illogical reason that eludes my understanding, many Christians believe our fair and righteous God has two sets of instructions for salvation. For an unknown reason I cannot explain, they think the teachings we follow depend on our heritage or whether we are a Jew or a Gentile.

I assure you that because we Christians cannot have it both ways, only one of the above two analogies is accurate, and the other is false. Positively, mistaken belief can affect our effort to win the grand prize of immortality, and please realize that commandment keeping erases myths.

Number sixteen > The death, burial, and resurrection of Yeshua are the most significant events in the history of Christianity, and the scriptures tell us that He was in the grave for three days and rose back to life. However, some Christians believe He arose from the tomb on Sunday, and others believe He arose from the grave on Saturday.

However, only one of these analogies is accurate, and the mystery is unveiled if we do the math from two different angles. One angle is from 3:00 PM on Wednesday, and the other is from 3:00 pm on Thursday.

Conclusively, all the above examples in this story reveal a division among Christians, which shouldn't exist. However, this division does exist, and it's because some Christians are Bible-savvy, and some aren't Bible-savvy, and this division proves Christianity has a lot of splinters.

Positively, I want you to know every division among Christians breaks the unity between brothers and sisters in Christ; in the same way, the truth is divided from a lie. Therefore, I feel compelled to warn you that wrong beliefs usually have consequences attached to them.

Indeed, I am sure that breaking unity among brothers and sisters in Christ reveals one of the main reasons for splintered Christianity. I assure you, splintered Christianity occurs whenever the original word of God suffers from deviations.

Therefore, suffering from the blindness of the mind is a tragedy; all the above examples in this story reveal many Christians are stumbling around in the darkness of the mind and are similar to blind sheep. Indeed, the terrible famine in the land we are suffering from isn't for food, but it's for a shortage of Bible authenticity.

Beyond a shadow of a doubt, the above examples in this story will give us something to consider if we are concerned about authenticity versus counterfeits. I firmly advise you to analyze and evaluate these examples.

I assure you that preachers and teachers worldwide teach every example mentioned in this enlightenment story. However, in all the above criteria, only one choice is correct, and because there's one truth, the other choices amount to false teaching.

I want you to realize that it's not the unbelievers and the false god worshippers causing splintered Christianity. However, splintered Christianity is a problem caused by teaching lies; the lies usually begin from the pulpit inside the house of God.

I hate to be the person who has to tell it point-blank bluntly, but this meaningful enlightenment story reveals part of my calling to write Bible stories. I am sure I would disappoint my great Creator God if I didn't try to shine a light on authenticity.

I assure you that the excellent word of God has been misrepresented too much by pretty and passive words from the pulpit. Sadly, I must tell you incorrect teaching has happened for many years, and misrepresentations do not please God. Because of this problem, I've written a revealing story called *Splintered Christianity*, which proves a difference in how man and God think.

Furthermore, compromising the perfect word of God has serious consequences, and compromises need to be corrected for our sake. Truly, it's up to you and me to get things right and not let men's traditions guide us in the wrong direction.

For the sake of love, I hope you'll be a Bible-savvy person for the rest of your life and will not be influenced by blind guides who preach and teach men's traditions. I hope you'll be strong like an oak tree and will not compromise the perfect word of God.

Indeed, I want you to realize exceptional advice and burn what I will tell you in your heart. Compromising the beautiful word of God is the same as sinning against the Ten Commandments, and acts of rebellion against His word will narrow our chance of receiving eternal life and a mansion in His kingdom. Truly, on a spectacular day in the desert, He gave us His covenant on Mount Sinai; the Ten Commandments concluded the whole matter, and because of their importance to Him, they are the *meat of Christianity.*

CHAPTER EIGHT
MY BIBLE ANALOGY

I call this personal story concerning the sincere feelings inside my heart my *Bible Analogy*. It reveals my understanding and how my thinking coincides with God's excellent word, and I am confident that the way we think is supposed to entwine with the commandments of God.

I've heard many concerned people say the God-inspired Bible has a history of being rewritten sixty-six times. This news is stunning to consider, and I assure you that rewriting the Bible so many times isn't something to take lightly, and it does concern many people and me.

As for myself, I am a bible lover, and the Scriptures impress me. However, I do not know for sure if sixty-six times is exact and accurate. But, I care deeply about the truth, and I like accuracy, and being rewritten by a man sixty-six times profoundly concerns me.

I've heard many people say some of the bible scriptures contradict each other, and some people also say correctness has gotten lost due to so much translation. For this reason, I conclude we have to scrutinize every word we read to see if it coincides with the character of God.

For the above reason, I will make an assumption. Although I do not enjoy making assumptions concerning the perfect word of God, and mainly because man's beliefs leave room for mistakes, I wouldn't like to misquote the word of God. However, here I go anyway because I cannot resist the chance to express my opinion.

In all my bible studies, which are many, I've found places within the scriptures lacking perfect clarity, and I am sure many Bible-savvy Christians have experienced the same clarity problem. Therefore, I firmly conclude that excellent clarity removes a lot of guesswork from interfering with authenticity.

Indeed, I like straight-forth and simple clarity on every subject within the Bible. However, the Bible has a lot of places lacking simple transparency, even though I know some things or specific topics may not be meant for everyone to understand completely.

However, I know when our understanding fails, it's times like this when many assumptions occur, and it's because of a lack of clarity. During this moment of lack of clarity, it might be better to move on instead of making assumptions.

The excellent King James bible consists of over seven hundred and eighty thousand words, and no man understands every word. Truly, we would be a fool to believe; we can make assumptions, and they'll all be correct. Sadly, I know our personal beliefs can make us look foolish when we interpret them wrongly.

However, I know one thing for certain, and I am sure: God cannot lie, nor does He have to lie about anything, and lying wouldn't cross His mind. This truth means if a contradiction man assumes to find within the Bible, then it's most likely made by man's interpretation.

Indeed, men of God make the wrong interpretation by accident, and it does happen when clarity isn't present. However, in their defense, I will say some things written within the Bible are analogies of men and are written according to their understanding.

However, because God has certain things He wants to reveal, many things written in the Bible are one hundred percent the perfect word of the Father and the word of the Son of God. I want you to know that their words are the pinnacle of all the other words.

Therefore, I conclude that when clarity fails on a particular subject, written by the prophets and the apostles. Then, I assure you, because of higher intelligence, it's better to go with the perfect word of God, written in red.

Mainly because the commanded word of God is told straight, I've realized that the word of God has greater clarity when written in red. If you'll notice, the red writing usually goes straight to the point in simple clarity.

This truth means that the word of God and His Son supersedes any man's words, and this truth includes the Apostles and the Prophets. Neither can God or His Son tell a lie about anything or be misleading about any subject. However, they will challenge us with puzzles to figure out.

Regardless of how doubting some concerned men are about the accuracy of the Bible and its every word, I firmly believe that the excellent Bible is God-inspired. I am confident that it's at least ninety-nine-point ninety-nine percent pure and correct.

However, some subjects are more complicated than others, and the problem of understanding is usually due to a lack of clarity. I am sure you'll understand what I am saying if you study the Bible regularly because it does have some hard-to-understand subjects.

As for myself, I study the bible regularly, and I do not believe the perfect and righteous Ten Commandments of God lack any clarity. Their simplicity means the Ten Commandments are easy to understand, and God didn't want anyone to doubt the definition of His Commandments.

Therefore, the excellent and perfect Ten Commandments of God deserve more attention than any other subject in the Bible, and to illustrate their importance, they were given to humankind under extraordinary circumstances that cannot be forgotten.

I assure you that the excellent Ten Commandments of God are perfect in every word; they are the conclusion to the whole matter and are words of iron. Positively, I conclude His beautiful commandments are unrustable iron and will not rust with time.

Furthermore, all Bible subjects are entwined with obedience or disobedience to the required Ten Commandments of God. I want you to know it took a brilliant designer to braid obedience and disobedience to ten individual Commandments.

The excellent Ten Commandments of God, incredible and superior to all other words written by any man, are the hinge pin on everything concerning every matter judged between righteousness and unrighteousness. We will be judged someday, after the death of our flesh and blood body, and our souls will hang on the balancing scales and be weighed by righteous or unrighteous works.

I assure you, this personal analogy story I am calling My Bible Analogy entwines the meat of Christianity and words of iron from the Heavens above. I want you to know an equation, to be exact: the meat of Christianity and iron words originate from God.

I guarantee you, and you do need to know, that the excellent God-inspired bible emphasizes the Ten Commandments of God more than anything else, especially anything I can say about the perfect word of God. The God-Inspired Bible is a gift to you and me, like a key He designed to open the Pearl gates in Heaven.

My analogies of how I perceive the Bible may not be perfect since I am a flesh and blood man. However, I guarantee you that the excellent word of God and His character are perfect, and for this reason, God is our model person; we should try to emulate Him daily.

Conclusively, we all make analogies concerning the meaning of the word of God, and it's better to make analogies than not. Mainly because God wants us to illustrate a hungry interest in His gospel, analyze His word, and do it to the best of our knowledge.

Therefore, a person not interested in making any analogies isn't showing enough interest in the required word of God, and I am pretty sure the beautiful Holy Ghost doesn't help the person uninterested in reading His road map to Heaven.

However, let's make our analogies through study and base them on the perfect word of God and not conform to the traditions of men. If we do this practice, the incredible Holy Ghost of God will gladly help us with our analogies.

CHAPTER NINE
AN OPEN CLAIM

This profound story, which I call an open claim, reveals a characteristic of loyal believers and represents how we should feel after seeing the light. After we realize that living in the light of a higher power is the only righteous and safe place to stand, we are ready to change directions and live the rest of our lives for the Lord.

An open claim means we aren't hiding our feelings from anyone, we've decided to be bold in the Lord, and we aren't ashamed to be thankful for our calling out of sin. It's certain; we should be glad our loving God called us out of our sinful lifestyle and gave us a chance to be a new person in Christ.

An open claim means our endeavors have shifted toward godliness, and the righteous gospel of God has replaced our desires for the ungodly pleasures of this world. Now that our hearts have embraced godliness as our priority, an open claim means we hate sin, have a new heart, and desire a fresh start in life.

Furthermore, if we are ashamed of the gospel of God and aren't faithful enough to openly declare our thankfulness, then sadly, I must say, we aren't where we need to be with God. Furthermore, His Son will be ashamed of us after our life in the flesh expires, and we stand before His Father in Heaven.

The following warning scripture is a revelation to remember and will help decide our future destiny. It concerns our loyalty to the Son of God and reveals Jesus Christ's thoughts concerning an open claim and being ashamed of Him. I assure you that being ashamed of Him is a terrible mistake we must account for someday.

Mark 8:38 Whosoever shall be ashamed of Me and My words in this adulterous and sinful generation; of him also shall the Son of man be ashamed, when <u>He</u> (Jesus) cometh in the glory of His Father with the holy angels.

In all honesty and absolute correctness, we cannot claim the gift of salvation unless we can proclaim Christ openly before all men. Truly, an open claim illustrates the number one characteristic proving we love the Son of God and believe in His excellent word.

Therefore, being ashamed to make an open claim means we aren't ready to let go of an ungodly lifestyle, and our hearts haven't entirely accepted the required word of God. Sadly, the being ashamed analogy means we haven't claimed Him as the righteous light in this dark and corrupt world.

Indeed, I want you to know that the open claim analogy doesn't have a middle ground. I assure you that no one is privileged to straddle the fence between a genuine claim and being ashamed of God and can pass by the Mediator in Heaven, and we are openly proud of God or ashamed of claiming God.

In the above scripture, the outstanding Son of God talks about returning to this Earth with the holy angels from Heaven. I believe He's talking about the end of the tribulation and Judgment time, and if we are wise, we'll fill our lamps with oil and look for His return.

I assure you that the holy angels have a job to accomplish, and they will separate the wheat from the tares. The tares will be bundled by the reaper angels and burned in the fire, and one of the reasons is that they lived precariously and refused to make an open claim.

Therefore, because the above declaration scripture is entwined with Judgement Time, I can expand on the definition of wheat and tares and their different character profiles. Maybe detecting their profile is as simple as understanding the mark of the beast or the seal of God.

Indeed, the wheat is symbolic of openly proud Christians who aren't ashamed of God and the beautiful word of God. However, the tares symbolize ashamed people who are too embarrassed to acknowledge God openly and proudly claim Him as their only God.

The tares are ashamed people who are too embarrassed and too liberal and will not put the word of God first in their lives, and when the Son of God returns in all His glory, the angels from Heaven accompany him. Then prophecy will come true, and the tares and the wheat will be divided and go in separate directions.

The Son of God clarifies in the above scripture that He'll be ashamed of the wicked tares and not accept them in His kingdom. This truth means the tares aren't His children, and He'll let the reaper angels mow them down, similar to wild grass cut with a sickle in an overgrown field.

CHAPTER TEN
TAKING A CLOSER LOOK

This declaration story, *Taking A Closer Look At The Word Of God*, requires our full attention, and it's meant to portray a closer look at our stomping grounds, concrete streets, and the rebels of society and reveal who mostly rules this unstable world.

Indeed, if we are willing to take a closer look and put the cruel and ungodly dictator nations on one side of the balancing scale and all the free nations on the other, then we analyze who controls this place we call Earth.

Then, I am pretty sure that the free nations would be like feathers on their side of the balancing scales, and the dictator nations would be heavy on their side. This truth means cruel dictators who control their nation by the threat of life and death wield a lot of control in this world, and democracy cannot be a part of our lives without fighting for it.

Beyond the shadow of a doubt, it's easy to conclude that there's quite an imbalance between the ratio of free and dictator-controlled nations. As much as I hate to admit it, a closer look reveals the imbalance favors the dictator nations.

This truth means all free nations better stay on guard, lest a wicked and robust dictator nation sees an advantage and conquers the free country. For this reason, I firmly warn you that strong dictator nations always exploit the weaker prey.

Beyond the shadow of a doubt, the evil and murderous Lucifer, the prince of this world, is the influence behind a cruel dictator, and he's a brutal dictator himself. Indeed, I assure you, even in a free nation, Lucifer controls the liberal and ungodly person.

This truth means a divided free nation cannot stand, and a free country's division is inevitable because of immoral liberal equality. I am pretty sure the definition of liberal equality amounts to Lucifer-influenced equality.

Liberal equality boils up within the bad seed, and the liberals care more about special rights than their free nation. I assure you it's shameful and disrespectful to God, and it's not wise to give liberal equality equal rights with God-designated things.

I assure you that God designed things; whatsoever they are, God created them, and they should supersede liberal equality in this world since planet Earth is a creation made by our Creator God. Furthermore, I want you to know it's the whole duty of man to live by God-designed things.

Within this struggling world today, an ongoing war never ends, and it's always the same scenario with the good seed defending itself against the evil source. I am sure that defending themselves is necessary for the good seed, or the wicked seed would terminate the believers in Christ.

A closer look reveals the evil seed, the ungodly liberals, as the root of all the troubles and violence on this Earth. If we look closely, we will see the love of money and the power attached to great wealth as the root of most conflicts and corruption.

A closer look reveals the bad seed as the cruel murderers and the ungodly people turned over to a reprobate mind. I want you to know the corridors of time have proven the bad seed is the thieves, the coveters, and the uncompassionate people on this Earth.

Suppose we could put the material treasures on this Earth in one pile belonging to the bad seed. Then we could put the treasures on this Earth in another, belonging to the excellent moral source, and then we could compare the amounts owned by the good and the bad seed.

Then, the pile of treasures belonging to the bad seed would probably be much more than the wealth belonging to the good moral source. I am sure wicked men love money much more than good men do, and corrupt men will murder for the love of money.

Beyond the shadow of a doubt, everyone living in this world, including both seeds, desires a comfortable nest egg and some savings for a rainy day. However, it's the bad seed that cannot get enough because they love money much more than they love the ways of God.

This true story, *Taking A Closer Look*, reveals that many insincere men and women will claim to love God, and if it benefits them among people, they'll say the right words with their mouths. However, sadly, I must say, conversion to the new person in Christ eludes them.

However, as much as I would like to think differently, I conclude that most men and women only know a little about Him and His everyday expectations concerning you and me. Sadly, most people fail to understand the honorable characteristics He expects us to illustrate among our fellow people.

I am sure everyone's heard about our Great Creator God, and knowing His name is enough information for the bad seed. The majority are spiritually blind and aren't concerned about honoring the God of Heaven and Earth and His designed character-building rules.

However, knowing His name doesn't mean we know Him; knowing He's the Supreme God isn't significant enough. For this reason, this encouragement story I call *Taking A Closer Look* advises everyone to protect their souls; please look closely at the word of God.

I assure you that the excellent word of God needs to be studied and followed like a road map to save your soul. The word of God provides the ultimate information concerning most things, regardless of whether they are good qualities or bad things.

The excellent teaching word of God divides the good seed from the bad seed. For identification, the word of God also divides everyone called into nobility from whosoever isn't called into the family of nobility.

Furthermore, taking a closer look is good advice concerning everything we do in this life and every decision we make. However, a carefree attitude reveals the characteristics of an unconcerned mind. Sadly, I must say, indifferent people usually fail to see the big picture, and they do not realize they are being evaluated for entrance into the Kingdom of God.

Whether unconcerned people are good or bad or believe in Christ or not in the Son of God doesn't matter because indifferent people never take a closer look, even concerning the essential salvation requirements.

Positively, a closer look is the formula for a personal defense mechanism, and not taking a closer look reveals a recipe for disaster. And sooner or later, no closer look at the word of God will result in a soul-crushing disaster.

CHAPTER ELEVEN
FILLED WITH WISDOM

This dedication story, *Filled With Wisdom*, is designed to recognize superior work to benefit humanity throughout the portals of time. This awareness story illuminates and recognizes a beautiful accomplishment in this crude world, surpassing all other literary works since the beginning of time.

Even though it's taken a lot of time and many generations and devout men of God to fulfill this incredible accomplishment. This recognition story isn't about them or the effort they made and died to advance. However, it's about a finished work they contributed to in some way or another.

This extraordinary and beneficial miracle accomplishment isn't about any person. However, it's about our precious Bible, and because it's the will of God, our necessary Bible reveals a divine history full of supernatural accomplishments.

Positively created for our benefit, our beautiful Bible became filled with our Almighty God's wisdom, and His knowledge is pure, undefiled, and exceptional, and we need to understand our Bible. Otherwise, our lifestyle and the ability to be a gentleman will not improve, and we'll remain crude individuals all our lives.

Our excellent Bible warns us of evil and ungodly ways men shouldn't consider doing, and it tells us about the Ancient of Days, the Ancient One, and our future destiny. Truly, we will learn about our great God if we are concerned for our soul and its last habitation place.

Our Bible tells us about spirit creations, places called Heaven and Hell, life and death, and what happens to all of us after the end of our flesh. We are foolish if we do not seek to understand these essential things coinciding with our lives, and because the God of Heaven and Earth loves us, He gave us a weapon to satisfy and protect our souls.

The outstanding and excellent Bible is a unique, one-of-a-kind book, much different and more personal than all other books. I guarantee you no other book in this crude world compares to our God-inspired Bible, which represents God's image and everything He represents.

The beautiful Bible tells us about a pure and undefiled God, perfect in every way, and it tells us about a corrupt and wicked devil. If we are wise and care about our soul, you, me, and everyone else should seek to know their many character differences.

The informative Bible tells us about the wheat growing in the field, and the Bible says the Wheat is symbolic of the loyal children of God. I assure you God's hot and on-fire children always seek to know all they can learn about their Supreme Creator God.

The excellent Bible tells us about the tares growing in the field, and the bible says the tares are symbolic of the wicked children of

Lucifer. Sadly, the children of the evil Lucifer aren't interested in knowing the commanded word of God or walking on a righteous path.

For the protection of our soul, the Bible tells us about two prophesized destination places where the believers and the unbelievers go after the death of their flesh. The believers believe in these two different places, and the unbelievers do not.

Even though it's pretty apparent, the wheat and the tares are growing together in the same field now, and man cannot separate them. But I assure you, a division will occur sometime in the future, and it'll take a Supernatural God to separate the tares from the wheat.

Indeed, there's a coming time in the future when the holy angels of God who live in Heaven, called the reapers, during the end time. They'll come down from the sky above, glorious and more muscular than man, and will have a sharp sickle in their hand and a severe separation job to do upon the Earth.

The reapers will separate the tares from the wheat to benefit everlasting peace, and they'll bundle and burn the tares, and evil and wickedness will cease on the Earth. After final judgment, it'll be a good day for the wheat and a bad day for the tares.

The Bible makes it extremely clear concerning the destiny of the children of God, and I want you to know that the peaceful children of God will not have to spend eternity with the wicked children of Lucifer. This wonderful truth is why the mighty reaper angels will separate the wheat from the tares.

I assure you that not spending eternity with the wicked tares is good news for everyone if they love the righteous word of God and hate ungodliness of all sorts. Because I understand the Bible,

I am sure the beautiful King in the kingdom of God will restrict every form of ungodliness.

However, this is terrible news for the wicked person because the kingdom of God is a luxurious place, and the pits of Hell are hideous for the soul. Indeed, corrupt people and evil angels will be the residents locked away in the recesses of Hell until they are judged by God and burned in the lake of fire.

Furthermore, these serious things I am telling you concerning Heaven, Hell, and Judgement are easy to understand if we read our Bible and learn about them. However, learning about them must be our heart's desire, or we'll not study our Bible and know about them.

Indeed, I hope you realize how much God wants to protect our souls. Our excellent Bible is our information center from our Creator God. The Bible and its commandments define nearly everything considered righteous and unrighteous to teach the right way.

Beyond the shadow of a doubt, all believers firmly believe that our Supreme Supernatural God created everything we see with our eyes. I want you to know He's the beautiful Creator of our excellent Bible, and we should enjoy every word written within it.

Positively, God has methodically poured His heart into the Bible and revealed all the details of His expectations concerning us and our lifestyle on Earth. I guarantee you that our precious Bible should be considered an extension of the thoughts of His wonderful heart.

Mainly because our incredible Bible speaks chapter after chapter and verse after verse from the heart of God, and if we give it much consideration, it's easy to conclude that it took a lot of effort to make the God-inspired Bible a finished accomplishment.

I assure you that if we want to know the secrets and the mysteries locked away inside the heart of God and be one of His friends, we must submit ourselves to His word before we are ready to live in the next life. Truly, all we have to do is read our Bible and consider it a letter of love; He's written to all His children living on this Earth.

I guarantee His beautiful Bible is wisdom-filled, exceedingly excellent, valuable, and desperately needed. It will fill our hearts with the necessary knowledge to secure the gift of immortality, and His righteous knowledge is a gift from a super-smart heavenly God.

I want you to know that we are equal flesh and blood people in the eyes of our Supreme God, and the wonderful word of God tells us that He illustrates no favoritism for certain people. No partiality of persons means He shows no difference between people or races.

However, I want you to realize the truth about God and know that everyone who is dedicated to God and living by His required ways that He favors with divine blessings and protection. These loyal followers are His select people, and He values them exceedingly greatly because they are dedicated and loyal to Him.

This acknowledgment of the Bible story, monumentally essential to understand, I call *Filled With Wisdom*. It's also a testimonial story dedicated to God's written word, and because of my love for His word, I sincerely declare that His word is my best friend.

Positively, I want you to know that our God-inspired Bible can erase myths and half-truths and increase our understanding of His expectations by many folds. Indeed, the God-inspired Bible is a myth-buster, a dream enhancer, and the most helpful book ever written to benefit humanity.

The Bible is the book of God, the road map leading into His kingdom, revealing the rules of a righteous designer. Without the bible to study, all the people living on this Earth would probably be living ungodly, and they probably wouldn't know any better, and that's a fact of life.

Conclusively, every person fortunate enough to own a God-inspired Bible should treat it like one of their most prized possessions because the beautiful bible is precious, a prized possession, and a soul-saving book for whoever desires to live forever.

I assure you that silver and gold aren't as valuable as our excellent Bible, and the information written within it exceeds the intelligence of flesh and blood men. Indeed, on Judgment Day, I would rather stand before God and have a Bible in my hand than have a pocket full of money.

CHAPTER TWELVE
THE WORD OF GOD VERSUS SPINACH

I call This meaningful story, *The Word Of God Versus Spinach,* an illustrated metaphor story designed upon the foundation of truth. Because it's unnecessary, no Bible scriptures are used to prove anything in this story. However, the characteristics of a character are evaluated, and simple logic is the foundation for this story.

I assure you that loving spinach or hating spinach compares with the analogy of loving the gospel of God or hating the word of God. Even though spinach doesn't correlate with the word of God, the concept I will reveal to you does compare, and our likes and dislikes will be illuminated by the word of God and the spinach analogy.

Positively, I am one hundred percent sure understanding the wonderful God-inspired word of Yehovah is extremely important, and I guarantee you that understanding His commanded word has benefits attached, much more than eating spinach.

I assure you that understanding the perfect word of God

makes us wiser about what's right and wrong and what's holy and unholy, according to our divine Creator God. I want you to realize our Creator is in charge of judging everyone and all the angels in Heaven and on this Earth.

Beyond the shadow of a doubt, possessing wisdom about the requirements for salvation will benefit us on Judgment Day more than any other type of wisdom, and it will take study time to fall in love with His word. Truly, searching through the scriptures for His excellent commands illustrates our magnetic pull toward His wonderful word.

However, we must apply what we learn about the word of God to our lifestyle because there are requirements for salvation. His commandments are excellent character-building requirements, and the infallible conditions He requires from us prove that God wants us to develop a good character.

Furthermore, I want you to realize a monumental piece of advice: Know that no person should stand before our great Creator God and be Bible ignorant. Positively, we are foolish to stand before Him unlearned and unsaved while our Supreme God decides our eternal fate.

On Judgment Day, our character and the lifestyle we record during the days of our lives will matter immensely more than anything else. I want you to know that during our judgment time before His throne, we will wish we had supported our Creator God to the utmost.

I want you to realize a fact before your breath of life ends: The lifestyle we choose to live will be scrutinized by the word of God concerning where the soul goes after the flesh's death. For this reason, I am warning you we only have a limited time to remove ungodliness from our lifestyle.

Therefore, regardless of how little concern some men living in the flesh show for their souls or care about the place they'll call home in the next life. Nothing will deter judgment from above; judgment will be based on the word of God, and we'll be judged by the things written in the sacred book of life.

The important heavenly book of life contains a complete record of you and me, and the secrets of our lives will be open on Judgement Day. Truly, the creation of such a miracle book proves that we are seen from Heaven and monitored while living in the flesh every minute of every day. I am telling you, it's not Santa Claus watching to see if we are naughty or nice.

Indeed, if we are concerned about winning the grand prize of immortality, our soul should be given excellent protection, even more so than our life in the flesh. Lest our soul ends up in the pits of Hell because we didn't show enough concern and care for the place, it ends its journey in the afterlife.

Positively, the perfect word of God, including the Authoritative judging Ten Commandments, is the armor and the shield of protection for our eternal soul. However, it's up to you and me to wear our shield of protection and utilize its benefits to secure our future in the Kingdom of God.

It should be pretty apparent to everyone; we have the choice of caring about where our soul goes or not about where our soul goes. We should consider this choice about our future residency before the Son of God opens the important judgment book of life in Heaven.

I assure you, and you shouldn't have to be told by me, it's a terrible shame to waste our life on the sinful ways of this world.

Especially when we know we have a date with judgment, and Lucifer's evil ways will destroy our souls and erase you and me from long-term existence.

Furthermore, please be aware that the gift of salvation isn't automatic. Please make no mistake or imagine wrongly that the sinful ways of this world will destroy our ability to live forever. This truth means we better be determined to fight against the temptation to sin daily for the rest of our lives.

Positively, acts of sin are dream killers, and choosing to live in sin isn't any different than saying no to the offer of immortality. However, we have a choice, and we can decide to be fruitful men and women on this Earth, or we can be fruitless and barren and die a lost person.

Indeed, if I tell you, a pattern can be established, illustrating the direction of our lives, and I tell you the way of our life is an indicator based on the word of God and the desires of our hearts. Then, I am saying men and women who are in love with the word of God, who believe it's essential, and try to live by it, decision after decision.

They are wise and fruitful men and women who show concern for preserving their souls. Their love for the word of God means that protecting their inner spirit matters to them, which is the conclusion the wise person learns and doesn't forget.

However, the unfruitful and bible illiterate men and women living in this unstable world are destroying and wasting their eternal souls because they will not allow the God of Heaven and Earth to be their Councilor, Savior, and protector of their souls.

God's excellent and revealing word indicates a specific detail, a severe warning concerning all acts of sin. The explicit warning never changes, and it tells us that the works of evil and darkness are wasteful and fruitless, and the results of living sinful will destroy the soul.

Still yet, as illogical as it is to sin, and as Bible ignorant as it is to sin, and as foolish as it is to oppose the wisdom of my Creator God. Most worldly people do not seem overly concerned about where their soul goes after their flesh's death.

Anyway, no long-term pleasure in committing any sin is worth more than preserving our soul and extending its life forever. However, short-time sinful pleasures, or anything gained through acts of corruption, will not compare to everlasting life in the kingdom of God.

Indeed, for an example to consider when a concerned professing Christian tells most sinners your soul is at stake in this game of life. Then, it's a truthful warning from a concerned heart about your soul, and I firmly assure you that committing acts of sin puts our souls in danger.

However, as illogical and complicated as it is to believe, most sinner people aren't affected by those honest and meaningful words of warning. Sadly, this critical warning means that some sinners do not want to change and aren't showing enough concern for their souls.

Anyway, I assure you that all concerned Christians must warn sinners about the consequences of losing their souls. Truly, I am one hundred percent sure that we Christians are doing God's will simply by being His voice, crying out to the lost, and asking them to change and claim Christ as their Savior.

Positively, I want you to know that all sinners traveling upon the bi-ways of life need to be worried about their future habitation place. They must be warned about judgment based on God's required word, and no one escapes from the All-Mighty Judge.

Positively, it defies logic not to believe in the afterlife and not care about protecting and preserving our souls, especially since some souls will be destroyed permanently because of unrepented acts of sin and rebellion against His required ways of life.

However, you and I have limited influence, and we cannot force anyone to pick up the cross and love the beautiful gospel of God if they do not want to. Nor can our will for them be dominant over their will, and we cannot force the lukewarm and the cold person to be hot and on fire for the perfect word of God.

Therefore, an illustrative metaphor, as accurate as anyone's analogy, uses God's word and spinach. A person's will is like forcing your children to eat spinach when they do not want it, and when they eat spinach, they are forced to eat they still dislike it.

Positively, this analogy means you and I can only enjoy eating spinach if we like it, and it's the same way with the word of God. Some people will not enjoy His gospel because the cold and lukewarm people listen to their hearts, and we cannot force them to be hot and on fire for His gospel.

Therefore, regardless of our concern for the lost person, their concern matters the most. Therefore, the analogy of spinach versus God's word is the same because we cannot force someone to love the word of God if they do not want to enjoy it.

This truth means that regardless of how much danger the soul is in because of acts of sin, we cannot force an ungodly person to love our Creator God. Truly, we are shortsighted; if we wrongly believe, we can instill love in an unloving heart.

Therefore, I wholeheartedly conclude that the inability to love the word of God is a terrible flaw, and it must be our heart's fault since our heart's reigns guide our thoughts. Furthermore, I am confident that the nature of our hearts decides all our feelings for God.

Beyond the shadow of a doubt, the old saying is true, and the old saying means we can lead a horse to water, but we cannot make the horse drink the water—no more than you, and I can force a kid to like spinach if the kid doesn't like spinach.

This truth means we have no control over the other person's heart, and everyone has a mind of their own, the same way we do. Put yourself in the sinner's shoes and imagine a reverse scenario; consider the unbelievers trying to convince us not to love God and us being the horse refusing to drink the water, and then our understanding of their unwillingness to change will increase. Undoubtedly, the heart has a mind of its own, and the rebellious heart parallels the stubborn man and woman refusing to accept the gospel of God.

Chapter Thirteen
THE INSTINCT OF THE HEART

Our incredible Creator God, alias the outstanding Potter Man in Heaven, knew us from the foundation of this Earth. Because He's immortal, He has the advantage of long-term memory. However, because of the way He designed us, we cannot remember beyond life in the flesh.

Therefore, I want you to realize that knowing us from the foundation of this Earth means we've been alive for thousands of years, and I firmly believe that we were untested heavenly creations before we became flesh and blood Earth creations.

However, when our mother's water broke, immortality put on mortality, and the memory of our former life was erased. This truth means that regardless of our image during our stay in Heaven, it's easy to conclude that an incredible body transformation has occurred.

Positively, at a specific time decided by God, our spirit was sent to this Earth and reborn through the womb of a flesh-and-blood woman. Because of our transformation from an angel to a human, all our trials and temptations mean we'll be tested and tried in this jungle world until we return to our Creator, God.

Indeed, while we live on this Earth, our invisible spirit is embodied inside a transformed form of dirt. A precise observation proves that this Earth is our new environment until the day the flesh dies, and after that, our spirit moves onward to another place.

This planet Earth is more or less a challenging place, where we are void and disconnected from the intellect and the memory of our past. I assure you, a forgotten memory of former things is the will of the Supreme Supernatural God concerning me and everyone else.

Therefore, we were born without former knowledge from above and did not know we were immortals in a previous lifetime. This change leaves us with the instinct to follow our heart and hope; our intuition leads us back to God and the place we were in the beginning.

Indeed, when we feel a desire pulling us toward the word of God, we cannot understand what is tugging at our hearts. Then it's probably the Heart's instinct, pulling us back to the beautiful God we've always loved, even from a former lifetime.

Beyond the shadow of a doubt, the beginning of our lives was newborn babes born without intellect, and testing ground Earth is crucial to everyone's understanding and much-needed discipline. I guarantee you; if our Creator God wants us here for a short while, then it's for the good of everyone.

I am pretty sure our Creator God knew this was the only way to reveal the true nature of a man and a woman. I believe that the actual character of our heart needs our realization, and we need to understand the ungodly temptations and characteristics we can fall prey to in this world.

Furthermore, I hope you realize this realization is because of God's blessings, and all people living on this Earth are tested and tried through the beautiful gift of free will. Therefore, regardless of good or bad, the characteristics we pick up along the way result from having free will.

On planet Earth, all people will face the reality of their character, the revelation of the image they create through free will, and what comes naturally to them. It's easy to conclude that after being given free will, the works of our hands will do as our heart desires them to do.

It appears correct to believe that some men and women instinctively and inherently choose to be moral, clean, and goodhearted. But for some unknown reason, thanks to our Creator God, choosing to live godly seems to be a built-in character quality.

However, it also seems correct to say that some men and women inherently choose to be immoral, unclean, and prone to commit various abominations. Sadly, it seems fitting to say some men and women cannot help themselves and do not know why they live the ungodly lifestyle.

Throughout our God-inspired Bible, the scriptures reveal the good and the bad, the godly and the ungodly, and paint us two opposing pictures. One picture is of good and moral men and women who wholeheartedly delight in keeping the excellent Ten Commandments of God.

However, sadly, I must say, the other picture isn't so good, and it's not a picture to admire. It's a terrible portrait; no person should be in at all, and I ask you, how could anyone delight in knowing they are indifferent to the Ten Commandments and their character's image is anti-godly?

The anti-godly character image will always be a picture of wicked and ungodly men and ungodly angels and false prophets being corrupt and guilty of practicing and teaching the traditions of men. Furthermore, the ungodly image fits whosoever isn't loyal to the word of God.

It's absolutely for sure; ungodly men and women from all walks of life are rebellious to the word of God and not interested in distinguishing between the clean and the unclean. For this reason, I am asking you, is it possible they are following the instincts of their heart?

It's also ungodly men and women with a seared conscience, guilty of refusing to distinguish between the holy, the unholy, and the profane. For this reason, I'll ask you again: Is it possible that wicked people follow the instincts of their hearts?

Positively, ungodly men and women know how to work abominations to their advantage, and it's an art form they proudly practice. Sadly, we know that wicked men and corrupt women devise evil schemes, and it's true; they do not let abominations hinder them from achieving their goals.

The wicked person looks for weak spots in the other person, and they thrive on the innocence of good people, and the love of money is one of their prime motivations. Indeed, eyesight proves that ungodly people will do terrible things to increase their prosperity.

Concerning the ways of this world, ungodly people are cunning like vipers, and they'll wait for the opportunity to strike and destroy innocent prey. Sadly, the emotion of mercy rides in the back seat and their options to corrupt people ride in the front seat.

Honestly, I am pretty sure the hot iron searing the conscience illustrates a common characteristic among those who live an ungodly lifestyle, and you and I should realize this world is full of both men and women guilty of having a seared conscience.

The searing of the conscience means that the mind and heart are deaf to the voice of the Holy Spirit, and this means that the soul is numb and uncaring about God's good ways. Sadly, I must say, once the heart is hardened, there may not be any way of reversing a seared conscience.

It could be possible; my Supernatural Creator, the God of Heaven and Earth, knew in advance some of His creations wouldn't change for the better. It's possible; Lucifer and the rebellious angels proved this analogy to my Creator God, and He knew the nature of many people would turn out to be insensitive, uncaring, uncompassionate, and unmerciful.

Therefore, our wonderful Supreme God created safeguards to detour men and women from being wicked and uncaring. For this reason, He gave us believers His righteous laws, His perfect Ten Commandments, and His chastisement.

However, there is a high probability almost all men and women might end up lost because they cannot find our Savior God of their own accord. Sadly, if the conscience is seared beyond repair, developing a new heart is improbable, and so is finding our Savior God.

Indeed, a place called Hell is waiting for ungodly men and women with seared consciences, and this means that people lacking any respect for the gospel of God or their neighbors will end their lives in the darkness of Hell. When the gates open, their spirit will be marked by the beast and called Lucifer's children

The ungodly person with a seared conscience will use insincerity as a maneuvering tool, and they'll do terrible things and deceive anyone for the love of money. For self-protection, you and I better learn the signs of the ungodly living among us and avoid the deceivers in this world.

Indeed, I suppose there are different degrees of ungodliness because of significant and small compromises. For this reason, I must warn you that the ungodly person with a seared conscience will keep climbing the ladder of corruption to compete with a higher degree of ungodliness day after day.

Furthermore, please be aware and do not believe men and women not having a seared conscience will walk the line of perfection. I firmly warn you that most people in this jungle world will do ungodly things and deceive for personal gain.

However, regardless of the degree of ungodliness we exhibit or the ungodly things we submit ourselves to daily. History proves that our wise and righteous God will let all men and women discover the many ungodly things they'll commit to doing in the flesh.

He lets us, flesh and blood creations, discover through trials and tribulations how corrupt, heady, and high-minded we can sometimes be, especially when we lack a righteous and powerful Most High God and His commandments to keep our consciences in check.

Therefore, it's a great advantage; if the instinct of the heart pulls us toward our Creator God, it inherently motivates us to love the perfect word of God. Although, it's pretty possible; if we do not inherit this instinct, we'll not feel a pulling toward our Great God.

However, it's a disadvantage if the heart's instinct is seared with a hot iron because A Hot Iron is a numbing to ungodliness tool used to destroy the conscience. If the instinct to love God isn't instilled within our hearts, then our degree of committing ungodliness will increase beyond acceptability.

Beyond the shadow of a doubt, on Judgment Day, or our day of recognition, the holy book of life will open when men and women stand before God. Indeed, the hidden will be known, and everyone will account for themselves and know their transgressions against the word of God have been recorded and saved for Judgement Day.

I am prone to believe that rose-colored glasses will not help us, and most men and women will be ashamed of themselves, some more ashamed than others. Especially after they realize they've lived a foolish lifestyle void of a godly, controlled conscience.

Indeed, on Judgment Day, all men and women will be forced to realize that none of us are perfect, that none of us have served our great Creator God to our best degree, and that we'll all be ashamed of not trying harder to live a godlier lifestyle.

Therefore, since I know the above statement is one hundred percent true, I fully conclude that a higher degree of goodness cannot be achieved unless we have discipline and entwine our conscience with the righteous gospel of God.

Beyond the shadow of a doubt, our testing upon this Earth is essential to us, and why should we believe our character doesn't need testing? Our testing will reveal our godly and our ungodly way of thinking, and so you'll know we'll be resurrected on the other side of death, an open book.

Our testing intends to illuminate our flaws and reveal how lacking and the small amount of love we truly have for one another in this cruel world. Especially when we are left to our own devices and are untrained and not taught the importance of the righteous word of God.

Without a doubt, our nature is primarily carnal, but our hearts can change the same way our age varies if we genuinely desire to be a changed person. Truly, if we see the light shining from the Heavens above, we better step into the light and stay within the light shining from Heaven.

It's one hundred percent for sure; everyone on this Earth has a destiny, regardless of age or lifestyle. Sooner or later, we will meet our Great Creator God face to face, regardless of whether or not we fulfill our destiny to His commanded specifications.

Positively, we all have a one-way ticket out of this world, but most of us cannot cash in until we walk through the arena of life. This truth means we better learn about God before it's too late, and to save our souls, we better teach ourselves to live by the perfect ways of the Lord.

Furthermore, I strongly advise you to try hard to be a winner of immortality and not be a loser who will receive the condemnation of damnation. I want you to know walking outside the light of God coincides with receiving the judgment of condemnation and, eventually, damnation.

I suppose believers and unbelievers have instincts of the heart, but their instincts are as different as positive and negative. It could be true that the heart's instincts have more control over our actions than we can imagine, and who among us could say our heart lacks instincts?

Our instincts may be significantly affected by how obedient, rebellious, close, or distant we were to our Creator God in our previous life. Unbeknownst to most of us, we did live a previous life and knew our great God from before.

Our previous life, our limited memory cannot recall, entails another time when we were living in Heaven when we knew Him or during the wicked first Earth age, before the excellent cleansing flood. Because the corridors of time are a mystery to us, we likely knew our great God at least two times before this life.

As for myself, I do not know if more testing, trials, and temptations can overcome the heart's instinct. However, I firmly believe that inherently, the soul loves God, or the heart doesn't love God, but I am confident that our heart will not feel something it doesn't want to feel.

Therefore, this story reflects my opinion, and I firmly believe that the instincts of the heart are more in control of our lifestyle than men and women might imagine, one way or the other. I firmly believe the instincts we inherited from a previous time could be one of the reasons this Earth is so diverse.

However, I know that if the heart instinct doesn't feel the pull to love God inherently, we may be unable to carry the cross back home to the special place where our spirit began its journey.

Indeed, I hope you walk in the light all the rest of your life and instinctively find your way back home to God and the place where you belong. After all, Heaven is the original place of birth and the beginning of your existence.

CHAPTER FOURTEEN
RATTLE SNAKE OR DEMON

I was fourteen years old and living in the coal fields in Pond Fork, West Virginia, when this personal story happened. Squirrel season was beginning the next day, and for an odd reason, my best friend and I were pretty excited. We wanted to miss school and go squirrel hunting, and our reasoning was illogical.

We'd talked to our parents several days before and hoped to receive their permission to hunt squirrels. However, we weren't successful, and neither of us seceded in getting permission to miss school and go squirrel hunting in the woods.

For the above reason, I am not proud to admit it, and I sincerely regret skipping school. However, my friend and I devised a foolish plan of our own, and during the day before squirrel season began, our not-so-wise plan to hunt squirrels went into action.

My friend and I secretly packed our hunting clothes in a plastic bag, and we took our shotguns and carried them across the shallow creek. While on the other side of the creek, we picked a good hiding place and covered our hunting gear under the leaves.

The following day, we rose at our regular time, as if we were going to school, and we arranged to meet at the bus stop. However, we didn't catch the big yellow bus, and we didn't go to school. Although, we were exuberant and looking forward to the day ahead.

Positively, we took off our shoes, waded across the creek, and uncovered our hunting clothes and shotguns on the other side. Then, up into the mountains, we journeyed hunting squirrels. We planned a long day and expected to have fun wandering the hillside.

I can remember that particular day well and will not forget it. It was a beautiful, picturesque morning. The sun rose slowly, breaking through the trees and piercing through a dense mist like millions of bright arrows raining out of Heaven.

Indeed, I remember thinking about how different nature looked during this early morning time in the mountains. The morning sunshine lifted the dew off the ground, creating a dense mist that rose above the trees. My friend and I, happy to be in the woods, were walking up a narrow path.

I was in front, and we were going toward a special place called the brown possum farm near the top of the mountain. However, about halfway to the top of the mountain, a dead tree had fallen across our path, leaves and tree limbs cluttered the ground.

I crossed the clutter of dead tree limbs first, and my friend behind me screamed snake, snake, and I hadn't seen the snake. However, I knew for sure that I was close to the snake, and immediately, I was afraid. I turned around and swiftly ran back toward my friend, and my heart was beating fast with fear.

When I returned to where my friend stood, he saw my fright

and started laughing as if it was funny to see me frightened by the rattlesnake. Because he was laughing, I thought he was playing a mean joke on me and was trying to frighten me.

I got mad at him, and I didn't appreciate being frightened, and I said, why did you scare me by screaming snake, snake when there wasn't a snake? My laughing friend replied, Paul, you walked over the top of a fat and long stretched-out rattlesnake lying in the path.

Furthermore, my good friend said, when I screamed snake, snake, you turned around and crossed back over it. I didn't believe him because I didn't hear the snake rattle, nor did I think I could cross over a fierce rattlesnake twice and not see it.

Indeed, we eased back up the path to see if it was still there, and it was still there, all stretched out and not moving, and for sure, it was a giant rattlesnake. I raised my 410-gauge shotgun slowly; I cocked the hammer, carefully aimed, and pulled the trigger.

Positively, the angry rattlesnake's reaction to the shotgun blast was more frightening than walking across it twice, and nothing could be More Terrifying than walking across and shooting the snake. However, I want you to know that both these incidents with the rattlesnake were equally scary.

However, what occurred next was unexpected, sending my heart speeding toward the red line. I have to say, this was the giant, maddest, and liveliest rattlesnake I've ever seen in my entire lifetime, and I've seen many giant rattlesnakes.

Immediately after pulling the trigger on my 410-gauge shotgun, I knew buckshot had hit the rattlesnake, and I wasn't ready for what happened next. I stood there frozen in fear, and it happened within a few feet of my face. Because the airborne snake was close, so I thought the giant rattlesnake would fall and land on my head. Truly, I never moved one muscle until the plight of an injured rattlesnake was over.

Indeed, I remember how the enormous angry rattlesnake I shot with buckshot came furiously alive. I want you to know that it had awkward, lightning-fast movements as it rose into the air, before my eyes, above my head, and extremely close to my face.

I am sure I could've reached my hand out and touched it if I had been courageous enough to attempt touching the giant rattlesnake. However, I didn't feel so brave at this life-and-death moment, high in the mountains and far from home.

I didn't know a fierce rattlesnake could exceed its audible boundaries and exhibit frightening sounds of distress mixed with the sound of anger. I assure you, I've never heard any snake make sounds like this injured rattlesnake made as if screaming in pain.

However, I want to reveal an unusual mystery: This injured rattlesnake swiftly rose into the air, extremely close to my eyes. It was making a weird noise piercingly loud, thrashing wildly, and rattling furiously simultaneously.

It was a hurt rattlesnake in distress and mad as a demon from Hell, and the odd thing about the incident was it never fell back down. However, this injured rattlesnake kept rising slowly into the air and thrashing wildly before my eyes, and within two or three feet of my face, I was witnessing my potential life-and-death moment.

I assure you I didn't kill the first squirrel that day in the mountains, but I had the feeling I had shot something evil, who was a natural-born killer. I believe this natural-born killer was placed in my path to kill me, and I firmly believe it was a demon-possessed rattlesnake. I am sure the odds of me being alive today and writing this story are astronomical.

I hope and pray you'll be spared life and death situations and never have to fight with the powers of darkness the way I have during my lifetime. I hope you'll never have to experience the many dangerous situations I've encountered throughout my adventurous years of living.

Indeed, a demon-possessed timber rattler carries much poison, and I was caught in a dangerous situation. I am confident that I would've died from the venom of the snake bite before I could get medical attention in the valley below had the rattlesnake bitten me.

Imagine my plight being much worse if I had stepped on the rattlesnake instead of crossing over it, and if I did step on it, I probably wouldn't be writing this story. On that dangerous day in the mountains, you could say I was a lucky boy or the merciful God of Heaven and Earth was watching over me.

Beyond the shadow of a doubt, I know the odds were against me crossing over the colossal rattlesnake twice and not being bitten. Furthermore, I firmly believe the odds are even more incredible that I didn't step on the rattlesnake, as I crossed it twice.

Positively, I believe a higher power was watching over me and ensuring I would live another day to fulfill my odyssey. Truly, I know I owe my life to God, and I will repay Him by writing the most incredible collection of Bible stories ever written by anyone.

Furthermore, if you have doubt and do not believe, an invisible demon spirit could enter into a rattlesnake and possess it. Then, consider the times of Jesus and the traitorous Judas Iscariot being possessed by Lucifer and the possessed people He delivered from demon spirits.

I assure you, the wonderful New Testament bible stories prove that demon spirits and the evil spirit of Lucifer enter into and possess certain people. I am sure because animals and humans are flesh, evil spirits will enter animals and us if we let our armor down.

Indeed, Lucifer's spirit is a fierce hunter, and he cannot kill with physical strength. But he does take control of unclean people and animals, and through them, he conquers and destroys. I want you to realize in the Garden of God in Eden, Lucifer was and still is the Snake of Old.

CHAPTER FIFTEEN
THE ANCIENT ONE

From the beginning of time, possibly billions of years ago, during the time of the angels, and even so in Heaven, during the First Earth Age, and within this Second Earth Age, including every second we live and breathe as time marches forward without interruption.

The great and marvelous righteous God of Israel, exceedingly excellent and wiser than all men, never changes His point of view concerning the order of things. I want you to know that His order of things is infallible and designed to be perfect, and He's the pinnacle of wisdom, and achieving perfect righteousness is His goal.

His unflawed character and righteous point of view concerning our character and lifestyle are still the same today as they were at the beginning of time or since the creation of angels, men, and women. Achieving a Christ-like status means we've learned to conform to His ways.

Positively, He's the Ancient of Days and the Potter Man of

all living flesh and shapes our future in many ways. Sometimes, we haven't a clue concerning the reason; the clay we are made from shapes a new way, but the clay gains strength and becomes stronger with whoever pleases Him.

I assure you that the passage of time hasn't changed His expectations concerning His creations of clay, and He still expects us to live righteously and not be rebellious to His written word, designed to create ladies and gentlemen out of forms of clay.

Indeed, He's our brilliant Creator God, and why should He expect otherwise, and why should we want to do otherwise? Therefore, I am asking you, what's the purpose of having a righteous God if He doesn't expect His created people to uphold righteousness?

I want you to know the exact or only reason why I call Him the Ancient of Days or the Ancient One. Because He was alone initially, there weren't any creations before Him, and His age is unknown. For this reason, He's called the Ancient One.

In His ultimate wisdom, He doesn't have to rethink things or change anything He decreed or commanded in the past. Because His superior knowledge is without flaw or mistake, and because He wants to perfect our character, you and I are expected to emulate Him the best we can.

I assure you, and I am sincerely proud to say, He's a perfect and excellent Supernatural God, and no evil devil, angel, or flesh and blood person compares to Him. We should take His commanded word exceptionally seriously and entwine it to all our decisions.

He's our Creator, and His superior wisdom accumulated through billions of years of experience; He gladly shares with you, me, and everyone else. His kindness illustrates the knowledge of a

Creator God, and we are silly to challenge or oppose the reason for any of His excellent decrees.

Furthermore, I guarantee my God is responsible for creating the Heavens, Earth, and all living things. Whether they are in the sea, on the land, or flying through the air, we could correctly say this Earth is His Garden Place. Bible history tells us He planted a garden, and from that point forward, living things fertilized themselves.

Positively, when He declares certain things or animals are unclean, unfit, or an abomination. Then, His decree is absolute, and He's never wrong, and who are we to challenge His word concerning the things we know, not whether they are harmful or good?

Please be aware that our wonderful Most High God will not be close to someone or share a personal relationship with anyone if they reject His advice. Nor will He be close to any man or woman, guilty of not distinguishing between the clean and the unclean.

I assure you, my Creator, God expects all of us believers in Him to put a difference between the holy and the unholy and the just and the unjust. I want you to realize that He wouldn't ask us to take this firm stance if it weren't the right thing to do.

In most cases, the people of Israel are our barometer, and we can use story examples about them to understand right and wrong. Because of all they've been through, we can use story examples about them to understand what's acceptable to God and what's not pleasing to God.

Indeed, the great nation of Israel has experienced much suffering, and it is an example nation for the rest of the world. We could correctly say that Israel is our definitive guide, and it is a nation of people set forth through many story examples.

I want you to know story examples are designed by a higher power; their purpose is to guide us the right way and teach us to ride upon the high places of this Earth. However, before we can ride upon the high places of this Earth, we do have to entwine ourselves with specific God-designed rules.

Furthermore, I assure you that God has expectations and expects obedience to His word and from everyone who professes to believe in Him. Especially if we desire the unique gift of immortality, and eternal life is an exclusive gift reserved for hot and on-fire Christians.

Nor does He want us believers in Christ to submit ourselves to the wrong attitude or falsely believe that no man can keep all His commandments, and maybe we will break one occasionally. However, we will be good commandment keepers if we try to be one.

Indeed, it should be as clear as a blue sky; his teaching story examples were written for our benefit. Simply so, we'll not stumble around in the darkness of the mind. I assure you that He doesn't want His believers loyal to Him to lack Bible knowledge.

His remarkable story examples illustrate the reason for judgment, punishment, and wrath caused by rebelling against His perfect word. His Bible stories teach us to avoid these negative compromises if we learn what they are and know how to avoid them.

Indeed, because I am glad for the gift of Bible stories, I sincerely pray that God will bless the land of Israel and keep its people safe, mainly because they've shown us God's character through their many stories of righteousness and unrighteousness.

I assure you that, with all of the excellent story examples

in the Bible, I relate to everyone the subject matter in definition concerning our great and perfect God. It's the best way for me to describe God's character and reveal Him to this starving world that needs to know about Him.

It appears certain that none were before Him, and none before Him makes Him the Ancient One, who comes to us from the Ancient of Days. Indeed, the Ancient of Days is so elusive that numbers of years cannot be applied to them by anyone.

Therefore, if I am allowed the privilege to speculate, I believe He was formed from the powerful Living Coals of Fire since everything began with the Living Coals of Fire. I firmly believe they began life together, and He and they share an unbreakable bond, forever and today.

I want you to realize that the particular Living Coals of Fire are the Element of God, the Spark of Life, the Essence of Pure Energy, and the incredible and elusive Holy Ghost of God. I believe they were the breath of life; God breathed into Adam's creation.

Therefore, I believe all of them are the same, and they came forth from the Ancient of Days and are the holy of holies. All of them are still alive and living within the realms of Heaven, except for the spectacular moments when they decide to visit the Earth.

For this reason, the spectacular and supernatural Living Coals of Fire are the greatest mystery of this universe. They might be billions of years old, and we haven't a clue to reveal their age, not that their age matters.

God bless you, and I hope you intend to make the kingdom of Heaven your home and become supernatural and immortal, similar to the other heavenly creations. I hope and pray that you'll become like the angels or Christ-like, and I assure you, it's your true destiny to find your way back home to God.

In conclusion, this story of revelation focuses on the beginning of history, reflecting on an unknown time and the Ancient One. It reveals the origin of life and the power source, allowing us this moment in the flesh, and I want you to know that you and I better conform to our destiny.

Beyond the shadow of a doubt, we better take this brief moment in the flesh extremely seriously and walk cautiously among the ungodly because this test of life we are experiencing in the flesh isn't for the carefree, lighthearted, or passive person.

Truly, nonchalant people have a problem with God; not being serious about the perfect word of God identifies their biggest problem. The dedicated Apostle Paul advises us to run the good race and try extremely hard to win the grand prize of immortality.

I advise the same thing; being hot and on fire for the word of God reveals the right frame of mind, and being hot and on fire for the beautiful gospel of God enhances the inspiration we need to win the prize of immortality.

Good luck, and be determined to learn all you can about our Supreme Creator God. Before this story ends, I advise you: do not stand before the Ancient One and lack Bible accomplishments or hot and on fire heat for His beautiful word.

CHAPTER SIXTEEN
UNDESIRABLE DEFINITION

This concern story, which I call *Undesirable Definition*, is a multi-purpose story that illuminates awareness, provides a high level of enlightenment, and serves as a dire warning about our lifestyle. Please realize that you, me, and everyone alive should be concerned about this message.

I assure you, and you do need to remember that our temperature autobiography, recorded in Heaven, is personal to us. Because our degree of love for God will be judged someday, our autobiography contains everything we've ever said and done upon this Earth after our age of accountability.

Our temperature autobiography means everything to us and is summed up through three indicator words written by our Creator God upon the Judgment Scales of His design. Truly, for the benefit of absoluteness, no other words are required to identify how we will be judged.

Therefore, it's through the free will of our hearts that you and

I have the great privilege of choosing to be hot, cold, or lukewarm toward the perfect word of God. I want you to know these three profound judgment scale words wield power over eternal life and death.

Indeed, you and I cannot outrun, elude, or avoid fitting the definition of one of these three profound words. Beyond the shadow of a doubt, our heart controls the reigns of our pursuits. I want you to realize that many of our goals in this life indicate hot, cold, or lukewarm.

Regardless of which of the three words applies to you or me, our heart's desires determine our flesh's desires. This truth means our heart mainly controls us and controls the temperature rating upon God's brilliantly designed Judgment Scales.

His indiscriminate Judgment Scales, powerful and never wrong, are essential to our life-and-death temperature evaluation. However, most people don't seem to care or do not understand the danger of being cold or lukewarm toward the required word of God.

Positively, it's an easy analogy to conclude that if we spit something from our mouth, it's usually because of a sour taste, and we do not like it. This statement of truth means that all lukewarm and cold individuals are compared to a bad taste in our mouths.

Primarily, since the cold and lukewarm people are spewed from God's mouth, they're failing their test in life. I assure you that being spewed from the mouth of God indicates a bad taste or something not liked by Him. However, being spewed from His mouth means He will reject the lukewarm and the cold person and not allow them to live in His kingdom.

I guarantee you that the phrase expressing bad taste has a lot of meaning, and it does us a favor and illustrates a parallel definition of the undesirables. If we think clearly and understand what God is saying, how could we consider the Bad Taste phrase otherwise?

I know for sure, and it makes me tremble with fear to realize that the word undesirables has a strong implication. Truly, undesirables have a firm definition, which connects to the judgment of condemnation, and this is a severe analogy formulated from three judgment words.

However, the fact remains true, and anyone not accepted into the kingdom of God is a cold or lukewarm undesirable. Two of the three indicator words written upon the Judgment Scales of God represent the unwanted person, and whoever doesn't respect His Ten Commandments isn't allowed to live in His kingdom.

This truth means that only the word hot represents a desirable person, and my analogy is perfectly accurate, as blunt as it sounds. According to the infallible Judgment Scales of God, the hot and on-fire person in Christ identifies with the only saved person.

Conclusively, righteous judgment is the way it should be among everyone because all people should be hot and on fire for the moral word of God. Indeed, living within the kingdom of God are people dedicated to living by the righteous word of God.

Therefore, because I care about your salvation and the place, you'll live for an eternity. Before this dire short story ends, I hope you've learned the infallible word of God and how the word called desirable entwines with the required word of God in harmony.

However, sadly, I must say, the unfortunate undesirables haven't found harmony with the perfect word of God. Therefore, no fellowship with the commanded truth equals cold or lukewarm, and the cold and the lukewarm person aren't allowed access to the beautiful kingdom of God.

Beyond the shadow of a doubt, the cold and the lukewarm person are walking on dangerous ground. This truth means whosoever is undesirable walks on the broad road, having the wide gate, and the wide road goes directly to an unpleasant place called the pits of Hell.

Conclusively, I am responsible for writing this warning story. Still, God is responsible for giving us His three judgment words, and the analogy of hot, cold, and lukewarm are His warning words to all of us. If we could ask Him the question face to face, God, should I be serious about your word, He would say yes.

I assure you that our Creator God wasn't playing around when He gave us His commandments to live by forever. However, if you and I play around and do not take His Ten Commandments seriously, we'll end our lives as cold or lukewarm people.

CHAPTER SEVENTEEN
THE EYE OF THE NEEDLE

The Eye Of The Needle is a metaphorical story that hovers between the literal and the symbolic, similar to a mighty ghost guardian angel. I assure you, the Infallible eye of the needle works in conjunction with the required word of God, and both the needle and He see things the same.

The seriousness of this story reveals that the needle's righteous eye distinguishes between the hot and the cold and the lukewarm. The word of God assures us the temperature of anything must be hot before it passes through the watchful eye of the needle.

Honestly, because the needle's eye is perfectly fair, it doesn't recognize race, color, or gender. However, the eye of the needle sees everything, looks deep through the exterior of the flesh and deep inside the heart, and reads every word we are thinking.

I guarantee you that the righteous eye of the needle has a long history, and it's been around since the beginning of time. I am confident that the Eye of the Needle has established itself from the

Ancient of Days and has an immortal lifespan.

I want you to know that the righteous eye of the needle entwines with the Father, the Son, and the Holy Ghost, and the Eye of the Needle has roots in every living thing, especially in every person alive, hoping to live in His peaceful kingdom.

I am sure equal rights weren't as complicated as they are now as they were in Ancient Days. However, thanks to God's guidance, the needle's incredible eye distinguishes between necessary equal rights and fabricated rights.

I assure you the eye of the needle is never wrong, and it doesn't change its point of view the way some men do, and I want you to know that the eye of the needle puts godliness and righteousness first. For this reason, the Judgement Scales of God are called the Eye of the Needle.

Indeed, to uphold godliness, all of us should emulate the eye of the needle. Positively, because it's entwined with God's will, the needle's righteous eye is perfect. Because it's God's right arm, it doesn't allow ungodliness and unrighteousness to pass through its narrow filtering process of scrutiny.

The eye of the needle is similar to the right hand of God, and it's stronger than iron. It has power over life and death, and passing through the needle extends life, but not getting through the Eye of the Needle means death to the soul.

Conclusively, to preserve peace in Heaven, the eye of the needle keeps out the camels and lets through the sheep, and it's never wrong concerning identity. Furthermore, you and I symbolize a camel or a sheep, and I hope and pray we are the sheep.

The righteous eye of the needle divides two kinds of people, and the needle's eye stands in front of you, me, and everyone else. I want you to know that only people in love with the beautiful word of God can pass through the eye of the needle.

The eye of the needle is the strong hand of God between an ungodly rebellious place and an orderly place. The Eye of the Needle will ensure the same type of people go to the same place.

Beyond the shadow of a doubt, because of its righteous design and ability to judge character, the powerful and righteous eye of the needle will eventually establish a peaceful world similar to the realms of Heaven. Indeed, when the beautiful Son of God returns, the natural order of things will coincide with God's stipulated things.

The eye of the needle has one Master and one kingdom specially designed for whoever can fit through the eye of the needle. I hope and pray that you'll go through the eye of the needle and become a happy resident in His specially designed kingdom.

Chapter Eighteen
THE REASON LUCIFER WANTS US IN HELL

Many preachers and teachers give us different analogies, trying to figure out why; they believe Satan wants us to end our lives in Hell. I am sure we may never know the mind of Satan completely or the reason to explain his hate, but it's easy to believe the wicked Lucifer does want our souls cast into the pits of Hell.

For this reason, and because I am an extreme Bible study person and a theologian of the heart, I am hungry to know the mysteries of Bible-related subjects. Out of curiosity, I want to know what's happening below in the pits of Hell.

I believe it's appropriate for me to reveal my analogy concerning why the wicked Lucifer and the rebellious angels fight so hard to get our souls cast into Hell. I am pretty sure you'll agree that the demonic Lucifer wants to capture our souls.

However, before this revelation story goes any further, and because we have limited information about Hell, I want you to know that this is an assumption story since there's no absolute answer to this story written anywhere in the Bible.

Therefore, this mostly unanswerable Bible question called *The Reason Satan Wants Us In Hell*, leaves us pondering a great mystery. It's appropriate for us to be curious and wonder why the evil Lucifer wants us cast into the pits of Hell.

I assure you, there's no harm in trying to understand the reason; Satan wants us in Hell, even if we make the wrong assumption. However, I believe with all my heart that the wicked Satan does want us to end our lives in the pits of Hell.

Therefore, I must say that my assumption is as good or bad as any other preacher or teacher's, and maybe my belief is more accurate. However, I am curious to know the answer to this mystery.

Beyond the shadow of a doubt, it is undeniable that Satan fights us hard and wants us cast into the pits of Hell. It's not because he likes us, cares about us, or wants us for companionship, and I am sure he doesn't feel compassion for anyone and doesn't care about us or our permanent well-being.

For the above reason, this unusual story must begin in Heaven to obtain a good understanding. It'll have to include the basis for explaining the reason: the wicked Lucifer wanted the throne of our Great God and everything else in Heaven.

Indeed, if I say the wicked and murderous Lucifer wanted the throne of my great Creator God. Then, I am saying that the demonic Lucifer wanted to be the most influential person in Heaven and the new owner of its valuable and priceless possessions.

Not many Christians know about the *Living Coals of Fire*, and not learning about them narrows their ability to broaden their thinking. A lack of Bible knowledge means they cannot completely understand why the rebellious and evil Lucifer wanted the throne of God.

I want you to understand that the supernatural Living Coals of Fire have other names, such as the God Element, the Spark of Life, and the Breath of Life. They are all one and were created from the same substance as the beautiful Holy Ghost.

The Living Coals of Fire can make material objects animated and alive, and we cannot imagine the extent of their supernatural abilities. I am sure the Father, the Son, and the Holy Ghost are the only persons alive to be formed entirely from the Living Coals of Fire.

Beyond the shadow of a doubt, the wicked Lucifer and the rebellious angels wanted to control the Living Coals of Fire that live upon God's altar. Truly, the Living Coals of Fire is Heaven's valuable, prized possession.

Lucifer and the wicked, rebellious angels desired to be the mightiest creations among all the creatures God created. Sadly, I must say, their heart turned hard, their conscience was seared with a hot iron, and they warred against their Creator God for their heart's desire.

However, it's excellent and fortunate for us faithful believers in God; they lost their war against God and the good angels. But, unfortunately for us, they were cast onto this Earth, and sadly, I must say, we Earthlings are getting a taste of their rebellious qualities of character

I firmly believe that God put them here for a reason, and maybe He was hoping they would repent and change. However, they didn't repent and change and continued rebelling against God. Sadly, they took charge of the Earth and changed some of His created pure bloodline people and replaced them with their bloodline.

Honestly, I believe the bloodline changing illustrates the primary reason for the great cleansing flood. When the whole Earth flooded, the mixed heritage ceased to exist among flesh and blood creations. It's easy to conclude that because their presence isn't with us anymore, God removed the mixed bloodline.

Furthermore, God took Lucifer and the rebellious angels and cast them into Hell, and they remain there in their physical form to this day. I am glad to know the tremendous amount of the Coals of Fire their bodies had initially; they cannot use it to their advantage from within the pits of Hell.

However, we have a small amount of the same Spark of Life, giving them life. I believe the Spark of Life never dies as the flesh dies; it stays alive for an unknown time. The Spark of Life is our spirit, the only thing left after the death of the flesh.

Furthermore, Hell is the holding place for wicked people, and when their flesh dies, the spirit they possessed descends into the pits of Hell. When the life force of evil people descends into Hell, it's like sending a little energy to maintain their spirit.

I am sure the wicked Lucifer and the demonic rebellious angels want as much of the spark of life coming to Hell as they can, especially since they cannot access the Spark of life in Heaven anymore.

Furthermore, I want you to know that the Holy Spirit doesn't live inside the damned person; it separated from the spark of life long ago. Furthermore, the Holy Ghost will separate from us also after we become ungodly. Truly, the spirits locked away in Hell are transformed energies, not godly anymore.

The spark of life is possibly the same thing as having food to sustain them; food is a rare substance in the gloomy pits of Hell. The exact source of energy they were fighting to obtain more of in Heaven; they fight every day to get it delivered to them in the pits of hell.

Therefore, Satan and the fallen angels want you, me, and everyone else to fail God and end our lives in Hell. Causing us to fail God is for their benefit since benefiting themselves is what they do, and you and I are the pawns being tricked and seduced by the invisible spirits of the air, who prod us to reject the ways of God.

I assure you the wicked Lucifer and the rebellious angels want our spirit in Hell, and they'll work extremely hard to get us into Hell. Throughout every generation, they are working hard to get as many people as possible sent to Hell.

It's the only way they can keep supplying their need for the Living Coals of Fire since the coals of fire are not a natural element available in Hell. Anyway, I am not asking you to believe this assumption story; I am unsure how it can be true and whether my analogy is accurate.

However, this story reveals the primary reason: they influence us to reject and rebel against God so our spirit will be cast into Hell. Indeed, they do know for sure God hates sin, and not serving Him illuminates the reason for the pits of Hell, and getting us to sin gets us sent to them.

Conclusively, I am sure they still need the element they warred against God to obtain inside the temple of Heaven, and they are still fighting for it. A little bit lives within us. This truth means that if our spirit goes where they are, the demonic angels may obtain a small amount of the Living Coals of Fire.

Positively, I don't know whether my analogy is one hundred percent accurate, ten percent correct, or zero percent valid. Truly, I want you to know that this subject is a great mystery not revealed in the Bible.

However, this concerning story intends to give everyone a point of view to consider and a good reason not to go to Hell. We do not want to contribute our spirit to Lucifer's cause. For this reason, let's do right and stay out of the pits of Hell.

CHAPTER NINETEEN
THE SECOND DEATH

This revelation story concerns you, me, and everyone else, too. It's called *The Second Death*, which illustrates a dreadful subject not many consider while healthy and alive. However, everyone should give the second death much thought and try to avoid its consequences.

For some odd and illogical reason, most people will give much thought to trivial subjects and not much about preserving their souls. Although, I must tell you, and I want you to realize, protecting our souls is a million times more important than trivial subjects.

Indeed, like a blind person flying an airplane and hoping to land safely, most people want the afterlife to take its course as if everyone goes in the same direction. Sadly, most people think the mercy of God is automatic and will cover everything, regardless of the severity of our transgressions.

I assure you, and you need to realize it too. Eternal salvation with the Lord isn't an automatic gift; not everyone automatically goes to Heaven at the end of their life and lives forever. Furthermore, we are unwise gamblers to believe that ongoing wickedness will automatically be forgiven.

I assure you, and you should never forget, that automatic salvation is a colossal size myth, greater than bunny rabbits laying eggs. Please understand automatic salvation is conjured up within the imagination of an illiterate fantasy mind, void of accurate bible understanding.

For some illogical reason, few people want to be Bible-savvy and know a lot of details about the Creator God of Heaven and Earth, the afterlife, and the burning hot lake of fire. I assure you it's a disadvantage not to know about the afterlife and the sizzling hot lake of fire.

The following warning scripture concerning everyone looking for the correct answer is given to us by God, and it reveals a lack of knowledge, which is why some men and women perish. Truly, my great God wouldn't disclose this need-to-understand information if it weren't true.

Hosea 4:6 My people are destroyed for lack of knowledge: Because thou hast rejected knowledge, I (God) will also forsake thee.

Indeed, I venture to say that not many people in this jungle world know the consequences of being Bible illiterate, nor do they understand the *Second Death*. Sadly, it's because they will not study the God-inspired Bible, and this is the reason they lack gospel knowledge.

I assure you, we aren't driftwood floating around in the universe; we cannot drift around the word of God our whole life, and we cannot dodge accountability for our rejection. However, we can be assured that our day of Accountability will catch up to us.

Furthermore, if people believe the death of our flesh is Serious, they should look deep and consider the seriousness of the second death. I assure you, excuses will not help the Bible-illiterate person, and the *second death* will be much more tragic than the first death.

However, I suppose that most people do not like to think about death for illogical reasons, and when they think about death, the first death, not the second, grabs their attention. Truly, as Illogical as it is, to be forgetful, out of mind, and out of sight is the best solution to a problem many people want to avoid.

Positively, the problem with the out-of-mind and out-of-sight solution reveals a high degree of shortsightedness, and I must warn you because the second death is a serious matter. Brain blindness blocks many things we do not want to think about, and brain blindness will not give us essential biblical knowledge.

Indeed, if for no reason other than knowing about the consequences of the second death, knowledge of the second death gives us a foresight advantage if it inspires us to live closer to the required word of God. Furthermore, I am confident that the definition of a foolish person entwines with whoever rejects gaining biblical knowledge.

It's pretty obvious: the first death is the death of the flesh, and the second death incurs death to the soul. I believe that death to the soul is similar to going to sleep and never waking up, and it truly is sad to know that some people will not experience the pleasure of living forever.

The meaning of the following important scripture can be considered a warning or plain good advice to the living. However, the following scripture is a severe revelation, and we would be foolish not to take the following scripture seriously.

Seriously, these following few words John the Revelator speaks from the book of Revelation should set off alarm bells to all men guilty of opposing God's word and going in the wrong direction. Because when the hourglass is empty, no more time remains to repent and change.

I want you to know that going in the wrong direction and choosing to live an ungodly lifestyle will place a person's spirit in Hell with the rebellious demon angels, and everyone locked away in Hell will feel the sting of the second death. However, thanks to Yeshua, our Savior from the second death, believers in His Father only die once.

I assure you that the following informative scripture reveals some characteristics that can destroy our souls. For this reason, I warn you: the following character flaws profile the ungodly person, making the violator a candidate for the second death.

Revelation 21:8 But the <u>fearful</u> (means dreadful), and the <u>unbelieving</u> (not having faith in Christ), and the <u>abominable</u> (means terrible, wicked, evil, and corrupt person).

Revelation 21:8 And murderers, and whoremongers, and sorcerers, and idolaters, and all liars, shall have their part in the lake, which burneth with fire and brimstone: Which is the Second Death.

I assure you that the second death is reserved for evil and wicked, rebellious men and women guilty of rejecting God because they desire an ungodly lifestyle. Now we know, thanks to the Book Of Revelation, the above scripture reveals wicked men shall have their part in the lake of fire.

Indeed, for some illogical reason or another, it seems natural for most people to put the commanded word of God in the far regions of their minds until death closes in around them. It's for sure the progression of years and the age of the flesh will bring death to our thoughts, and it will come knocking on our door someday.

However, for some reason, not based on scripture evidence, most people believe they are okay with God even though they aren't enthused and inspired by the scriptures. I am pretty sure; that many people will think they're okay with God, and many will be wrong and still be damned.

The scripture in Second Thessalonians tells us that many people will believe a lie and be separated and damned for eternity. Sadly, it's easy to conclude that a lack of bible knowledge allows the mind to accept myths, lies, and whatever they want to believe.

I want you to realize that the second death is for every person determined to refuse, accept, and embrace righteousness according to the perfect word of God. Truly, we should tremble with fear whenever we rebel against God's required gospel.

Second, Thessalonians tells us that in flaming fire, vengeance is taken on those who do not obey the gospel of our Lord Jesus Christ. The scripture says that whoever refuses to obey the gospel of Christ will be punished with everlasting destruction, and for these reasons, we must endeavor to understand His gospel.

The word of God tells us about the fate of everyone who falls into the category of the second death scenario. Because He loves us, we are being told that ungodly people, alias the unbelievers, will not be resurrected until the thousand years of peace upon this Earth have expired.

After the thousand years of peace have expired, the prophesized time for the second death arrives. Then, it's destiny time, and the ungodly spirits locked away in Hell will be raised from their terrible imprisonment, just in time to be cast into the burning lake of fire.

However, whoever accepts the Son of God as their Savior, sincerely loves His commandments, and considers them beautiful and delightful will have their name written in the Lamb's Book of Life. They shall be residents in God's coming Kingdom and live forever in peace.

Indeed, I want you to realize this serious story called *The Second Death* is a warning to everyone. It's written to save lost souls from destruction and entwines with the Book of Life. Sadly, I must say, this story explaining the *Second Death* reveals where some souls end their lives.

This powerful story concerning the choices we make in this life, which I call the second death, reveals the seriousness of living a lifestyle in conjunction with the perfect word of God. If we do not live by His word, we'll be candidates for the second death.

In conclusion, avoiding the lifestyle God has planned through His commandments and not getting our name written in the Lamb's Book of Life means we have a prophesized destiny in the Lake of Fire.

This truth is the absolute word of God, as it's written in the Book of Revelation, chapter twenty-one, verse eighteen. Indeed, our Creator God does want everyone to know that automatic salvation is a myth.

I assure you that the greatest injustice we can do to ourselves would be to be passive or indifferent and reject the perfect word of God. Please realize this critical story reveals that ignoring our Great Creator God amounts to a self-imposed tragedy and permanent death to our souls.

Urgently, I advise everyone who reads this revealing story to please get on fire for the perfect word of God and love it immensely, mainly because the second death entwines with a destiny equal to falling off a rock cliff and going to a terrible place we should avoid going to for eternity.

I hope and pray that this revealing story concerning the second death inspires you to become a firm believer in the word of God, mainly because it will take a firm believer, hot and on fire, for the word of God to avoid judgment and the Second Death.

I assure you that it's our whole duty to live by the required word of God, and if we do not, we aren't upholding our commitment to God or taking our test in life seriously enough. You need to know that we are gambling on losing our souls if we prefer an ungodly lifestyle to His planned way of life.

Indeed, above all other things considered necessary, I want you to know that God didn't give us His Bible for fun or as a curiosity book. I assure you we would be foolish to believe we can blaze our trail through this life and then escape the second death.

Positively, there's a hurtful price tag for sin; God is the debt collector, and the second death wipes charge accounts clean. For this reason, we do not want to run up a sin tab big enough to keep our name from being written in the Lamb's Book of Life.

I want you to realize that the beautiful gospel of God is the image of God, a picture of His heart and character. I assure you that the beautiful word of God is the ultimate reading material, and only a fool will reject learning the commanded word of God.

So, you'll know the importance of His word is monumental;

my God is all-powerful and a Savior who will save us from the lake of fire. Eternal life is ours to claim if we reverence Him and keep His word, and if I were you, I would be a determined commandment keeper.

Daily, I would base all my decisions between right and wrong on the beautiful Ten Commandments of God and not be afraid to stand before Him on Judgment Day.

CHAPTER TWENTY

LOOKING DEEP OR PLAYING ON THE SURFACE

This straight-up enlightenment story concerns every believer in Christ, *Looking Deep Or Playing On The Surface*. It purposely portrays two kinds of Christians: passive and passionate, and we are one or the other. Truly, if you are wise and want to live forever, you'll passionately believe in Christ.

I guarantee you that playing around on the surface isn't enough for some Christians because some Christians love the righteous word of God, and they cannot look deep enough into the revelations of God. These types of Christians are passionate Christians who continually want more understanding of Him.

We cannot expect all Christians to exhibit the same enthusiasm for God's excellent word, but for our benefit, God does provide us with a deeper look at Him. However, we'll have to dive as deep as the deepest part of the ocean floor to find the deeper Him.

I assure you if we play around on the surface and neglect our opportunity to learn the conclusion to the whole matter. Sadly, I must say, we'll miss an essential part of life, and we'll never know our great Creator God well.

Conclusively, a Christian on fire for the word of God illuminates a Christian continually searching and looking deep for the authentic truth. However, we'll have to be a hot and on-fire Christian before our heart compels us to look deep for the wholeness of God.

Beyond the shadow of a doubt, playing around on the surface will only provide us a glimpse of our wonderful Creator God. However, glancing at Yehovah doesn't reveal much information, at least not enough to satisfy me.

Therefore, we'll have to look deep into the word of God before we can see the larger picture of Him and the wonderful character image He represents. However, when we see the larger picture of Him and are hot and on fire for His word, our obligations to Him will become apparent and extremely important.

Positively, we'll have to phase out the traditions of men and all acts of spiritual fornication whenever these compromises are revealed to us. Because looking deep, Christians do not want to be unfaithful to the word of God, nor do looking deep Christians want to be laid-back Christians.

However, I want you to know that by playing around on the surface, Christians are often unfaithful to God's original word. Because of playing around on the surface, Christians do not dedicate enough time to being solid and loyal believers in the Son of God.

Our study pattern versus consequences is a personal observation story, looking deep or playing around on the surface. It reveals wise warning words I've purposely taken from the great

Book of Revelation. The warning words in this revelation story must be remembered every moment we live and breathe.

I am positive that, looking deep, Christians understand the importance of the following revealing scripture. However, playing around on the surface, Christians overlook the importance of the following scriptures.

Revelation 22:14 Blessed are <u>they</u> (anyone) who do His commandments that they may have right to the Tree of Life and enter through the gates into the city.

Ironically, and for the benefit of higher learning, the last chapter in our Bible strongly advises us to keep the commandments of God. The commandments are for preserving peace, and keeping the required commandments of God is the conclusion to the whole matter, and keeping them proves extreme love for Him.

Furthermore, I want you to know that keeping the excellent Ten Commandments of God proves that we are hot and on-fire Christians, and we want to see the larger picture of Him. Furthermore, if we love Him, we'll seek to know Him exceptionally well through His word.

Beyond the shadow of a doubt, the perfect word of God divides and cuts asunder whosoever falls under its blade of truth. Truly, you and I cannot challenge the excellent word of God with alternatives and be correct, nor can we be successful at disproving anything He decrees.

Therefore, I want you to know that it'll be much better for us humans if we commit ourselves to live by the excellent word of God instead of wading around in the mud puddles of foolishness and to illuminate clarification; the mud puddles of folly are various sins.

However, none of us living in the flesh are perfect, but we still need to try to be as perfect in the word of God as we possibly can. Because they love God, hot and on-fire Christians who look deep into the word of God are trying hard to keep the authentic gospel of God.

However, if we fall short of perfection in the Lord and break a commandment, we are remorseful for breaking it. Then, thanks to our forgiving God, we have a relief formula that allows us to repent and change our direction in this life.

I guarantee you that our perfect Creator God knows we cannot be perfect, and He knows a mistake from deliberate sin. It's for sure; He knows we wrestle against the powers of darkness and gives us the privilege to repent and change whenever we make mistakes.

The perfect word of God should mean everything to us; if it doesn't, we'll suffer from a lack of Bible knowledge. However, if the word of God is meaningful to Christians and we love it, we'll be extremely cautious concerning what we accept and reject.

I assure you, looking deep for the meaning of bible related subjects is much better than playing around on the surface. I am telling you, seeing the larger picture of God is much better than getting a quick glimpse of Him.

Positively, a quick glimpse means our interest in His word is lacking, and we aren't focusing on His required word. A Quick Glimpse means we may be more lukewarm than hot and on fire, and a quick glimpse means we may be failing the eternal life test.

To win the valuable prize of immortality, I hope you are a deep swimmer, not concerned about staying in the water too long. I hope you'll dive deep into God's great and excellent word, and if you do, you are increasing the odds of winning the prize of eternal life.

I assure you, my wonderful God desires for you and me to look deep, be hot and on fire for His gospel truth, and savor the flavor of His commandments. I am sure the God of Heaven and Earth will respect a deep swimmer much more than someone playing on the surface. I want to warn you that your life is short when we parallel it to a vapor, and for this reason, put foolishness behind you and serve God with all your heart, mind, and soul.

CHAPTER TWENTY-ONE
BIRD IN DISTRESS

I've had many frightful encounters with snakes during the youth of my life, and I wish I could've avoided them all. I've been bitten by one during my youth while foolishly going into high weeds after a baseball. I've walked across a rattlesnake twice the same day while going into the mountains and rode across them on a bicycle for the thrill.

Positively, every time the opportunity presented itself, I killed the rattlesnake. I'd been fishing late at night while drifting down the river in a canoe and looked up, and the tree over my head was full of snakes, probably hundreds of them, and during moments like this, I moved out fast.

I've had river snakes try to climb inside my canoe during bullfrog hunting late at night, and I've had one get inside my house. I cannot tell you why; I've had many encounters with snakes, but it's for sure I've had a lot of snake encounters.

As a foolish young man, I made many unwise decisions, and I

would search for snakes among the rocks and catch them with my bare hands. Sometimes, I would grab two snakes at a time until my father saw me and gave my rear end a good reason to stop being foolish.

However, I will tell you that the hungry snake encounter in this story is quite different, unlike all my other snake encounters, and I assure you, I did want to kill the snake. However, the circumstances were too critical, and I didn't manage to kill it because the safety of a bird was more important to me than killing the snake.

In this story, the predator snake I encountered was hunting for a vulnerable meal, and the dinner included a defenseless bird in distress. During this rare moment on a lovely Saturday morning, hundreds of spectators were gathered at an archery tournament held at an old abandoned McClintock armory.

The McClintock Armory was located near Point Pleasant, West Virginia, near a disaster occurrence. Still, its location probably doesn't have a connection to the snake incident. However, the abandoned armory is close to where the Silver Bridge disaster occurred during a cold winter, only a few days before Christmas.

Furthermore, the snake incident at the archery tournament is close to the same geographic area where many Ohio people sighted the Moth-man. However, I didn't see him even though we were at a competition archery shoot amid his stomping grounds.

However, this rare and personal story isn't about me being in harm's way or the elusive and mysterious Moth-man. However, it's about hundreds of others, me, and all of us watching a predator snake charm a defenseless bird.

On this particular morning, I was anticipating a great day. I drove from Ashford, West Virginia, and went to Point Pleasant, West

Virginia, to compete in an archery tournament. It was between ten and eleven in the morning, and crowds gathered at the registration place, with everyone talking and getting ready for the competition. I was getting ready, the same as everyone else.

However, the tournament hadn't begun yet, and everyone was bunched together in the same place, parallel to a swamp area with dead trees. Suddenly, the loud crowd started quietening, and silence replaced the chatter from the entire group.

I looked to see what was happening and noticed the crowd focused on a dead tree amid a swamp area. Not one person among the archers spoke a word, and everyone was awed by the unusual sighting of a snake on a dead tree limb.

After I finally viewed what had the crowd's attention, it was a giant snake, its long body wrapped around a dead tree limb. It was easy to see that this hungry snake was confident about having the frightened bird for lunch.

The snake's head was perched upward in an **"s"** shape, and its head swiftly went in a left-to-right motion. The snake's tongue was sticking out of its mouth, and I could hear a constant hissing sound, continuously hissing without interruption.

The little bird was sitting on the end of the dead tree limb, and it was charmed and paralyzed and could not move. Besides the hissing sound from the snake, the only sound was a weak chirping sound from the frightened bird.

The small, frightened, defenseless bird chirped in distress as the confident snake inched slowly toward the paralyzed bird. As I watched this unusual event briefly, it was easy to see that the vicious snake was about to conquer, devour its helpless victim, and make lunch out of the little bird.

I want you to know my heart ached, and I felt sadness for the small bird, and I didn't want to see it become lunch for the snake. I felt desperation, as if a tragedy was about to occur, and I wished with all my heart that the little bird would fly away, but it couldn't.

I looked around at the crowd and thought someone would save this little distressed bird from the predator snake. However, I was wrong; not one person in the crowd attempted to rescue this little bird, but everyone in the group seemed as charmed as much as the little bird.

The moment of truth was only seconds away for the little bird, and I considered shooting an arrow at the snake. However, I knew the odds were against me shooting the snake with one of my arrows even though I was an excellent archer.

Anyway, I knew the bird only had a moment or two left before its life would end inside the mouth of a snake. My blood rushed, and my heart beat faster than usual, and the bird's life seemed valuable to me. I realized that not one person in the crowd out of hundreds of people was willing to save this little defenseless bird.

Therefore, as I stood amid the crowd, I concluded that it was up to me to save this little defenseless bird and not let the vicious snake take its life. So, I looked down on the ground around me for a rock, found one, and slung it across the swamp at the dead tree limb.

The rock whizzing through the air got the snake's attention and broke his charm on the little bird. After I broke the snake charm, the frightened little bird flew away, and not one person in the crowd of hundreds mentioned the incident all day.

However, personal satisfaction belonged to me on that day, and I felt happy for saving the little bird's life. I am sure everyone in the crowd wished it had been them, and I'll always be glad I saved the little bird from the vicious snake.

CHAPTER TWENTY-TWO
FILTHY RAGS

This exposure story concerning our character profile, *Filthy Rags*, is a metaphor depiction. It's not about the dirty clothing we wear or any clothing at all. However, filthy rags is a character definition word in this story, and I use the word to make a character comparison.

Filthy rags are another word to identify sinful and corrupt men, including some Christians. I want you to know that everyone not doing God's will is compared to filthy rags, and climbing to the highest pinnacle of perfection is impossible.

I assure you, the odds are against us always doing right. None of us is perfectly clean, and we cannot live every day and not occasionally fall into the dirt. If we say we never sin, then we are liars.

Therefore, regardless of how hard we try to stay clean and free from sin, we'll never achieve perfection while living in this world. However, because we love the righteousness of God, we should give it our best try anyway, and God does expect us not to sin.

The loyal prophet Isaiah assures us that none of us can escape the analogy of being compared to filthy rags. This truth means as much as we wish it were different, we are an inferior creation, and we'll always have unavoidable character flaws.

However, I must say, for the sake of some men and women who try extremely hard to live righteously and by the exact word of God. There's a big difference between falling short of perfection and pre-meditated dirty work.

It's for sure; falling short of perfection is one thing. However, planning and scheming to sin goes beyond falling short, but falling short doesn't mean we aren't trying to escape corruption. However, plotting and planning to sin means we've crossed the boundary line and gone beyond falling short.

I assure you that falling short doesn't mean we've slipped backward, dropped out of grace, and lost our salvation because we aren't perfect. However, falling short does mean we've made a judgment error, and Judgment errors need to be fixed before they become ungodly filthy rags.

Ungodly, filthy rags accumulate numerous judgment errors, and the more unfixed judgment errors we collect mean we aren't trying to wash our filthy rags. However, cleaning our filthy rags means we've sincerely repented and changed and want to live by the word of God.

Positively, I assure you, some of us try harder to live by the required word of God, tremendously more than ungodly people do. Even though all of us compare to filthy rags, there's a big difference between filthy rags and ungodly filthy rags.

My definition of filthy rags illuminates the inability to be perfect, even while trying to be perfect but falling short. However, my description of ungodly, filthy rags portrays evil and ungodly men and the wicked Lucifer going beyond the boundaries of falling short.

This truth means the definition needs clarification, and we need to know the accuracy of filthy rags. I am saying falling short and ungodly filthy rags have different boundaries. Because of the degrees of sin, filthy rags have different limitations concerning the depth and intentions of their filthiness.

However, I want you to know that ungodly filthy rags haven't any boundaries, borders, limitations, or restraints, and I am sure the deepness of their filthiness depends on their unclean and corrupt opportunities.

Therefore, I want you to know that a moral boundary line is drawn between filthy rags and ungodly Filthy Rags, and the severity of the sin isn't the same between the two definitions, and ungodly filthy rags is much worse than the definition of Filthy Rags.

Furthermore, I am sure that when the moral boundary line is crossed, filthy rags become ungodly, and the penalty placed on us is more significant when we cross the boundary line and commit premeditated sin.

We would be highly naïve to read Isaiah's scripture, saying that all our righteousness is as filthy rags. Then, we would erroneously believe that one person is as sinful as another, which would be like believing that one person is as clean as another. Therefore, I must tell you the character of people isn't equal.

For the above reasons, I want you to realize that a characteristic dividing point separates filthy rags from ungodly Filthy Rags. This truth means that the analogy of filthy rags isn't the same as that of ungodly filthy rags.

Conclusively, I guarantee you that the analogy of filthy rags intends to tell us none are one hundred percent good, and we've all fallen short of being perfect. I conclude that as hard as we try to be righteous people, we'll not fully live up to the ideal standards of God.

Anyway, I want you to know that my analogy of filthy rags intends to say we aren't equally ungodly because we are not. It's easy to see that some rags are stained a little, and some are ungodly and filthy.

The following explanation scripture, taken from the book of Isaiah, says sin will carry us away from God, similar to a leaf being carried away from a tree by a strong wind. This truth means we must reject sin to stay close to our beautiful God.

The following scripture reveals God's feelings concerning the house of Israel after they drifted away from Him. However, I am sure the following scripture can apply to any person or nation guilty of drifting away from God.

However, the following important awareness scripture doesn't stereotype everyone, and it's because every act of sin isn't equal in proportion. Truly, I guarantee you the ratio of sin identifies filthy rags or ungodly Filthy Rags.

The following informative scripture includes certain men who rebel and grieve God's heart. Being rebellious to His required word will cause Him much grief, and being undisciplined will create distance between God and us. Therefore, if you love Him, prove it by keeping His commandments.

Indeed, our excellent God-inspired Bible clarifies that being rebellious against God's perfect word has hurtful consequences, and committing contrary acts will make Him our enemy. You must realize and reduce your sinning; we are foolish to rebel against His perfectly designed decrees.

Beyond a shadow of a doubt, the following passage specifically reveals its meaning to rebellious and ungodly men guilty of troubling His Spirit by rejecting Him. Conclusively, forsaking Him parallels us to an out-of-control leaf carried away in a strong wind.

Isaiah 64:6 But <u>we</u> (meaning all the rebellious men of Israel) are all an unclean thing, and all our righteousness are as filthy rags.

Isaiah 64:6 and we all do <u>fade</u> (means die) as a leaf; and our <u>iniquities</u> (sins), like the wind, have <u>taken us away</u> (means carried us away from God).

If the above explanation scripture applies to you and me, you and I must abort whatever sinful things stand between our great God and us. I assure you, whatever stands between our wonderful Creator and us isn't worth having or doing, and the corridor between us shouldn't be cluttered with compromises.

Indeed, it saddens me, and I conclude that the above declaration scripture from the Book of Isaiah paints a sad picture of the human race. However, the analogy doesn't apply to everyone on this Earth and everything we do, and everyone cannot be stereotyped.

Indeed, our righteousness accomplished for God's glory cannot be considered filthy rags. I want you to realize that whatever we do in conjunction with the commanded word of God fulfills the definition of righteousness.

Therefore, obedience and love for the required word of God

exempt many believers from fitting the description of ungodly filthy rags. I want you to realize obedience and love for the word of God are good character qualities, and good character qualities coincide with godliness.

Beyond the shadow of a doubt, the saying, none good entwines with the definition of none are perfect; no, not one. Truly, I must tell you, love and obedience to God don't have faults or stains of filthiness, and whenever we do right, God will not consider our works compared to filthy rags.

However, not all of us can be stereotyped as ungodly filthy rags, and none of us flesh and blood creations are perfect. Therefore, love and obedience to the gospel of God sets imperfect people apart from ungodly filthy rags.

The loyal Apostle Paul speaks the following informative scripture, telling us that none are good, not even one person. I am sure the wise Apostle Paul and Isaiah both say we cannot fully live up to God's expectations.

Positively, I want you to know that the above statement is true concerning humankind as a majority. However, the closer we live to God's Ten Commandments, the more Christ-like we'll become. Maybe we aren't perfect models, Christians, but trying to be a model Christian should be our endeavor.

Anyway, I must believe a few firm believers live on this Earth, and they are earnestly seeking after our great God with all their hearts, souls, and minds. They aren't perfect, but they do not fit the analogy of ungodly filthy rags.

However, the strong-speaking Apostle Paul says it a little more absolute than Isaiah when he says none are seeking after God. I do not like to contradict a loyal apostle or have an analogy different from his, but we do see some Christians seeking after God all the time.

Indeed, the loyal Apostle Paul, a person I consider a holy prophet of God, leaves me a little confused in the following analogy, as he does in several of his conclusions because I know that I am seeking after my great Creator God.

Furthermore, I know that there must be multitudes of Christians seeking after God, the same as me. However, it'll be up to you to define this scripture, and you can find your understanding concerning the degree of its meaning.

Romans 3:11 There is none (means no one) that understandeth (the importance of His word). No one seeks after God (passionately caring about His word).

I believe the loyal Apostle Paul means we all are sinners to some degree, and it's because we are imperfect creatures while we live in the flesh. Therefore, the Apostle Paul may be talking only about the people of Israel living among him during the moment of the above scripture writing.

Simply because whoever we are in the body of Christ, we know we seek after Yehovah. However, we also know that we passionately care about His excellent word and realize that we aren't perfect followers and will make mistakes.

Positively, we make mistakes, which isn't going to change. However, our imperfections do not stop us from seeking God or fade our intense love for Him. I assure you, we would be silly to stop seeking after our wonderful God just because we fall short of perfection sometimes.

Therefore, the solid and questionable statement saying, none seeketh after God isn't entirely self-explanatory in the scriptures and can only apply to ungodly filthy rags. I want you to know if we drift too far away from our Creator God, where there's no barrier between godliness and ungodliness, then we are an ungodly, filthy rag.

It's one hundred percent true; we all fall short of the glory of God, mainly because we cannot fulfill the definition of being completely perfect. It's for sure; none of us flesh and blood people can measure up to the perfection of Yeshua.

Undoubtedly, the excellent Son of God was the only perfect man to walk on this Earth, and we cannot be ultimately like Him. However, many imperfect creatures enthusiastically worship Him, love Him, and seek to follow His word the best they can.

It's also an accurate analogy concerning every converted Christian; I am saying that a heart cleansing must occur after our conversion to Christianity. However, it's also true that growing in Christ isn't instantaneous with transformation, and it'll take work to grow strong in the Lord.

Therefore, we believers start out drinking the word of God as if it's milk until we can chew on the word of God as if it's strong meat. As for myself, I passionately love strong teaching, but being perfect will always elude me since I am imperfect.

However, our imperfections will make us sad, but they cannot kill our faith, even though our faults compare us to filthy rags. Regardless of our interpretation of Filthy Rags, whoever calls on the name of the Lord shall be a saved person.

Indeed, I want you to know that we will be saved from the judgment of damnation if we confess with our mouths that the Lord is the Son of God, alias Jesus Christ, who is Yeshua. The following declaration scripture says so, and I believe in the validity of the scripture, and so should you.

Therefore, if we believe in our hearts, our Creator God has raised Yeshua from the dead, and we think He represents the right way. Then we shall be saved from the burning lake of fire, even if we are compared to filthy rags.

Romans 10:10 For within the heart man believeth unto righteousness; and with the mouth, confession is (the stipulation) made unto salvation.

The above scripture and the commanded word of God are all about righteousness. This truth means that the foundation of righteousness must entwine with the thoughts of our hearts before we can claim the gift of eternal life.

Positively, faith cometh by hearing the word of God, and our faith fades away when men do not seek to know the word of God. This truth means that many men will perish for lack of Bible knowledge, and it seems reasonable to believe that the Bible-savvy person has the most faith.

Therefore, I assure you that righteousness cannot be ours to claim, and a higher degree of faith than average will not be achieved unless we know God's word. I want you to know that learning God's beautiful gospel is the formula for acquiring a solid faith. So, says the scripture written in Romans 10:17.

Honestly, if you care about your next life and want to live a life of immortality, then I advise you not to conform to the ungodliness of this world. However, be a new person transformed by renewing our mind, entirely entwined with the perfect word of God.

The concerned Apostle Paul assures us that God's beautiful

word renews our minds, and I know that righteousness emerges from a renewed mind whenever it is entwined with God's excellent and perfect word. Truly, I conclude, not all men are equally sinful and wicked.

Furthermore, it could be true we'll always compare ourselves to filthy rags in this life, but not all are similarly filthy. Truly, it doesn't take a genius to figure out that filthiness varies from person to person.

Therefore, I conclude that if we resist sin, we do not have to compare ourselves to ungodly filthy rags, and I assure you, the two definitions are a big difference. Furthermore, I am sure having a light stain is much better than having a heavy shame.

Conclusively, I want you to know that the conclusion to the whole matter is to reverence God and keep His righteous commandments. If we do this requirement and entwine our lifestyle to His commandments, no person can compare us to ungodly filthy rags.

Commandment-keeping separates us from the ungodly person, and commandment-keeping is the only effective cleaning solution that keeps us sin-free and clean. Always realize keeping His commandments illustrates our heart's desire to do the right thing.

Furthermore, I want you to know that the great barrier between filthy rags and ungodly filthy rags is the excellent and perfect Ten Commandments. There's no better defense or Barrier between godliness and ungodliness than the Ten Commandments of God.

Positively, I will reveal a perfect analogy and tell you if there's any light in this world compared to exceptional words. The excellent

Ten Commandments of God are brighter than the sunlight on high noon, and I am confident that the pinnacle of perfection was illustrated through His Ten Commandments' creation.

I guarantee you that metaphorically taking off our filthy rags and putting on clean clothes is the same as deciding to wear the infallible gospel of God everywhere we go and every day of our lives.

This truth means that the fight rages on in this world daily, and you and I are warriors against sin. I guarantee you: the less we sin, the cleaner our rags will be in the washing machine on Judgment Day. We can trade our filthy rags for a white robe on that day.

CHAPTER TWENTY-THREE
GOD DESIGNED ART

This informative story, *God-Designed Art*, entwines our Creator, God of Heaven and Earth, and us together. The art in this story isn't about pictures, sculptures, drawings, or pretty things made by man's hands. However, it's about our Creator God in Heaven and the works of His hands.

Positively, I want you to know that this personal story is about you and me and multitudes of others. I want you to realize that the gospel of God refines and improves artwork. God is the Art designer in this story, and we are God-designed art, even though we are an incomplete picture, needing work on our character daily.

I assure you the most beautiful art in this world is the loyal believers in Christ and whoever has learned to love the righteous ways of God. Truly, we believers are the special people who gladly submitted ourselves to the Potter Man's hands.

However, it's pretty apparent to me that some works of art are more beautiful than others, and some artworks do not turn out beautiful. It's because too many Christians love many abominations in this ungodly world, and I want you to realize that all abomination things are ugly artwork.

Therefore, we cannot be beautiful works of art if we live an ungodly lifestyle and continue to do terrible things. I want you to know that all the glitter in this unstable world cannot turn an abomination into a beautiful work of art.

This truth means that if we believers in Christ aren't willing to give all our hearts, minds, and souls to God entirely and live by His excellent Ten Commandments, Then I conclude that we are incomplete Christians, similar to unfinished artwork.

Indeed, if we want to be in a privileged position close to God, have a strong Holy Ghost friend, and hope for answered prayers, we must give ourselves to the Potter Man and be willing to let Him shape us into beautifully designed art.

I assure you that before we can transform and be beautifully designed art, we will need to do extra work and put our heart into it because transforming is a long, drawn-out process. Regardless of the effort, every Bible-savvy Christian knows the process is a wonderful journey, good for the heart and soul

Achieving the status of beautifully designed art is an endeavor we'll have to work on all our lives if we expect it to remain beautiful artwork. Be assured we will have to dedicate the works of our hands and every decision we make to a God-designed formula for righteousness.

Furthermore, we will incur many battles in the arena of life, and battles with evil spirits are designed to take away our beauty. I am sure most Christians can testify to having many battles with the powers of darkness, and all of our struggles with the spirits of demons are designed to destroy the Potter Man's work.

However, I want you to realize that every Christian must defeat the anti-Christ spirit before becoming beautifully designed art. But, I warn you, the anti-Christ spirit is the major stumbling block in this world, standing between us and God-designed artwork.

I assure you that the more we love our wonderful God and understand His beautiful and infallible word, the more we'll enjoy doing His will. With gladness, I testify that our character design will become more beautiful daily.

I hope you realize that God-designed art has nothing to do with the looks of the flesh or the smiles on our faces. His works of art have everything to do with the pureness of our hearts. I want you to know in advance that falling in love with His word prods Him to do better artwork.

Indeed, I hope and pray that my heavenly Potter Man will honor you and shape you into a showpiece of beautifully designed art. If He does, He'll also give you a home in His kingdom, and Bible scriptures reveal that His kingdom is another piece of beautiful artwork.

CHAPTER TWENTY-FOUR
ENTHUSIASTIC OR INDIFFERENT

This critical temperature of our heart story, *Enthusiastic Or Indifferent*, parallels the words hot, cold, and lukewarm, and considering our degree of love, this story reveals two different feelings we can feel for the required gospel of God.

I want you to realize the word enthusiastic insinuates that someone believes the word of God is electrifying and loves it. The word enthusiastic parallels the inspirational words called hot and on fire for the perfect gospel of God. However, the word indifferent coincides with the judgment words called cold and lukewarm.

Indeed, as we journey through this life indifferent to God's word, it doesn't matter much to the rebellious person. However, after the death of the flesh, I am sure illuminating the emotion of indifference to the word of God will matter more than anything else in this world.

This concern story coinciding with the temperature of our heart, called enthusiastic or indifferent, is a warning story. Because I care about the lost person, this story advises against the expression of being indifferent, especially since being indifferent reveals a non-caring attitude toward God.

This important concern story, critical to everyone, illuminates opposite responses characteristic of our emotions. I am sure you already know our feelings cannot lie, and our emotions reveal our feelings inside our hearts.

I want you to realize that the definition of passive isn't much different from indifferent. Furthermore, I am sure that a passive emotion to the required word of God amounts to nearly the same thing as an indifferent emotion.

I suppose the word indifferent is stronger than the word passive, but not much different concerning the feelings of the heart and not different enough to make a difference. I am pretty sure the indifferent emotion belongs to the ungodly unbeliever not bound by the gospel of God.

However, at any rate, being passive or indifferent concerning the word of God will cost a person their salvation and the grand prize of immortality. Furthermore, I do not understand how the passive and indifferent person could expect to receive the gift of salvation.

Indeed, throughout this story, I will use the word passive instead of indifferent most of the time. It's mainly because the passive Christian only has to take one more step backward before fulfilling the definition of indifference to His beautiful covenant.

I assure you that our Creator God designed us to be free thinkers. The wonderful gift of free will allows us to choose emotions and form our beliefs. Therefore, the feelings we express toward the required word of God reveal the good or bad feelings inside our hearts.

Indeed, by personal choice, we can be enthusiastic about God's beautiful word or passive or indifferent about His perfect gospel. However, we must know He's a supernatural God who will look inside our hearts and know our feelings for Him.

Beyond the shadow of a doubt, I know that my God approves of enthusiastic Christians determined to delight themselves in His perfect word. However, I am sure He disapproves of being a passive Christian, nor does He approve of anyone indifferent or doubtful about the truth of His word.

Apparently, and I hope I am wrong, only a few people study their Bible enthusiastically. Sadly, only a few will learn it enough to show themselves passionate and highly concerned about His required word and His excellent Ten Commandments.

I know that a passive state of mind, cloudy and forgetful, doesn't mean some Christians are indifferent to the word of God. However, too much passiveness illustrates a character flaw; being a passive Christian is borderline the definition of indifference.

It's for sure, and I want you to know that our relationship with God will go much better for us Christians if we are hot and on fire for His wonderful word. Truly, I am sure that being hot and on fire for His gospel is the key to opening up His heart.

Indeed, our great God will be pleased if we are passionate Christians hungry for His inspirational word. This truth is because every word spoken by the God of Heaven and Earth is Highly Passionate, and every one of His words has a helpful meaning attached to them.

Therefore, I am sure that a show of passion from anyone in

this world would meet the approval of our highly passionate God. I assure you that being passionate about His wonderful word creates good feelings between Him and us and parallels our hearts to His heart.

It is accurate to say that my God doesn't want us to be passive toward Him. Sadly, because of too much passiveness, only a few Christians realize the amount of passion our supreme God expects from everyone claiming to be one of His believers.

I want you to know that a lack of enthusiasm and passion for the beautiful word of God illustrates a good reason for an underdeveloped, passive Christian. Sadly, it's easy to conclude that the world of Christianity has many underdeveloped Christians.

I am confident that our Supreme Creator God is responsible for giving us His excellent and wisdom-filled Bible. He doesn't inspire a Christian to be passive or indifferent toward His perfect word, and I wholeheartedly conclude that we would be foolish to be Passive Christians.

I assure you, a passive attitude toward His Bible and His passionate words do not go together, and valuing passiveness is like saying we have a penny's worth of God. I am sure all hot and on-fire Christians in love with His gospel want more than a penny's worth of God.

However, I want you to know if His followers expect rewards of favor, divine protection, and eternal life. Then, I am sure, they better stoke up their heat and become passionate, hot, on-fire Christians.

Simply because passion is precisely the emotion my Supreme Creator God expects from all of us Christians every day of our lives, and even after becoming a spirit. Because it's true, I want you to know that fulfilling this obligation to God is easy if we've fallen in love with the perfect word of God.

Think not throughout this concerning story; I am bashing a passive Christian. Because I am not, and bashing a lukewarm Christian accomplishes nothing. However, I wholeheartedly say that a dollar's worth of Him is better than having a penny's worth.

I assure you that I must use a professing Christian as an example to illustrate passive or passionate Christianity, mainly because non-believers are indifferent people. Sadly, I must say, the unbelievers haven't got a penny's worth of Him.

This truth means that the unbelievers didn't invest any time in learning about Him or have no passion or enthusiasm for the required word of God. Indeed, a passive Christian person, lacking Enthusiasm and love for God's beautiful gospel, has also lost their direction in life.

Furthermore, a passive Christian is nearly borderline the definition of being indifferent and fits the description of an unbeliever. A passive Christian will show less resistance to the unholy and the unclean than a loyal, passionate Christian will.

Conclusively, when the day arrives, it's time for us to account for ourselves; the Mediator between God and us will remember our lifestyle. It's certain; when we stand before the Son of God, our Mediator will identify us as passive or passionate about His word.

However, Yeshua, the beautiful Son of God, is choosey about the person He represents and will only mediate for the passionate Christian. The indifferent person may not have a Mediator at the gates of Heaven, and He may tell the indifferent person, I know you not.

Positively, I warn you: always remember to protect your soul simply for acceptance at the pearly gates. At the Pearl Gates, I am pretty sure it will be much better to be an overdeveloped Christian than an underdeveloped Christian, and maybe there's no such thing as an overdeveloped Christian.

I assure you, there's a lot at stake on our journey through this life in the flesh, and the value attached to the excellent word of God is priceless. It's priceless because the test of life is a must-adventure every man and woman will submit to based on God's perfect word.

Positively, the excellent word of God is priceless to whoever loves it dearly and is willing to put their faith and trust in His gospel. I assure you, sincere believers found the great pearl in this world, and passing through the gates of the pearl will be easy for them to do.

I want you to know an essential piece of wisdom: the excellent word of God is incomparable, unmatched by gold and silver, diamonds and rubies. I guarantee this absolute fact will be proven true on Judgment Day.

CHAPTER TWENTY-FIVE
THE SPIRIT OF GOD AND US

I am calling this enlightenment story concerning you, me, and all other Christians, *The Spirit Of God, And Us.* This story reveals the link and the strength of the connection between God and us, and we are one of many links, making up a long chain of believers in Christ.

This revealing story illustrates that you and I are the keys to having a strong Holy Spirit, a weak Holy Spirit, or no Holy Spirit living within us. I assure you that we can do certain things to increase the strength of our link to His Spirit, and we should prioritize strengthening our bond with Him.

Indeed, we can believe our Father raised His Son from the dead, and we can believe that Jesus gave His life for you and me to be saved from the lake of fire. However, those beautiful things alone will not make the Holy Spirit strong within us. This truth means to add more than simply or only believing in Christ; you and I need a strong Holy Spirit to complete the makeup of our faith.

I guarantee we have an evil adversary in this world, and he doesn't want you and me to have a strong Holy Spirit. Our adversary is Lucifer, alias Satan, the Serpent of Old, and he's determined to separate us from the love of God.

I assure you that the wicked Lucifer will do everything possible to keep the Holy Spirit within us weak and hindered from being helpful. The wicked Lucifer will try his best to prevent us from having access to the Holy Spirit entirely if he can.

Therefore, every day of our life, we'll have to fight with the invisible spirit of Lucifer if we desire to keep the presence of a strong Holy Spirit within us. I want you to know there are certain things we need to understand before we can defeat the wicked spirit of Lucifer.

Our fight with Lucifer isn't casual, passive, or meaningless like a Grade School child's fight. Be assured we'll have to pull off the gloves, get down to bare knuckles, and be as vicious as a boy named Suzie before we can defeat the invisible spirit of Lucifer.

Otherwise, I want you to know that Lucifer's spirit will walk all over you and me, and he'll kick us around and laugh at us for being weak in the Lord. Truly, it will be much better to understand his tricks, defeat him, and not give him a reason to laugh at us.

Therefore, if you and I aren't willing to fight for a strong Holy Spirit and do the required things we need to do, then I want you to know that our spiritual journey will be tremendously impaired, and we'll probably not have an influential Holy Ghost teacher.

However, this fight against the wicked Lucifer will not be a bare-knuckle fistfight and will not depend on physical strength. However, it will be a battle of wits, and our wits will entwine with our morals and values based on the required word of God.

I assure you that our obedience to God's wonderful word will be pitted against the traditions of men and the ploys and tricks of Lucifer. Indeed, we better realize that the evil Lucifer fights to win, and so should you and I fight to win.

Furthermore, even though this battle with Lucifer challenges our wits and ability to avoid sinful temptations, this battle of the mind between us and the spirits of darkness will still be as vicious as any battle we've ever fought.

Indeed, when it all boils down, and the root cause is exposed, this challenging battle of the mind we war against with evil spirits. It's a battle for closeness and companionship with our Mentor, the beautiful Holy Ghost of God.

I am confident that if our heart is focused right, all Christians will desire to be close companions with the Holy Ghost of God. However, companionship with the Spirit of God isn't handed over to us on a silver platter.

Companionship with the wonderful Holy Spirit is not presented in a pretty box or wrapped with a colorful bow. The beautiful Holy Ghost isn't our fighter, and He doesn't fight our battles for us, but we will gain strength through the knowledge of His word.

Therefore, keeping companionship with the beautiful Holy Ghost of God will require all our strength and determination. I warn you, we will have to want companionship with Him above all other things if we expect to hold onto and keep Him in our hearts.

Positively, I want you to know that the incredible Holy Ghost is our teacher of wisdom and discernment, and He will teach us how to defeat the devil's wiles. Simply so, our companionship with God will grow in strength daily.

I assure you that the excellent Holy Ghost of God desires that we be active and not be a dead limb void of benefits to the Tree of Life. This truth means that as long as we live and breathe, we have work to do for the glory of God.

I want you to know that the excellent Holy Ghost of God doesn't allow us to sit back in a rocking chair or watch Him fight our battles for us. He'll not allow us to use Him; let us sit back and watch Him do everything for us.

Indeed, there's no such thing as rocking chair Christianity, nor any Christianity allowing us to retire in a rocking chair and rock our way to heaven without fighting a few battles with Lucifer. However, he'll likely battle us harder after we become loyal Christians.

Therefore, we should brace ourselves for demonic battles and the many temptations of sin, and when the bell rings, we should come out swinging. When I say we should come out swinging, it's a way of saying we should fight the temptation to sin and be as vicious as a boy named Jane, Mary, or Sue.

CHAPTER TWENTY-SIX
NO FAVORITES

If we are created equal in the eyes of God, and He shows no difference for persons, and we are in the driver's seat of our destiny? We were His sons in Heaven and knew Him personally before being born here through a woman's womb.

Then, indeed, there are no exceptions to the rule, and race, color, or gender are all bound by the exact requirements. This truth means there aren't any special exemptions concerning God-given stipulations, and I want you to know the Ten Commandments He gave to Moses on Mount Sinai are His stipulations.

If the above two sentences are accurate, I believe they are true; according to perfect fairness, no favorites are the best way to portray us all. Therefore, knowing this statement to be accurate raises His righteous word to the pinnacle of importance.

This impartial story, which I call *No Favorites* in the eyes of God, portrays Him as a fair and righteous Judge, not swayed by color or gender. This truth means we are in the driver's seat of our destiny and should be glad we'll be judged on our own merits.

This impartial story linking all of us to God's word illustrates God's expectations, which are the same for everyone living on this Earth. Truly, personal favorites aren't a part of His selection process, and God will treat us equally.

However, I am telling you that commandment-keeping and love for the perfect gospel of God are a particular part of His selection process. I want you to realize that these are the two character qualities He desires from all of us who want to live in His kingdom forever.

With all its beautiful scriptures, the much-needed Bible is a portrait of God's design to point men toward righteousness. Living a righteous lifestyle pinpoints His expectations of us. Indeed, living a moral lifestyle proves that we've conformed to His heart's desires.

As elegant as the stars in the sky, the great Bible is our infallible Prep Manual for this testing ground on Earth. The word of God tests and tests us every day. After the death of our flesh, the beautiful Prep Manual can be handed over to someone still alive.

Indeed, knowing life in the flesh is short means we only have a limited time on this Earth to conform to God's perfect Prep Manual. For this reason, we better not be noncaring or passive about accepting the righteous ways of the prep manual.

I assure you, and you need to know, that God will not like it if we reject His prep manual. If we do, it'll be like failing one of our most important obligations to Him, and I firmly warn you that my all-mighty God isn't passive concerning our obligations to Him.

Indeed, because of its God-designed destiny, the excellent prep manual will still be among humankind throughout every generation following us. The prep manual never dies with old age, nor will it disappear or hide from among us earthlings.

I am pretty sure that even within the realms of Heaven, the excellent and perfect Prep manual will always be the most revered book among all books written by a man. I assure you the importance of the prep manual coincides with the need for food, water, and the air we breathe.

Positively, the purpose of the informative prep manual is easy to conclude. It's to illustrate the difference between rebellion and obedience and sin and righteousness. The excellent prep manual, exceedingly perfect and grand, makes all these distinctions.

I assure you that the excellent prep manual doesn't lean to the left or the right and doesn't play favorites. However, the superb prep manual containing the perfect word of God defends righteousness and evaluates all men and women on their own merits.

Our excellent prep manual encourages us to do good work among all men, and we are the extension of His hands and must perform good work. Indeed, doing accomplishments to benefit people is one of His many desires; our righteous and compassionate God wants all of us to do.

Concerning our ability to know the right way, our excellent Prep Manual, full of wisdom and divine guidance, symbolizes a sharp two-edged sword. Furthermore, it's obvious that the beautiful prep manual has duties to fulfill, and we can partner with it or avoid it.

Positively, the beautiful prep manual, the pinnacle of all books, cuts and divides the godly from the ungodly, the clean from the unclean, and the learned from the unlearned. I want you to know if we do wickedly, the Lord's two-edged sword will seek us and cut us.

Many people will cherish and love their prep manual, seeing it as a Special Road Map God designed to lead them back to their place of origin. I assure you, the map readers are the wise people living on this Earth who despise sin and love God's righteous ways.

Indeed, many skeptics and unbelievers will be appalled by the prep manual and all its excellent advice from God. Sadly, I must say, the skeptics will hate and despise it, call it a fairy tale manual, and not put much validity in it, if any.

However, some dedicated men and women are hungry for wisdom, and they'll spend their entire lives trying to live by the prep manual and enjoy the challenge it presents us. As for myself, I am glad to say I am deeply in love with the prep manual.

Most of this world's population will spend their entire lives rejecting the prep manual, and sadly, I must say, they'll not allow themselves to be challenged by the excellent word of God. I firmly conclude that these people are rebellious to God's will.

Regardless of which category we fall into, it plays no favorite among men and women concerning God's excellent prep manual, and we can love or despise our prep manual, and the choice is ours to make.

I want you to know that God's righteous and incredible prep manual has many enemies, and their names coincide with the definition of rebellion and unbelief. I warn you so you'll know in advance: the enemies of the prep manual are the enemies of God.

Beyond the shadow of a doubt, rebellion against His word and unbelief are two major stumbling blocks. They stand between the learned, the unlearned, the saved, and the unsaved, and who will and will not enter His kingdom.

This truth means the excellent prep manual is the pinnacle of honest advice. It's beyond comparison to any other book and provides the only cure for the plague of damnation and sin. I want you to know that the remarkable prep manual parallels miracle medicine.

However, we do have to understand our prep manual and absorb its contents before it can help us overcome sin. The excellent prep manual is my best friend, and I hope you feel the same way about the beautiful God-inspired Bible.

Positively, the brilliant prep manual exceeds the boundaries of all other books written by the hands of men, and the beautiful contents of the righteous prep manual are unmatched by any other reading material ever written in this unstable world.

I assure you that the stories in our prep manual are unique, rare, and more accurate than the sun's pattern. The prep manual's history goes back further than the history of precise recording on any subject. I firmly believe that some articles inside the Prep Manual were written in Heaven before they were written on Earth.

I guarantee you that the excellent prep manual of my Creator God has a serious mission to fulfill. It speaks to every generation, past, present, and future, and it's easy to conclude that the corridors of time aren't a barrier to the prep manual.

Indeed, I must admit that my heart is captive to the God-inspired Prep Manual, and my love for it is loyal. As I write these Bible-related stories, the God-inspired prep manual is my greatest inspiration many generations after its beginning. I sincerely testify that because of my love for His Word, the prep manual has a powerful hold on me.

Conclusively, this heartfelt testimonial story, I call no favorite people in the eyes of God, lifts and illuminates glory and edifies the excellent Prep Manual of my Creator God. I am glad to say that this story proudly lifts the prep manual before the eyes of every person alive.

However, I want you to realize that the excellent prep manual isn't beneficial to the dead, and there aren't copies circulating in the Pits of Hell. For this reason, you, me, and everyone else better study the Pep Manual while we are still alive and can claim a Savior.

Sadly, I must tell you that this world is unstable in all four corners of Earth. It's because people have lost their interest in the prep manual. Truly, they parallel a cloudy sky, a desert without rain, and raging seas and oceans. However, the world could be calm again if everyone followed the prep manual.

CHAPTER TWENTY-SEVEN
HOPELESSLY IN LOVE

Love is splendorous, and many people fall in love with many things; as for me and my heart, I am hopelessly in love with the word of God. I can honestly say nothing enthuses me more than to learn something new about my wonderful God.

His wonderful word goes through my mind when I am asleep and consume my thoughts throughout the day. I sincerely testify that nearly all my thoughts revolve around God's great and perfect word, and nothing pleases my heart more than to know I have a great Creator God.

I gladly get up in the early morning hours to give my heart to the beautiful word of God, and because I love the truth, I am under the authority of God's great wisdom and love it more than all other words. Every day, because He's my source of admiration, I search far and wide to learn a new mystery about Him.

I happily conclude because I've learned a better way that I am married to the beautiful gospel of God. I am unmarried, but still, yet, I am married, and because of my great love for the word of God, the gospel of God is my great love, and I eat it, drink it, and love every word of God.

I believe His scriptures and miracles are true, and He has a place prepared for you and me. My heart desires to attend the marriage feast of the Lamb and witness the love between the bride and the bridegroom. I am proud to say my faith in Him is greater than the mustard seed, and I will move mountains to be a member of the royal family of God.

I assure you, being in love with a mate is one thing, but being hopelessly in love with a righteous way of life is another thing, extremely special and unique. I am in love with the gospel of God, and the desires of my heart are married to His righteous ways of life. Within the kingdom of Heaven, everyone living inside the Pearl Gates loves His honest ways.

My wedding ring is the excellent Ten Commandments I love dearly, superior to all other words. I am proud to say the bridegroom is my loving King, and my loyalty is to both of them. I sincerely say I am hopelessly bound to Christ by an invisible and unbreakable chain, even though we cannot see the chain with the naked eye.

However, just the same, the intangible chain between Him and I is unbreakable, and my love for Him will determine the chain's strength. Truly, to satisfy my heart, I hope the chain between Him and me strengthens with each passing day.

I am captivated by His wonderful word, and I gladly follow Him because His unbreakable chain pulls at me, and my heart cannot resist following Him. Now, I can tell you after all these years of searching, I've discovered the excellent love ingredient.

The unbreakable chain between God and me is sincere and

formed from the substance of love, and the emotions radiating from my heart are mightier than the strength of steel. After all my years of searching, I finally realize that I am where I want to be with my wonderful God.

I sincerely testify before all men; I love the link between Him and me, and for the glory of God, the connection between Him and me gains strength every day. I am happy to tell you that my love for God multiplies as my knowledge about Him increases.

Furthermore, I boldly say love is the strongest and the most unbreakable chain among all chains, and the strength of steel will not compare to the power of sincere love. I guarantee you that the master link is the Son of God, and I am only one link among many links.

I proudly testify before all men that I would be lost if I didn't have the unbreakable chain of love between God and me. Now that I've found His love, I must hold onto it. I do not want to lose it or do anything to weaken the link between Him and me.

I am passionately and hopelessly in love with the perfect word of God, and I am happy to say I am married for life to His gospel. Again, I proudly testify before all men that the intangible substance of love is more valuable than the tangible substance of silver and gold.

Therefore, I am not ashamed to say the breaking of bread and the gospel of God are the delights of my heart, and I am confident I'll go to my grave believing in Him. I want you to know that living in His kingdom is my heart's desire and greatest expectation.

On the wings of a snow-white dove, God sent down His pure, sweet love, and the wonderful gospel of God is the pure sweet love from above. I am proud to say I love the pure, sweet word established from the Heavens above, and nothing else is more precious to me.

Furthermore, another name for the precious Son of God is the Word, and the Word is God. I want you to know that their sweetness came through Him, and He and the Word are the perfect matches. The chain of love started with Him, and the following scripture illuminates the superior bond.

John 1:14 And the <u>Word</u> (Jesus Christ, or Yeshua) <u>were</u> <u>made</u> (means became) flesh, and dwelt among us.

Bible history reveals that grace and truth were illustrated through His kindness toward all people, including His enemies. Therefore, we beheld His glory, the glory of the Father's only begotten Son, full of grace, truth, and genuine brotherly love. While alive, the Son of God walked to and fro on this Earth in the flesh, and I can correctly say He was a hero among believers in Him.

Beyond the shadow of a doubt, Bible history proves that He was in the world and made the world, yet most of this world knows Him not. Sadly, I must say, many people will go to their graves, and they'll never discover Him.

Indeed, most people in this world don't know Him unless they are hopelessly in love with the beautiful word of God. It's easy to conclude that most people do not appreciate Him and aren't in love with His life-saving gospel.

Furthermore, when I sincerely say I am hopelessly in love with the word of God, I am saying His word is as solid as concrete. I am glad for His strong word, standing tall for righteousness, and even the oak tree, or things made from iron, aren't as strong as His gospel truth.

Positively, I am hopelessly in love with the Father, the Son, and the Holy Ghost that dwells among men. Hopelessly in love means my heart is overflowing with love for the priceless gospel of God, and I cannot receive enough of it to satisfy my hunger.

Therefore, concerning the feelings of my heart, the perfect word of God is similar to a continuous waterfall. The scriptures symbolize the waterfall, and I am happy to say that the waterfall supplies me with a never-ending magnetic pull toward Him.

Conclusively, the pursuits of the flesh reveal our treasures and the priorities hiding inside our hearts, and I guarantee you: the desires of our hearts choose our Treasures and Priorities. Indeed, whatever we consider a treasure, there will be our heart since one cannot separate from the other.

The wonderful word of God is my great pearl, a beautiful pearl I found in this turbulent world, and it's the pillow I rest my head on at night. It's easy for me to say that the beautiful word of God is the pinnacle of the most delicate pearl among pearls.

I sincerely testify that the beautiful word of God is my sword and armor, and for my benefit, His gospel is my fortress; God designed to protect me from the poisons of this world. For the glory of God and my advantage, I lean on His word every day.

Positively, I am hopelessly in love with the beautiful word of God, and I am bound to His word by strong emotions radiating from my heart. It's easy for me to say that nothing compares to the excellent word of God if our heart has chosen it above all other things.

Furthermore, it's correct to say that beauty is in the beholder's eye, and every person loves it from the heart. Because this statement is true, I gladly choose to be hopelessly in love with God's infallible word and excellent counsel from the heavens above.

Positively, I believe the beautiful gospel of our great Creator God is more beautiful than the flowers that bloom in the spring. Because of my unwavering analogy of beauty, I am sure God's excellent and beautiful word is the root of all beauty.

The perfect word of God is a gift from the heavens above and given to everyone before me, and I accept it, too. It'll be a gift given to everyone coming after me, and we are foolish if we expend our lives and do not take advantage of our heavenly gift.

Therefore, I urgently urge you not to waste another day, and do not fail to fall in love with the word of God and hold it tight, every minute of every day. I am confident that the word of God is alive, and it's more than a great philosophy or paper and ink.

I am sure that being in love with the beautiful word of God will be our proudest confession on Judgment Day, and it'll be the one thing we'll not mind telling our great Creator God we've fallen in love with completely.

Furthermore, falling in love with God's beautiful and required word illustrates my heartfelt confession daily, and I sincerely testify that I would feel unfaithful if I forgot it on some days and didn't put it first every day.

I am hopelessly in love with the word of God, and for the benefit of receiving eternal life, I hope you are too. In a metaphoric way of speaking, the required gospel of God is our stairway to Heaven, and the steps on the ladder going into the land of Utopia are His perfect Ten Commandments.

Indeed, I want you to know one crucial thing before this love story ends: God's gospel is the image of God, and the bread of life is the beautiful word of God. Without falling in love with it, our recommended daily requirements will be lacking.

This personal story called *Hopelessly In Love With The Word Of God* describes a lot of Christians. For the glory of God, I hope you can say that you are hopelessly in love with the word of God, too, because illustrating reverence to His word is the right way to live and die.

CHAPTER TWENTY-EIGHT
IN THE PRESENCE OF GOD

This awareness story concerns every person living on this earth. I call it Living In The Presence Of God. It reveals the bold truth and the absolute facts of life. We should wake up every morning thankful and purposely realize that the presence of God is all around us.

Even though you and I cannot see into the spiritual world or know the number of spirits trying to influence us, it doesn't mean the spiritual world doesn't exist, and it doesn't mean the intangible spirits of good and bad angels cannot see everything we do.

It's easy to conclude that everyone alive in the flesh has limitations, and we live within the boundaries of this material world. This material world is a specially designed, tangible, and natural place where everything visible can be touched and felt.

However, I want you to know that the invisible world surrounding us is a different world and much more significant than this one. The world I am talking about is outside our reach and touch, invisible and intangible, and it's called the spiritual world of God. I assure you, ghost spirits of angels are everywhere in the spiritual world.

Therefore, and for an illustration, if I compare the spiritual world of God to anything intangible on this planet, it would be the invisible wind, mysterious and unpredictable, circulating every inch of the Earth.

I assure you, and it's important to know that my great God created the spiritual world. My Supernatural God decided to separate the tangible from the intangible, and even though these two worlds entwine together, they are separate worlds.

The definition of tangible is explained by eyesight and touch, while intangible is explained by unseen and mostly unfelt. I want you to know that you and I have a God-designed destiny, and we will be residents in both worlds before our journey through the unknown ends.

Therefore, because we see and feel what we touch, it's obvious that this material world is tangible. However, the spiritual world is intangible and invisible, similar to the wind and air we breathe. Our Creator God is the one connection to both worlds, crossing barriers and breaking the law of nature.

Therefore, I want you to know that as we live and breathe upon this Earth, we do so in the presence of God. I assure you, He can be tangible or intangible, a part of the spiritual or real world, and it's pretty possible we could entertain Him unaware on a sunny afternoon.

However, I want you to realize that regardless of whether He's tangible or intangible. He's all-knowing and all-seeing, and His presence is everywhere. He could be walking or sitting next to us, and we wouldn't know it's Him in the proximity of our presence.

He knows our spoken and unspoken thoughts hidden within our hearts, and somehow, beyond our comprehension, our great Creator God is powerful enough to monitor everyone on this Earth simultaneously, and His eye watches us.

He's one hundred percent supernatural and knows every imagination and desire to pass through our hearts. Therefore, I am warning you: there aren't any secrets we can hide from Him. You and me, and everyone else, are an open book; our God can read and always reads our hearts.

You would think by now, after thousands of troubled years passing before us, humankind would've concluded to accept God completely. However, eyesight proves that giving ourselves to God and His word entirely hasn't happened yet, even though it defies intelligent logic not to accept God completely.

It's for sure; it seems patterned in every generation; the never-ending epidemic of rebellion constantly plagues my supreme Creator God. Truly, being rebellious to the King of kings and His perfect word reveals our most terrible character flaw.

Even though my Supreme God warns humanity about the perils of rebellion throughout His guiding Bible, Lucifer still wields much influence over most of this world's population and purposely influences rebellion against my Great God. Sadly, he snatches the word of God from people's minds daily because he's invisible and supernatural.

It seems correct to say that most men and women forget and do not consider the seriousness of the consequences of being rebellious to His commanded word. For this reason, I want you to know that this is a terrible flaw capable of causing us much trouble with God.

Indeed, most people living in this world, including many passive Christians, have patterned compatibility. Sadly, they forget or do not care; they have a purpose: obeying God's truthful word and not giving His word much thought is the pinnacle of foolishness.

However, the teaching word of God only applies to His concerned children, who are dedicated and loyal to Him and desire to live in His kingdom forever. Sadly, I must say, men and women of unbelief aren't concerned about the test of life and death, and regardless of the reason, this world is full of unbelievers who refuse to take the test of life.

I assure you, although you should already know, it's an unchangeable requirement for His children to love and hunger for the required word of God, and part of our testing in this life will reveal the degree of our loyalty to God and show if we are hungry for His beautiful word.

Furthermore, I want you to know that His children should meditate on His righteous word day and night and strongly believe in the validity of His word. Truly, having faith to accept that He's one hundred percent truthful gives us an edge to believe in all His promises.

It's for sure; we cannot be a hot and on-fire child of God, keep our old rebellious nature, and show no concern for His required gospel. We would be foolish to believe that a child of our great Creator God doesn't have to be a new person in Christ.

Positively, and regardless of the words men and women speak, rebellion against the things of God is unacceptable, and he will not tolerate acts of sin. Assuredly, penalties will be attached to rebellious acts against His gospel, and we would be foolish to believe otherwise. For this reason, my wise advice is to live a godly lifestyle.

Indeed, if we desire to be a child of God, it will be better for us to start practicing immediately and not be rebellious against His life-saving words. We live in God's presence every minute of every day, and nothing we do in the light or dark goes unnoticed by Him.

I assure you, He's as close to us as the invisible wind, the air we breathe, and the dirt underneath our feet, and yet, He's undetectable. It's easy for me to conclude that because of His design, you and I aren't allowed to see Him unless He opens the windows of Heaven.

Positively, we can start reading the unusual book of Genesis and end our search in the book of Revelation, and everywhere throughout the Bible, He'll ask us to obey His word. It's not because He's a dictator God, but because He wants us to do right.

Indeed, a common denominator comes into the light within nearly all of His story examples. We'll find our Most High God, and He'll repeatedly say to reverence Him, and submitting ourselves to His required word reveals the right way to reverence Him.

He'll tell us if you fear, it means reverence Me, serve Me, obey My voice, and not rebel against My required commandments. Then, His hand shall be helpful to us as we perform all our fruitful and good works on the Earth, and He will bless us according to our needs.

However, because our God of Heaven and Earth can withdraw His mercy, the following important scripture reveals another side of God. The other side of God shows His hand will be against us, regardless of whether we profess to believe in Him.

Therefore, I want to warn you strongly there's a price tag for being rebellious to His word, and the following scripture tells us this statement of truth. Truly, I want you to realize that memorizing the following scripture is high on the chart of importance.

1 Samuel 12:15 But if you will not obey the voice of the Lord, but <u>rebel</u> (means resist) against the commandments of the Lord, then shall the hand of the Lord be against you.

This enlightenment story, *Living In The Presence Of God*, tries to reveal that the spiritual world is full of influential ghost angels. This story also illuminates a precaution because the spiritual world observes the material world, and I want you to know that some blessings and recompense have strings attached.

Positively, the material people created from the dirt of this Earth cannot affect the course of the spiritual world, and it's pretty obvious; we humans are powerless tangible creations, unable to change the littlest things in the supernatural world.

However, I want you to realize the same statement of truth isn't accurate about spiritual creations who see the big picture better than we do. Because Spiritual Creations have some supernatural abilities, they can intervene in our affairs and affect the daily walk of our lives.

Conclusively, when the above scripture tells us that the hand of the Lord will be against us if we rebel against His commandments. Then, the scripture tells us that God can intervene in our affairs anytime He wants to, and many scriptures prove He can intervene.

Therefore, the presence of the Lord is an undeniable fact of life, and He's been present with every generation before us, and He will be after us. Truly, we who love righteousness and hate acts of wickedness should be glad for His constant presence.

Even though each of the story examples is different from chapter to chapter, the message from God is nearly always the same. Because my Creator God is unchangeable throughout every generation, the corridors of time prove that His ways are superior and righteous, and nothing needs to be changed.

This truth means that He established the order of things long ago, and regardless of the generation, He always expects His children to reverence Him, obey His commandments, and delight themselves in His perfect word. I am asking you, can anything rival this righteous expectation?

This informative story is based on His gospel truth, Living In The Presence Of God, which is only believable if we believe in the Intangible Spiritual World and an unseen God. Furthermore, I want you to know that we are spiritually blind if we do not have the faith to believe in the spiritual world.

For example, the intangible wind and the intangible spiritual world are more alike than most people realize. However, because all relationships with God aren't on the same level, each of us individually will have to form our conclusion concerning the presence of God.

I assure you, as you already know, that lifestyle choices belong to us, and right or wrong, all of our decisions will be formed by the thoughts of our hearts. It's our privilege, given to us by our beautiful Creator God, and it's called the gift of free will.

Furthermore, I guarantee you that learning all we can about Him creates an intangible bond, and we can feel His presence in our hearts. I hope you firmly believe in Him without seeing Him in person; if you do, it indicates exceptional faith.

CHAPTER TWENTY-NINE
TIME IS WASTING AWAY TO IMPRESS GOD

This analogy of the truth is a heartfelt story everyone needs to understand; I call *Time Is Wasting Away to Impress God.* It's a direct-to-the-point story, and the title of this story means to express the importance of the subject. Because the hourglass empties after a specific time, we better profile ourselves correctly before God's eyes.

The above statement is an accurate analogy and sums us up from our youth until death. Every day we live and breathe on this Earth, we should ask ourselves, what shall I do with my time today, and what acts of goodness shall I accomplish as I journey to my new home?

I am sure sometimes we can say our time was well spent today and wasn't wasted away on unimportant things. So, you'll know this story defines things that aren't important, such as sinful and corrupt acts and compromises contrary to His Ten Commandments.

This foresight story intends to warn everyone and say that

God is watching us from above and recording the works of our hands. I assure you, He's concerned about how we spend our time and whether or not we are wasting our lives away.

The great preacher is our example of a man who wanted to be more impressive than everyone else and look grand and wise in everyone's eyes. However, trying to be more impressive than everyone else usually amounts to self-imposed vanity, and it usually takes a lot of money to impress most people.

Being highly impressive means building bigger things, having a beautiful house, and looking proud of ourselves. Having these things is okay, but we can be proud of ourselves without having the best of everything.

Being more impressive than everyone else usually means having the best of everything to make ourselves look good, and gaining a highly impressive profile before men mean having the best cars, the most expensive food and clothing, beautiful furniture, and bigger parties.

However, all the things that make us impressive before men do not make us Impressive before the Son of God since material wealth doesn't impress Him. Someday, we must impress Him since He's the beautiful mediator between God and us.

The highly resourceful Son of God didn't try to impress anyone with the best of everything while He lived in the flesh, and He could've easily impressed kings if He wanted to use His power to generate wealth. However, He didn't want to and didn't seem to own much materialism.

Impressive people usually desire to be associated with other Impressive people who share their vanity character. For this foolish reason, vain people are drawn to material things and do not associate much with poor people.

However, vanity people usually hang out with the upper class, as Belshazzar did on party night. For vanity reasons, this makes them think they are better than other people, and these kinds of people do not impress God since He's picky about impressions.

In most cases, impressive people cannot keep from being vain and usually have a much too high opinion of themselves. They typically think of themselves as better than they are, and nothing good is gained by having better-than-thou feelings.

The vanity things men do to be impressive before others may be achieved through ungodly accomplishments or by taking advantage of someone else. However, our Creator God will trouble our hearts if we impress incorrectly.

Therefore, we should consider the consequences before we set our sights on being impressive, and we should ask ourselves, who do we need to impress? Do we need to impress other men and women, or do we need to Impress our wonderful God?

Since most impressive men are vain, I must tell you vain men rarely try to impress God. However, they live unthinkingly and ungodly and think impressing God is unimportant. Indeed, most men would rather impress other men than our great supernatural God.

Furthermore, I am sure it's easier to impress men than to impress our all-knowing, intangible, and quiet God. Truly, the ability to impress men doesn't require God-made stipulations and rules, and usually, all it takes is materialism and money to impress other men.

However, I want you to know that if we intend to impress God, we'll have to do it through His gospel requirements, and having lots of money isn't one of His requirements. God asks what a man shall profit if he accumulates millions or billions of dollars and loses his soul

His unchangeable gospel requirements are that everyone live by His perfect word, keep His commandments, and be hot and on-fire Christians. Indeed, if anyone lives by His perfectly designed word and puts Him first, their acts of reverence will impress Him.

However, putting my Creator God first will not impress many men if they would instead leave God out of the picture. But leaving God out of our plans usually means putting God first isn't necessary or the desire of impressive men if they are determined to impress with material wealth.

This observation story, meant to reveal an imperative need called *Time Is Wasting Away To Impress God*, is also a warning story. It says that our hearts aren't right with the God of Heaven and Earth if we would rather impress other men than Him.

Conclusively, putting our Creator God first means our love for Him is the strongest desire in our hearts, and being a child of His means our heart embodies His Spirit. I hope you realize we aren't impressive before God if His Holy Spirit isn't living within our hearts.

Furthermore, the facts are clear: We must impress God before He allows us residence in His kingdom. But it'll not be impressive when we stand before Him as a do-nothing, lukewarm person. For this reason, time is short and wasted if we aren't trying to impress God.

My advice to everyone is urgent: get on fire for His word, eat it up, and be highly Bible-savvy. It's the right way to carry His cross to Heaven, and if we impress Him, He'll be waiting for us at the open Gates of Pearl.

Therefore, because of its significance in this world, I would like to end this story by telling you a monumental truth. The name of this story I call *Time Is Wasting Away To Impress God*; it's the pinnacle of all facts if we want to be one of the immortals granted the privilege to live forever in His peaceful kingdom.

CHAPTER THIRTY
REBELLION ERASES GOD

Here we are, a full-grown people living on this Earth in the flesh, and we are making our own decisions and blazing our trail through life. However, we didn't start this way initially, and it takes a long time to grow into an adult and walk through the crossroads of life.

Therefore, this awareness story will have to start from the beginning; even when we innocently left our mother's womb, and even during our earlier years of life, as the corridors of time raced before our eyes, we lived innocently through much of our youth.

However, living as an innocent person has the destiny to change with age, and during each passing year of our life, our innocent way of thinking is less and less. We'll start making decisions at some point and time in our lives, and they'll be based on reasons other than innocence.

However, it would be much better if we could live innocent from our youth until we die. However, sadly, I must say, we cannot live our entire life as Innocent as a child. Sadly, not being able to live as an innocent person means we may not be able to be as close to God as we want to be.

This truth means that our Creator God is much closer to us when we are innocent and living pure at heart. Sadly, the gap grows wider between God and us after we lose our innocence, and it's a hurtful tragedy to humankind because this corrupt world will not let us live innocently.

It's easy to conclude that almost all flesh and blood creations do not start making foolish and ungodly decisions until our innocence departs from our hearts. Truly, as much as I hate to say so, personal experiences prove a piece of our soul dies after our Innocence Departs.

I call this declaration story concerning many people among us *Rebellion, Erases God From The Picture*. It entwines itself together with foolish decision-making after our innocence has departed. However, innocents departing from our hearts doesn't have to mean our godliness leaves, too.

I assure you, an innocent mistake or wrong decision isn't nearly as bad as one made on purpose. But I want you to realize that purpose violations against the required word of God erase God from our picture.

Purpose violations against the required word of God have a solid and concrete definition, and it's called rebellion against God. For a moral learning purpose, I want you to know that every sin committed upon this Earth amounts to rebellion against the required word of God.

I assure you that rebellion against the required word of God illustrates a breach of contract. This truth means that breaking commandments breaks down a binding agreement between Him and us, and our covenant agreement with Him means that God expects us to be commandment keepers.

You should consider that breaking the binding agreement between our Great Creator God and you and me has consequences. I want you to realize that breaking a covenant with Him and living unrepented and unchanged has everything to do with whether or not we'll receive an invitation to live in His peaceful kingdom.

I assure you that rebellion against the word of God should be considered an eraser, and disobedience could be the reason; salvation is erased from our picture because there cannot be a portrait of Him and us together in His kingdom when rebellion against His word is the picture of our image.

Furthermore, I want you to understand that the only way to stay close to the will of our Creator God is to obey the voice of God, and His voice speaks clearly through His righteous Ten Commandments. Indeed, whenever we read them, He talks to you and me.

Positively, obedience to the righteous word of God is the only way to overcome a rebellious heart. Otherwise, the terribleness of sin will overpower and destroy obedience, and our wonderful God will be erased from our picture.

In this short story, we need to understand as accurately as the sun's pattern, which I call *Rebellion, Erases God*. It's an awareness story, saying don't rebel against the required word of God. Otherwise, closeness with our great Creator God will elude us like the sun missing during the night.

This truth to remember is an awareness story, and it's trying extremely hard to expose humanity's number one problem with our great Creator God. Please realize this so you can make corrections. I am telling you that acts of rebellion against His perfect word are our number one problem.

I hope and pray that you'll be strong like an oak tree and avoid doing the things the great Creator God disapproves of us doing. I hope your walk through this life will entwine with loving the opportunity to carry the cross of Yeshua wherever you go, day after day.

I assure you that when our testing in the flesh is complete and finished, our appointed time comes to leave this testing ground on Earth. We'll proudly stand before our great Creator God as sincere, hot, on-fire Christians, and we'll be glad we separated ourselves from the ungodly temptations of this world and remained loyal to Him.

I want you to know that Christians are destined to live hot and on fire. They will be the common denominator among the population in His peaceful kingdom, and we can be one of them. However, we'll surely have to be hot and on-fire Christians to become residents of His kingdom.

I hope to see you there, living in God's presence, wearing a beautiful white robe, walking on streets of gold, and drinking pure water as it flows from the throne of God. I want you to know if God allows us to live in His kingdom forever, it'll be because we gladly carried the cross from Earth to Heaven.

I guarantee you that scratching the surface of God's beautiful word is nothing compared to going deep into the heart of His revelations. The deeper we go into His righteous word, the hotter our fire burns for His ways.

Furthermore, God's presence is felt stronger whenever we are close to the heart of His conclusions, and I know that Bible-savvy people always develop strong feelings for the King of kings. Indeed, I am telling you that the more we learn about Him, the stronger our feelings will be for Him.

However, we can lead a horse to water, but we cannot make him drink the water. This truth means the way we decide to live our lives is ours to choose, and our wonderful God will not interfere with our hearts' desires. However, please remember that *Rebellion Erases God From Our Picture.*

Therefore, with the most significant consideration for our portrait with God, I am telling you sin is our enemy and the enemy of our image with God. For this reason, repent and be forgiven; God will have to be in our picture before we can escape the fires of damnation and live in His kingdom.

CHAPTER THIRTY-ONE
AFTER MEETING YESHUA

This opportunity story illustrates a special moment I am calling *After Meeting Yeshua.* It reveals the caring Son of God being considerate to everyone and Him offering us the excellent opportunity to be a new and different person. Because our salvation matters, and we want to live in His kingdom, we better accept His offer.

This thankful story portrays a change of heart and a new person free from the bonds of our sinful past. This remarkable character change occurs after meeting Yeshua, and I am sure Yeshua is the reason for a better type of people in this world.

I assure you that we do not have to be one of the twelve apostles before we can experience the freedom to become true believers. The twelve apostles of Christ, average and ordinary in the beginning, are examples of people who changed after meeting Yeshua.

Suppose you'll recall the life of the twelve apostles before they knew Yeshua, alias the Son of God, our Savior, from the judgment of damnation. Then, you would know for sure; they were an ordinary Joe and fishers and lived average lives, similar to everyone else, you and me.

However, after meeting the outstanding Son of God, the thoughts of their hearts changed, and they preached with exceptional wisdom. It was divine wisdom, thoroughly entwined with righteousness and wholly based on God's great and authentic word.

Furthermore, after finding Yeshua, their old life was a part of their past, and they never looked back. After meeting Him, they possessed exceptional knowledge and understanding they didn't have before meeting Yeshua, the glorious and perfect Son of God.

I know they were blessed and given exceptional understanding, more so than we are given knowledge after finding Yeshua. However, our wonderful God will provide us with much insight if we surrender our hearts to Him and diligently follow Yeshua's teachings.

I am a witness and genuinely able to say that God has given me much understanding since I found Yeshua. Since I found Him, I've written over twelve hundred individual Bible stories, and I didn't have the skill to write them until I found Yeshua.

This truth means that our gift of divine knowledge and the ability to understand God's mysteries depend on our finding Yeshua. Although this true analogy may seem illogical to unbelievers, it's an accurate analogy concerning our understanding of heavenly wisdom.

Therefore, our gift of divine knowledge is a supernatural gift given to us by the beautiful grace of God. I want you to know religious knowledge is an extraordinary gift given to any believer, able to say sincerely; I found Yeshua. Furthermore, Yeshua is the perfect pearl a man locates in the field and sells all he has to own a new habitation place.

Indeed, I am thankful to reveal this new direction in my life story After Meeting Yeshua. It entwines with the beautiful gift of grace, and together, they mold and shape a new you and me. Please realize that true conversion to Christianity means we've been given the gift of grace because of Yeshua.

However, I want you to realize that we do have to find Yeshua before receiving the gift of grace. Sadly, I must say, there's no gift of grace for anyone until they find Yeshua, and this combination is an absolute formula designed to bond us to a salvation Savior.

I assure you that the amazing grace of our Creator God, compassionate and merciful to believers in Christ, amounts to much more than the gift of pardon from the judgment of sin. Indeed, the wonderful gift of grace is why Yeshua forgives our mistakes.

Positively, I want you to know that our great and merciful God is the reader of every person's heart. He gives the gift of grace to everyone that loves Him and is willing to do His will. The gift of grace is provided to them whenever they desperately seek after Him and claim Him as their one and only Savior.

Even though the gift of grace erases the judgment of sin, it isn't a license to sin nor does it give us a good reason to be a relaxed Christian. I assure you we would be abusing the gift of grace if we used it to relax our stance against acts of sin.

Simply because the beautiful gift of grace can be lost even more quickly than we found it if we relax in our God-given convictions, and not any amount of grace allows us to be a part of the works of ungodliness or to be a lukewarm Christian standing in the doorway between two worlds.

Positively, we cannot straddle the fence between sin and obedience and still please God. However, God's mercy and gift of grace will allow us to repent and change whenever we fall short of righteousness. Truly, we will make mistakes and sin occasionally, even while trying to be perfect, and I am one hundred percent sure that we all fall short of being perfect.

Furthermore, I know that compromises will trouble our hearts when we sin, and a troubled heart has the potential to shape us into better men. I wholeheartedly conclude that being troubled over sin is a step toward godliness.

Indeed, this meaningful story concerns our relationship with the Son of God *After Meeting Yeshua*. It reveals exuberant Christians, hot and on fire, as the only people seeking His designed ways of perfection and wanting to be Christ-like forever.

However, because it's an unavoidable crisis, unchangeable and absolute, I want you to know that this awareness story also reveals a disturbing fact. This truth means all Christians are still battling the flesh, a world full of sin, and living among it daily.

Therefore, I conclude that we can find Yeshua and be proud to be firm believers in Christ. However, we'll still fall short of perfection and sin occasionally, and because it's unavoidable, we'll live among wickedness daily.

Indeed, this enlightenment story has hinged on my analogy concerning the time *After We Discovered Yeshua*. However, it's time for me to turn this informative story over to a higher authority, and the higher power is a much wiser person than me.

I sincerely confess I believe every word the loyal apostle of

Christ reveals in the following scripture. The loyal Apostle John is a higher authority than I, Paul Castle, and John was an extremely close personal friend to Yeshua, the Son of God.

Therefore, the following few scriptures are as accurate as this Earth's rotation and require our full attention. They explain God's love and mercy much better than I can, and the following few enlightenment scriptures speak to us also after we find *Yeshua*.

1 John 1:7 But if we walk in the light, as He is in the light, we have fellowship one with another, and the blood of Jesus Christ, His Son, cleanseth us from all sin.

1 John 1:8 If we say we have no sins, we deceive ourselves, and the truth is not in us.

1 John 1:9 If we confess our sins, He is faithful and just(ready) to forgive our sins and cleanse us from all unrighteousness.

1 John 1:10 If we say that we have not sinned, we make Him a liar, and His words are not in us.

The following revealing scripture is given to us by the great preacher man, and he's responsible for explaining the conclusion to the whole matter in simplicity. The great preacher man paints a clear picture as he explains our obligation to our Creator God.

The next matter of factual truth, scripture explicitly talks about all of us; even if we try to be Christ-like, we cannot fully obtain perfection. I believe the following scripture parallels all of us Christians, and I say this because we all fall short of fulfilling God's expectations.

Ecclesiastes 7:20 For there is not a just man upon Earth, that doeth good, and sinneth not.

This realization story concerning the new person we've become, called *After Meeting Yeshua,* is an awareness story that illuminates a particular moment in our life. This story portrays us Christians abounding with love for the beautiful Son of God, regardless of the person we were before our conversion to Christianity.

However, I want you to know that as hard as we try, we'll still sin occasionally and fall short of His expectations. Even though we are ashamed of our sins after compromising the word of God, this revelation of our character proves that we cannot be perfect every minute of every day.

Therefore, I am sure it makes a Christian extremely happy to dodge as much sin as possible, and I hope you manage to avoid transgressions against God. After all, avoiding sin is what we desire to do after meeting Yeshua, our excellent teacher of righteousness.

CHAPTER THIRTY-TWO
TAKING OFF THE ROSE-COLORED GLASSES

This unusual true story, *Taking Off The Rose-Colored Glasses*, concerns all flesh and blood people. It illustrates a symbolic way of life that characterizes our character. This truthful story will challenge us to look into the mirror or place ourselves under a microscope.

This metaphor story, *Taking Off The Rose Colored Glasses*, has an expanded analogy. It entwines the blindness of the mind, and I want you to know that the blindness of the heart and mind is a spiritual flaw. The definition of a spiritual flaw means we are blind concerning the will of God.

This exposure story called taking off the rose-colored glasses hasn't any scriptures to support its conclusion. However, I conclude that understanding the meaning of this story is the main thing. For perfect clarity, this story's analogy represents an indisputable fact of life and profiles many people.

Rose-colored glasses symbolize seeing but not seeing until we open our eyes completely. After we open our eyes to the world of God, we'll see the whole picture in clarity, not blurred by an imaginary illusion conjured up from the imaginary part of our brain.

I call this awareness story as accurate as the rivers flowing in one direction only, *Taking Off The Rose-Colored Glasses.* This story does the unusual and looks into the realms of an invisible world. The unseen world is much more active than we imagine, and enemy ghost spirits live in it. The demonic spirits are the power of the air determined to influence us to do wrong.

This informative story is meant to expose a terrible problem in this world: Taking Off Rose-Colored Glasses. Rose-colored glasses reveal a supernatural world, much different from our tangible world. Demonic supernatural forces are the residents of the intangible world we'll fall prey to if we wear rose-colored glasses.

Rose-colored glasses represent a lack of Bible knowledge and understanding concerning the invisible supernatural forces we battle against daily. Indeed, I want to warn you: We, inferior flesh and blood people created from the dust of the Earth, cannot defeat demonic spirit powers if we wear rose-colored glasses.

Rose-colored glasses represent an illogical point of view, not clear thinking, and a double standard, unwilling to see both sides of the fence. Truly, I conclude that wearing blinders as the horses did in the old days is similar to wearing rose-colored glasses.

Rose-colored glasses are symbolic of a thick barrier prohibiting total godliness. Rose-colored glasses represent spiritual blindness and the mind clouded by dense fog, hindering the ability to see from God's point of view. This blindness occurs because the ways of God are hidden by the darkness of the mind when we wear rose-colored glasses.

I want you to know that rose-colored glasses lack the strength of clear vision and represent a passive or indifferent attitude. Truly, a passive attitude can't separate the holy from the unholy, the clean from the unclean, the just from the unjust.

Rose-colored glasses represent compromisers, fickle people, and a seared conscience not bound by righteous convictions. Sadly, people who sway in the wind, bending left and right and going with the flow of things, are carried away by a strong current, not taking them in the right direction.

Rose-colored glasses represent unstable ground and the inability to stand firm on the absolute word of God, and whoever wears rose-colored glasses does not believe strongly in authenticity. A weak or non-believer can't be similar in strength to an oak tree, day after day, and I am proud to say that oak trees do not wear rose-colored glasses.

Rose-colored glasses are consistent in one thing: they have a godliness flaw and make no difference between the approved things of God and the unapproved things. Nor do rose-colored people differentiate between the righteous and the unrighteous or the hot and the cold.

Rose-colored glasses show no difference between men's traditions and the authentic word of God. However, rose-colored glasses will shade the truth from the light. Sadly, I must say, rose-colored glasses veil many things, including ungodly compromises they shouldn't hide.

Rose-colored glasses cannot distinguish the difference between one God and another god and the correct requirements for godliness. However, they adapt to vain philosophies, and the foolish imaginations men and women conjure up inside the runaway mind.

Furthermore, I know that the wild imagination conjures strange things within the mind, and I warn you that myths shroud the brain when we wear rose-colored glasses. It's for sure; Rose-Colored Glasses cause the heart much sorrow and a loss of godliness and closeness to God.

Lucifer and the rebellious angels wore rose-colored glasses when they thought they could conquer God and take His throne by force. Lucifer still wears rose-colored glasses; if he wrongly believes, God will overlook his works of darkness and not cast him into the burning lake of fire.

I assure you: the cold, the lukewarm person, and all liars guilty of stretching or misrepresenting the truth are wearing rose-colored glasses. If they wrongly believe, they'll not be cast into the burning lake of fire with the rebellious and wicked Lucifer and his army of rebellious angels and be erased from permanent existence.

The cruel and murderous Egyptian Pharaoh wore rose-colored glasses when he imagined his army could stop the Hebrew people from leaving the land of Egypt. It's easy to conclude that the blindness of the mind caused him to be a foolish Pharaoh.

The foolish Egyptian Pharaoh, cruel and hardhearted and a worshipper of other gods and goddesses, was blind to the supernatural power of my Creator God. The Pharaoh wore rose-colored glasses when he thought he could safely pursue Moses and advance to the other side between two high walls of water at the Red Sea.

The hardened-hearted Egyptian Pharaoh, foolish and a terrible tyrant, was wearing rose-colored glasses when he wrongly believed that Jannes and Jamborees could mimic the supernatural powers of my great Creator God and equal His incredible abilities.

The enemy Philistines wore rose-colored glasses when they thought they could kill Samson in man-to-man combat. They didn't realize their disadvantage and didn't know no man could defeat the mighty Samson in a man-to-man battle.

The boisterous giant Goliath, too confident in his size and not wise in the brain department, gladly fought for the enemy Philistines. He wore rose-colored glasses when he thought he could easily defeat the young David in a man-to-man battle.

Indeed, since the beginning of time, all the evil men in this world and all the hounds in Hell have been wearing rose-colored glasses. If they wrongly believe, they'll somehow escape the wrath of my great Creator God. For the above reason, I warn you not to wear rose-colored glasses.

I guarantee you that rose-colored glasses are a handicap, a hindrance to whoever wears them and submits to their ungodly influence. Surely, I don't doubt that rose-colored glasses are a product manufactured in the demonic spirit world, and I conclude that no one should wear rose-colored glasses.

Mainly because nothing good comes from wearing rose-colored glasses because they are flawed and cause good eyesight to have impaired vision, even though the person wearing them may not have impaired vision at the time.

Rose-colored glasses are an untouchable and intangible product, and the devil, alias the snake of old, called Lucifer, creates them. Truly, I want you to know that the wicked Lucifer encourages everyone to wear rose-colored glasses, and all his servants wear them daily.

Rose-colored glasses do not have glass lenses and wire rims. However, I warn you: they block the more excellent light from reaching our hearts. I want you to realize distress, calamities, and all sorts of troubles are unavoidable to whoever wears rose-colored glasses.

I guarantee you, even though I shouldn't have to tell you, our wonderful Father, His Son, and the Holy Ghost do not wear rose-colored glasses. Furthermore, no one is allowed into His beautiful kingdom if they wear rose-colored glasses.

Positively, our wonderful Father in Heaven does not want you and me to wear rose-colored glasses, and it's because rose-colored glasses mirage a false illusion. In the same way, the hot sun affects our eyesight and perception of things in the desert—sort of like being in the desert and seeing a lake of water, not there.

Somewhere near the top of Mount Sinai, God gave Moses and us the Ten Commandments, and He fully expects us to base our lifestyle on them. Indeed, we are wearing rose-colored glasses; if we falsely believe, we aren't required to live by the Ten Commandments of God.

I want you to realize that rose-colored glasses aren't worn only to cover our eyes. However, their spectrum is broad; rose-colored glasses cover our hearts, minds, and eyes. Surely, anything possessing this kind of power isn't good, and they have an evil origin and compatibility with the Snake of Old.

The analogy of this story reveals rose-colored glasses will not block out the sunlight, but they will block out the gift of discernment from the Holy Ghost. For this reason, I conclude that rose-colored glasses are an on-purpose design to hinder the Holy Ghost.

Rose-colored glasses do not offer us any good qualities or God-designated benefits. Still, Rose-Colored Glasses will cause headaches, heartaches, and a loss of honor and cause us to accumulate unwanted adversaries.

I want you to know that rose-colored glasses will not help our autobiography with the God of Heaven and Earth. I am sure the personal Book of Life will not speak favorably about rose-colored moments, and there's a high probability whoever wears rose-colored glasses will not have their name written in the Lamb's Book of Life.

Furthermore, if the ever-expanding definition of rose-colored glasses has compatibility with another explanation, it would be the definition of a rose-colored imagination, an untrue or dreamy imagination. I warn you: a rose-colored imagination will block out things, not wishing to be truthfully seen or things seen from two different points of view.

Beyond the shadow of a doubt, I can correctly say that rose-colored glasses magnify the imagination into a big fantasy world. Truly, it would help if you realized that our imagination's abilities will not compare to honest thoughts based on perfect clarity.

In my analogy concerning rose-colored glasses, I look for some positive attributes for their defense, and I cannot find any. Therefore, I must conclude that anyone wearing rose-colored glasses has a foresight problem, and they risk a lot by wearing them.

I assure you that rose-colored glasses will cause this world to look different than it Looks in perfect black-and-white vision. Sadly, I must say, we cannot worship God correctly and be pleasing before His eyes if we are wearing rose-colored glasses endowed with the power to alter the truth.

In conclusion, my supreme Creator would advise us to remove

our rose-colored glasses and see everything without using blinders. I know our caring God doesn't want us to believe imaginary things or live unthinkingly.

I want you to know that this teaching story called *Taking Off The Rose-Colored Eyeglasses* can identify a flaw in our character, and it's written by a real-life, experienced author who cast his glasses away years ago. The author concluded that he didn't like rose-colored spectacles and the blind spots they created.

I advise everyone to face life straight up and with a clear mind. Otherwise, we'll never see things as they are or from a godly point of view until we remove our rose-colored glasses. The sooner we do, the godlier we'll become, and the better we'll blend into society.

CHAPTER THIRTY-THREE
THE PARADOX DILEMMA

This declaration story, *The Paradox Dilemma*, portrays indecision based on two opposing choices. For example, the paradox dilemma profiles a person faced with Indecision when a decision must be made for correctness's sake.

Indeed, another example is quite unusual to consider since godliness should prevail. But it's a logical parallel and concerns the inability to make a serious or moral choice, especially when the mind lingers at the crossroads and doesn't know the right way to proceed.

Consider a concerned person, believer or not, standing between two worlds and having the choice of stepping left or right, but into one world only. They must make an important choice, one way or the other, because they realize they cannot live on the middle ground forever.

Positively, their desire to change course means they've lived in one world for part of their life, their mind cleared, they saw the light, and they didn't like the old world anymore. However, they've decided to live in the new world to improve their lives.

This scenario is *The Paradox Dilemma*; we are caught between decisions. I want you to know that a split decision isn't acceptable to our great Creator God since He expects us to choose His world or the ungodly world, and being fickle will not work with God.

Positively, a decision between one world and the other must be decided by us, even though it may seem right to live in both worlds. Truly, every person converting to Christianity must step out of one world and into another because we cannot stand in the middle of the doorway and still be acceptable to God.

Another example to consider, and this time, I'll use a hungry animal for an illustration. However, please be aware that this illustration is a parallel example. Imagine a hungry cow standing between two hay bales; the cow looks to the left and right. However, the cow stands in the middle too long and starves to death because the cow cannot decide which hay bale to eat.

The paradox dilemma has an expanded definition and can include many opposing things causing indecision. However, the paradox dilemma in this awareness story entwines the perfect word of God and the flawed traditions of men.

I assure you that the perfect word of God and the traditions of men are opposing points of view between God and man. I want you to realize that it's not a little thing to reject the word of our Great Creator God and then accept a counterfeit alternative.

Positively, many Christians observe men's traditions for years before they finally realize they are opposing God's perfect word. Indeed, whenever Christians realize they've been following men's traditions instead of God's authentic gospel, it creates a paradoxical dilemma.

The paradox dilemma upsets the order of things; the mind is confused, a compromising situation is exposed, and corrections are required. However, no Corrections mean we've accepted our compromising position, spiritual blindness is unveiled, and a challenge presents itself.

Positively, the paradox dilemma reveals a challenge to conquer and overcome, and standing at the crossroads isn't acceptable. The paradox forces a decision concerning whether to keep observing the traditions of men created by men or fall in line with God's original and perfect word.

A paradox dilemma tries to lean to the left and the right, illustrating a situation that appears to be acceptable. However, the alternative isn't acceptable; no more than a leaky boat in deep water, a leaky roof on a rainy night, or a lie standing between the truth.

I assure you, and you need to know, that a paradox dilemma always occurs whenever two viewpoints collide. Sometimes, both points of view seem correct, as if correctness can coincide with either way of thinking, regardless of whether or not it does.

Indeed, a paradoxical dilemma is God's sacred and holy fourth commandment versus men's traditions. This example means the seventh-day Sabbath Day of the Lord versus the first day of the week, the Sun-day Sabbath Day of man.

There's a paradoxical dilemma between God's Sabbath Day and man's manufactured Sunday Sabbath Day. Truly, the indecision of being unable to separate the two Sabbath Days from each other amounts to a paradoxical dilemma if we require authenticity.

Furthermore, and for the benefit of a closer relationship with

God, I encourage you to solve this paradox dilemma of man because the truth matters. I am telling you, the reality in this matter must coincide with the required fourth commandment of our great God, or the matter will not be solved.

Another example of a paradox dilemma reveals a common practice; nearly everyone is guilty of this violation. It's the decision to eat the unclean swine when the God of creation tells us not to eat it or touch its carcass.

Indeed, people illustrate this unclean violation at the dinner table, during breakfast, and at supper time, and we all know it's a personal decision to eat the flesh of the unclean swine. Furthermore, it's obvious men and women worldwide always eat the swine's flesh.

Therefore, as our knowledge of God increases, newfound truths emerge, and the decision to oppose God's infallible and perfect word and do what we are told not to do creates a paradoxical dilemma. Truly, to be specific, the word of God compromisers are the people experiencing the paradox dilemma.

I assure you that when any Christian person stands between the required word of God and the traditions of men and feels like a choice must be made between the two options, it's similar to the hungry cow standing between two bales of hay and suffering from indecision.

However, I know for sure that we aren't hungry cows, but sometimes, we emulate the confused condition of the hungry cow. This truth means there are moments when newfound truths create a paradoxical dilemma between decision and indecision.

For an example to consider, we need to understand that the most significant event in the history of Christianity is, without a doubt, the Son of God's death, burial, and resurrection if we celebrate His rising from the grave, life after death, and a Savior that delivers us from permanent extinction.

The fact that we are symbolic of the doorposts covered by the blood of the Lamb, who suffered death upon the cross, means we believers in Christ are privileged because the death angel will pass over us. After all, the merciful blood of the Lamb covers us, and we are sealed with His blood.

For the above reasons, including a show of respect for God and His wonderful and caring Son, we should put correctness before incorrectness and call Yeshua's voluntary death, burial, and resurrection the Second Passover.

Indeed, we shouldn't be guilty of calling the death of Christ by the ungodly pagan name Easter. I guarantee you that entwining colored chicken eggs to the resurrection event defies Christian intelligence. Truly, I want you to know that this tradition of men isn't Biblical.

Therefore, there's a severe paradox between the pagan word Easter and the holy and correct word called the Second Passover, and this identification error proves that Christians need to study our Bible more intensely.

Another example of a paradox dilemma is noticeable through the spectrum of the imagination, and it's so commonplace this paradox is passed around more than salt and pepper at the dinner table. It's the assumed rapture, an end-time event yet to come, seemingly correct to many Christians and incorrect to others.

Conclusively, anything assumed has the probability of being incorrect, and the collision of indecision fits the definition of a paradox dilemma because both sides of the rapture debate seem correct when only one side can be right. I want you to realize the wrong belief fits into the category of an imaginary dreamy imagination.

I assure you that many Christians believe we sleep in the dirt grave until the rapture occurs, and they believe the Rapture is an escape plan implemented by God. However, other Christians believe we go straight to Heaven in spirit form, after the death of our flesh, if we are a hot and on fire Christian.

Positively, I want you to know that both sides of the resurrection theory produce a good debate. However, indecision is the winner or the loser, and the paradox dilemma means we cannot decide which way to believe.

Therefore, Christians cannot combine the rapture and resurrection theories into one absolute conclusion. Being caught between two opinions is a paradoxical dilemma because of the rivalry between decision and indecision, godly or manmade.

In all actuality, I want you to know that this entire world suffers from a paradoxical dilemma. This truth is because there is always an alternative to the truth or godliness. Because of alternatives to the truth, it's easy to conclude that this is a confusing, paradoxical world.

Beyond a shadow of a doubt, conflicting liberal and conservative values are the main reason this world suffers from a paradoxical dilemma. This truth is simply because the liberals and the conservatives are both headstrong and believe they are correct concerning controversial issues.

However, their inability to be conclusive and know something for a fact creates a paradox dilemma, and maybe the human race isn't intelligent enough to know absolute truths. Truly, we all know for sure that the conservatives and the liberals have opposing points of view and rarely see the other side.

Another example can confuse the mind, and this example is highly controversial among many Christians because many preachers call this the grace age. Obviously, in their mind, the excellent gift of grace invalidates or supersedes God's laws and commandments.

However, many Christians believe God's laws and commandments are still as valid today as they've always been, and for the benefit of godliness, they are still an everyday requirement. However, a divide certainly exists in how some Christians define the gift of grace, and I am confident that the wall isn't likely to fall.

Therefore, the boundaries of the gift of grace aren't the same in every Christian person's analogy. This truth truly means a paradox exists between the unlimited grace believers and the limited grace believers, and a lack of Bible knowledge is one reason for many paradoxical dilemmas.

This eye-opening, serious, and important story, the Paradox Dilemma, has an awareness objective. It aims to spotlight ungodliness and suppress godliness, and I am sure this world needs a great God capable of solving the paradox dilemma.

Positively, I want you to realize that this story revolves around decisions and indecision and illustrates how some Christians believe differently. Even though our excellent Bible never changes its point of view, some Christians do, and the traditions of men manifest into Christianity from man's point of view.

Therefore, I want you to know that this revealing story parallels nearly everyone worldwide. However, this story does not intend to solve the differences between the examples of paradox dilemmas I've purposely chosen to illustrate within this story.

Conclusively, this eye-opening story only intends to illuminate the enormity of today's paradoxical dilemma between men. Positively, we all have gray areas in our lives, and the gray regions teeter between decision and indecision, even if they shouldn't.

Therefore, indecision coincides with a cloudy mind or the inability to see things in black and white. Indecision proves that the paradox dilemma is closer and more personal to us than we realize. However, I know the original word of God can solve the paradoxical dilemma.

Indeed, before this story ends, I must say that men have different opinions on the same subject for many reasons. However, I want you to know that there's never a good reason to oppose the wonderful word of my great Creator God.

Positively, for the benefit of satisfying the appetite, you do need to know a fact. The excellent word of God is the bread of life, and all other bread is imitation bread. Furthermore, I want you to realize that the beautiful gospel of God is the image of God, and His gospel deserves the utmost respect from us.

CHAPTER THIRTY-FOUR
A LACK OF MOISTURE

This explanation story concerning the unbelievers, *A Lack Of Moisture*, isn't exactly literal, and water isn't the subject I am talking about in this story. Still, I will give you a parallel concerning a lack of moisture. This story hasn't anything to do with dampness, wetness, a lack of rain, or plants welting away and drying up in the heat.

This lack of moisture story is symbolic, and for the benefit of painting a picture, it entwines with a significant metaphor meaning. This symbolic story we need to understand will parallel a lack of moisture to something alive but dying from dryness.

In this declaration story, extremely meaningful, to the point, and symbolic of many people in this confusing world, I am saying that the hot and on-fire Christians have moisture, and quite the opposite; the lukewarm and cold people are drying up because they lack Moisture.

Moisture is the main ingredient, prolonging life, and a lack of moisture slowly destroys life, and eventually, dryness will defeat life. It's the same way with the life-giving word of God since the required gospel of God illustrates the ability to provide everlasting life.

Therefore, please understand that not knowing God's required word resembles a plant lacking moisture, and it's because life dries up and dies because it doesn't receive the right essentials. The literal part of this story reveals that life will permanently end if we go to the grave unsaved.

Many people say; I know God as if knowing He's God automatically grants them safe passage into the kingdom of God. However, I assure you that knowing God is our Creator isn't the formula for eternal life, and the gift of salvation through grace isn't based on us knowing God is God.

Even Lucifer knew my God of creation, and he knew Him exceptionally well, and he's prophesized to burn in the lake of fire, and there's no grace prophesized for him. Lucifer is our example angel, revealing the beautiful gift of grace isn't designed to save everyone.

Sadly, I must say, many preachers and teachers teach the assumption that once in grace, always in grace, as if the excellent gift of grace cannot be lost. I want you to realize once in grace, always in grace isn't an accurate analogy, and this truth is revealed to us by the author in the book of Hebrews.

I assure you that because of the requirements attached to eternal life, a believer in Christ can lose their salvation one day. If they forget they need moisture and aren't careful about their choices between godliness and ungodliness, we are warned to be cautious about making bad choices.

Written by the unnamed author in the informative book of Hebrews, the author's message is a profound statement of caution, and his truthful warning to every Christian should be embedded into our memory. Truly, we are foolish people if we wrongly believe demonic spirits cannot snatch away the wonderful gift of grace.

Positively, the above warning paragraph means that sin shouldn't be taken lightly because all acts of sin lack moisture. I want you to realize that acts of sin stunt spiritual growth, like a lack of moisture causes slow growth and stunts the development of all plants.

I want you to know that the brilliant author responsible for writing the book of Hebrews tells us to walk carefully in His word unless we fall from grace. Surely, walking carefully among the wolves means walking cautiously every day. I want you to know choosing to live a careful lifestyle means we are living by God's commandments.

Walking cautiously in this jungle world means we are concerned about our souls, and we've decided to live by God's righteous Ten Commandments. Otherwise, what has moisture today can dry up and fade away even faster than the sun's light, giving way to darkness.

Furthermore, it would be a terrible loss if we slipped and fell from the grace of God and lost our promised heritage. Then, we would be similar to Esau, the rebellious son of Issac, who was denied the promise of the firstborn and lost his promised heritage because he lacked moisture.

The interpretation of the critical message in the Book of Hebrews, taken from the God-inspired author, is straightforward, especially after the Apostle cautions us. Once in grace, always in grace, isn't an accurate analogy.

I guarantee you that our wonderful God, who demands a righteous people, is serious about us keeping His required word. The reason for judgment is designed to separate careless sinners from believers in righteousness, concerned enough to repent for sin and change.

I assure you because I care where you'll spend eternity, I want you to know there's no such thing as automatic salvation, and everyone doesn't automatically go to Heaven after the death of their flesh. Because the ungodly person goes somewhere else besides Heaven, and sadly, I must say, it's at the bottom of the elevator going to the center of the Earth.

Apparently, for some illogical reason, silly, silly, foolish, many Christians consider judgment lightly as if it isn't meant for them, even if they live a life of sin. This mistaken belief parallels being blind, even with good eyesight.

I guarantee you that the reason for judgment is to separate careless sinners from someone concerned enough to repent for sin and change their lifestyle to be entwined with the word of God. Be aware and know if careless sinners do not repent and change, a separation day will divide them from the wheat.

Positively, I want you to know that sin is sin, and Christians aren't exempt from the judgment of sin and are no different than unbelieving sinners. However, a sincere Christian can repent, change, and receive forgiveness for sin, and by God's amazing grace, this is their gift through the blood sacrifice of Yeshua, the Son of God.

I guarantee that my great God doesn't display double standards or bend the rules for anyone if they refuse to conform to His required commandments. I am confident that our best eternal life policy is to be a commandment keeper because He allows commandment lovers to live in His kingdom.

Therefore, it's a one-hundred percent accurate statement, the wise author of the book of Hebrews proclaims. When he tells us to walk carefully, lest we fall from God's beautiful grace, this is one crucial scripture we better not forget. Because sin is our enemy, and grace given can be grace taken away, and a foolish compromiser isn't cautious enough to protect the gift of grace.

Beyond a shadow of a doubt, various acts of sin are why many Christians fall from God's grace. This truth means that constant sinning and the gift of grace do not go well together, and we would be foolish Christians to believe otherwise.

Positively, the following warning scripture concerning the slippery road of life illustrates how carelessness and a lack of thankfulness can erase the gift of grace. I conclude that the gift of grace shouldn't be abused or stretched too far out of definition.

I assure you the above statement is an excellent example to remember and not be forgotten like Esau forgot. The rebellious brother of Jacob, Esau, was careless and lost his inheritance because of carelessness, unthankfulness, and a lack of moisture.

The following enlightenment scripture, profiling a man on a slippery road, reveals a sobering declaration. The declaration points to a lack of moisture and godliness; these terrible character qualities will cause a wide gap between our Creator God and us.

Indeed, this serious metaphor about lacking moisture has a meaningful declaration: We better not lack moisture for our benefit. Indeed, for everyone's enlightenment, I must say that a lack of moisture and the definition of ungodliness mean the same thing.

Hebrews 12:16 Lest there be any <u>fornicator</u> (that's accepted strange gods, or have been polluted by immorality) and lust or profane (means became a godless, sensual, and unclean) person, as Esau, who sold his birthright for one morsel of meat (means food).

Esau was careless, thankless, irreverent, and disrespectful and didn't exhibit the right kind of honor and loyalty toward the God of his fathers. For this reason, he couldn't obtain favor with our great Creator God or step off the slippery road going downhill.

I assure you: an assumed heritage, whether it's the land of Israel, in the kingdom of God, or within our household. It doesn't mean an assumed inheritance is absolutely one hundred percent for sure, day after day unless we put the beautiful word of God first.

Indeed, an example to consider is Esau, a brother older than Jacob. However, Esau is characteristically different from Jacob, and the scriptures insinuate that Esau was a strong bully and thought he could take what he wanted by being forceful.

Esau erroneously assumed he would inherit the promise of the firstborn. However, Bible scriptures prove that Esau was wrong. Therefore, to keep Israel out of the wrong hands, the inheritance passed from Isaac to Jacob and will not be given to Esau, the firstborn.

Positively, Esau was godless and uncaring. He was rebellious to God's commanded ways, and his heritage wasn't valuable to him. Otherwise, he wouldn't have sold it to his brother Jacob for food and would've applied himself to God's required ways.

Possibly, Esau failed to obtain grace because of his ungodliness, entwined with acts of rebellion forbidden by God. Bible scriptures reveal that he lost his divine blessings and promises, but he did receive a barren wasteland instead of milk and honey.

Indeed, the wrong type of examples that Esau portrays in this story should be a warning to us if we are indifferent and lack moisture. Indeed, lacking moisture means not taking the word of God seriously enough, and a lack of Moisture will result in a careless walk on the ungodly ground, and God will not bless a person who dried up on the inside.

This story's other example should always be remembered, lest forgetfulness overcome us like a thief at night. We can fall from God's grace and lose our inheritance in the kingdom of God if we become unthankful.

This eye-opening story, which requires our full attention, is called *A Lack Of Moisture*. It has nothing to do with water and plants. However, I want you to realize that this critical story has everything to do with staying in or falling out of grace.

This eye-opening story concerning our failure to do right, a lack of moisture, symbolizes not having a good relationship with our wonderful God. I want you to know that His righteous Ten Commandments are heavily laden with moisture, and they will accelerate our growth in His word.

Conclusively, this story should end with good advice, and I want you to know that self-examination is good for us. Truly, every time we see a plant suffering from a lack of moisture, we should look into a mirror and make sure a Lack of Moisture isn't an image of us.

CHAPTER THIRTY-FIVE
BETTER PEOPLE

This undebatable short story, which I call *Better People,* is an enlightenment story that reveals a fact most people already know, and if you don't, you should. There are formulated things, not secret or hidden, and are perfectly designed to shape us into Better People.

Even though everyone should already know no one is perfect, this accurate analogy includes all Christians. However, because I've learned the secret, I can accurately say that extraordinary things created by my great God can shape us into better people.

Therefore, because of the specialness we seek, this short story looks into the heavens above, specifically at our great and righteous God. His wisdom is beyond compare, and He sits upon the throne in Heaven, inside His grand temple on God's holy mountain.

I assure you that our wonderful and caring God, who sits on heaven's throne, gave us the formula for creating better people. Because He wants the best for us, He hopes we'll utilize His infallible design for perfection every day we live and breathe in the flesh.

Furthermore, everyone alive and living on planet Earth should desire to be better people; we should try to live a godly designed lifestyle, especially since a Christian lifestyle entwines the formula for creating better people.

Beyond a shadow of a doubt, we aren't alone in our quest to become better people; God gave us His Holy Ghost to help us. He wants us to become better people before we meet Him at the Judgement Throne and be ladies and gentlemen while we live in this crude world.

I guarantee that the excellent Holy Ghost is our Mentor, and He will share the right kind of wisdom and knowledge with us. Because He cares about our souls, He will increase our armor's strength if we allow Him to guide us correctly.

As our fathers found out before us, the infallible ingredients that strengthen our armor are found in God's perfect word. However, we are in control of our decisions, and it's up to us to wear the word of God and use it as body armor to protect our souls.

I want you to know that God's wonderful and perfect word is a killer arrow and a sin-preventer. For the sake of preserving righteousness, the word of God can kill the ungodly doctrines of Lucifer, designed to prevent us from being better people.

Positively, without the analogy being debatable, if you are a serious Christian and hope to overcome Lucifer's ploys and tricks. Then, the required word of God must be the bread you eat and the crutch for steadying your walk daily.

God's excellent and righteous word must be the pillow we rest our heads on at night, and it's because the beautiful and infallible word answers all our sin problems. I am confident that the word of God is the only formula for creating better people.

I assure you that there are no sin problems in this world; the strong word of God cannot correct or prevent them from happening. Furthermore, if you think about it, you'll have to conclude that commandment-keeping prevents sin. I am sure nothing prevents acts of corruption better than obeying His commandments.

This meaningful declaration story called Better People reveals His expectations of us. This true story purposely gives my wonderful Creator God credit for showing us the only formula designed to transform us into God-designed, better people.

However, I want you to know that the Better People formula has a powerful and cruel adversary, and he doesn't like the Better People formula. The evil Lucifer has a procedure designed to keep us from being better people, and his recipe is called ungodliness.

Beyond the shadow of a doubt, the rebellious and wicked Lucifer hates the required word of God, and it's easy to conclude he's the main reason the word of God is disappearing from among men. For this reason, I warn you we will have a few battles with him.

However, the fact remains true, and this God-designed analogy is unchallengeable. I assure you, there's nothing else in this world able to transform men and women into better people other than the perfect word of my Creator God.

Positively, I want to believe with all my heart that everyone on this Earth should want to be a better person. However, I am sure we cannot be better people without opening our hearts and accepting guidance from our great God.

Beyond the shadow of a doubt, the superior teaching of the beautiful Holy Ghost is a Christian guiding Spirit. His moral education, Special to all other instructions, is one of the primary reasons Lucifer hates Him and us.

Conclusively, I am exceedingly proud to say that the excellent gospel of God, superior to any other character-building essentials, contains the right ingredients and is guaranteed to transform us into better people.

Positively, some things are worth more than gold, and the great Ten Commandments of God provide an excellent service to all of humanity. I assure you, His commandments are the heartbeat of every good thing, and better people are a creation from their wisdom. I hope you are a covenant keeper determined to improve your character daily.

CHAPTER THIRTY-SIX
SCRUB BRUSH AND SOAP

This personal-to-everyone story, illuminating the lifestyle we choose to live, is called *Scrub Brush And Soap*. It's an illustrative story, and it parallels me and everyone else who lives daily in the sunshine and the rain.

Indeed, this is a metaphor story designed to coincide with actual reality, and metaphors illustrate how we can get saved one day and be unsaved the next. And I assure you, our salvation with the Lord isn't so secure; it cannot get lost the following day.

This expressive story, reaching into the depths of the soul, *Scrub Brush And Soap, illustrates the unclean man repented and changed by God's beautiful and powerful grace. Since the beginning of creation, the Lord's objective has been to clean us up and mold us into new creatures.*

This parallel to everyone's story also illustrates that falling away from God means we can be scrubbed clean today and dirty tomorrow. I assure you, when the sun comes up in the morning, so does a new set of challenges.

In some ways, a scrub brush and soap represent the weak, passive person who slides in and out of sin; a scrub brush and soap parallel to the man by the wayside who hears the word of God and receives it with joy.

However, his joy weakens and fades away sometime after that because the wayside man's heart wasn't wholly converted. Sadly, it's because the devil cometh and taketh away the wonderful word of God and removes it from his heart.

This truth means various temptations stand in our way, day after day. Truly, whenever the word of God becomes heavy, and a burden to our lifestyle and the joy of the Lord disappears from our hearts, we'll fall away and get dirty again.

Therefore, our conversion to Christianity is similar to washing the dirt away, putting filthiness behind us, and making you and me cleaner. However, falling away from God is similar to throwing the scrub brush and soap away and preferring to stay dirty.

The following informative scripture was taken from the great book of Hebrews, and it reveals a warning about playing in the mud puddles of sin and getting dirty again. The wise author of the book of Hebrews tells us sin knocks on our door, and we better not let it in.

The following extremely serious scripture reveals that men can receive the gift of grace and fall from grace for various reasons. This truth means we have a great responsibility to ourselves because we are the caretakers of our beautiful gift of grace.

Beyond the shadow of a doubt, the beautiful Holy Ghost and the gift of grace go together like a scrub brush and soap, and when they are entwined together, they'll make a cleaner Christian out of everyone they work through.

However, please remember, and do not fail to remember, that the same God responsible for giving us the Holy Ghost and the valuable gift of grace can and will take it away from us if we do not appreciate the Holy Ghost and its excellent and beautiful gift.

This truth means that whenever the wicked devil steals God's Special and holy word from our hearts and minds, our memory fails us, and we cannot retain His wonderful and righteous word; our dwelling inside of us must be unclean.

An unclean heart means that the Great Holy Ghost and the wonderful gift of grace have nowhere to live within us. Because too many ungodly things are cluttering the way, we've failed to maintain the beautiful Holy Ghost in a godly living environment.

The above environment analogy, absolutely correct and vital, reveals the primary reason for the following awareness scripture. Without directly saying it, the following explanation of scripture advises us to use soap every day and not fall away.

The following enlightenment scripture can be considered a warning to anyone not thankful enough for the Holy Ghost and the gift of grace. The words diligently used in the following scripture mean that the gift of grace isn't so lenient; we can continue being careless sinners.

I assure you, and you should know, that it takes solid spiritual armor and a heavily fortified heart, firm in His word, to protect the dwelling place of the Holy Ghost and the needed gift of grace from being snatched away.

Conclusively, the perfect word of God is our spiritual armor and sin deflector. The evil devil is the wicked one, trying hard to steal the word of God from our hearts, and the rebellious Lucifer is an expert thief, self-trained to snatch the word of God away from weak in the Lord men.

The wicked Lucifer is our prime example, illustrating an angel falling away, and a scrub brush and soap will not wash his dirt away. Sadly, after all these thousands of years since the angel rebellion in Heaven, he's still a dirty Lucifer.

The following three examples are metaphor illustrations, illuminating a similar robbery committed by Lucifer's ghost spirit. After reading them, it'll be easier to identify the wicked Lucifer as a word of God thief.

Number one > The word of God tells us that if the seed falls by the wayside, then the fowls of the air will devour it.

Number two > However, if the Seed falls upon the rocks, it'll wither away from a lack of moisture.

Number three > However, if the seed falls among the thorns, then the thorns will restrict the seed's ability to grow. The three paralleling examples of men reveal a metaphor, and the metaphor shows we have a demonic ghost spirit problem.

Beyond the shadow of a doubt, the thorns the beautiful Son of God is talking about are ungodly people, not strong in the righteous word of God. It's easy to conclude that the word of God cannot help or grow strong among ungodly people.

I want you to know that the above three metaphor examples illustrate the seed as the excellent word of God, and it's easy to see that the needed word of God is struggling to grow strong within most people's hearts.

The above three examples illustrate the required word of God is ineffective because the seed wasn't rooted in good ground. For this reason, a scrub brush and soap must be used if we expect to keep the heart from falling away.

This next need to remember scripture illustrates a dire warning and great words of wisdom concerning why men and women fall away. If we remember the words in the following scripture, it'll be easier to keep from falling away.

I assure you that the author responsible for writing the book of Hebrews doesn't want us Christians to believe that once saved, always saved is the truth. The author of Hebrews tells us, without saying it directly, to reverence God and keep His commandments.

Hebrews 12:15 <u>Looking</u> (means walking) diligently (means walking carefully) lest any man fail of the grace of God (means fail to be thankful to God for their heritage of eternal salvation, and fall from grace).

Hebrews 12:15 Lest any root of <u>bitterness</u> (between man and God) springing up trouble you, and <u>thereby</u> (is the reason) many (people be) <u>defiled</u>.

I want you to know that the word defiled means changed for the worse, lost, corrupted, and unclean, and becomes godless. Because whenever godliness is forgotten, ungodliness prevails, and thankfulness to God isn't an emotion of the heart.

The word defiled means that an unclean person becomes godless and unthankful for the promise of eternal salvation. When men and women exhibit these characteristics, their hearts are defiled, and darkness blocks the light.

The word defiled means we've lost our faith and quit putting the word of God first. This truth means that our minds and hearts are drifting into sin, which means we are further away from the peaceful kingdom of God.

Therefore, indirectly, the above author is saying grace given can be grace taken away. This truth means the seed only grows in good ground, where the roots can grow strong and deep. I am confident that the Seed only grows strong in the Bible-savvy person.

Conclusively, the unknown author is responsible for writing the excellent book of Hebrews. He points out the absolute fact when he reveals that we must continually walk with God to stay in His grace, and picking up the cross of Yeshua and carrying it illuminates a continuous walk with God.

Positively, I want you to realize that the unknown author uses the word carefully as an illustration and warning word. You must know that the warning word concerns us and our ability to retain the beautiful Holy Ghost.

Therefore, a scrub brush and soap will only keep us clean if we use them daily, or we'll get dirty and fall away. The word diligently means we must stay exuberant and loyal to God to avoid falling from His presence.

Conclusively, I want you to know that a fall from grace amounts to losing our heritage in the kingdom of God. Being defiled is always the reason for our fall; the warning means we better stay clean daily.

Positively, because of extreme importance, I want you to realize that a defiled heart cannot retain the beautiful Holy Ghost and the gift of grace. A defiled heart lacks the qualities of godliness, and the Holy Ghost and the gift of grace will not live in an unclean place.

Without a doubt, the thorns, rocky ground, and the fowls by the wayside mean that our hearts failed to root in the word of God. Sadly, when the heart doesn't root into good ground, the word of

God will not grow strong within us.

This truth means that when the seed does not grow, there's a problem with the heart, and a scrub brush and soap cannot clean a defiled heart, especially if the heart's owner doesn't cultivate the seed and feed it the essentials for continuous growth.

The thorns and the rocky ground mean we didn't respect the seed or show it enough concern to keep it growing healthy and strong. Please realize the fowls of the air are our enemy, and they're symbolic of us letting ungodly people steal our hearts away from the commanded ways of God.

In conclusion, I want you to realize that a scrub brush and soap only work if we stay away from rocky ground, thornbushes, and the fowls of the air. All three of these illustrations mean we better avoid sinful things.

In this symbolic story, *Scrub Brushes And Soap* says it's our responsibility to water and fertilize the seed and protect it from being snatched away by robbers. I conclude that we'll have to fall in love with the word of God, or we'll not be able to protect the seed from robbers.

Positively, the bread of life is the commanded word of God, and eating it every day illustrates the clean and scrubbed brushed way. Indeed, eating the bread of life illuminates men and women who are determined not to fall away from the authentic gospel of God.

CHAPTER THIRTY-SEVEN
THE SPRING THAT NEVER RUNS DRY

This enlightenment story, *The Spring That Never Runs Dry*, is more accurate than the sun's pattern. It entwines and expresses the literal and illustrates it through an illustrative example. This story says our lives are missing godliness if we don't develop a love for God's word and drink from the spring that never dries.

Therefore, before this revealing story starts, I want you to know that the spring that never runs dry isn't about water, wells, or bubbling over wet locations. Truthfully, the spring that never runs dry is everywhere a believer in Christ is thirsty.

I want you to know that the beautiful spring that never runs dry is connected to a divine source. The spring that never runs dry is about the righteous word from the Heavens above, which flows from God's compassionate heart. My God is bubbling over, full of incredible wisdom, love, and righteousness.

The excellent word of God sprung up from His incredibly passionate heart, and His heart commanded Him to share with you and me His superior wisdom. Because of His love for us, He poured out the knowledge in His heart through the best of words.

I assure you that because of many recorded biblical events, we know His heart commands His thoughts and actions. Furthermore, it's a beautiful blessing in our favor to have a righteous God, bound and entwined to His own honest heart.

Truly, I want you to realize that His superior and righteous thoughts were passed from Him to the prophets, apostles, and His beautiful Son. Because a new world is on the horizon, He wants us to learn the correct way from Him and all His servants and be ready for the new horizon.

I am sure His excellent and righteous thoughts are constantly taught in every generation. Because He cares about our spiritual development, it will remain the same until His beautiful Son returns in the last days.

Conclusively, we must stop, look up, thank our great God, bend down, and drink from the spring that never dries. After tasting His delicious waters, I am sure we'll not be full and thirst over and over for the beautiful word of God.

Bible scriptures reveal that the spring that never runs dry symbolizes the rock in the desert. The rock is where pure water flowed forth during the time of Moses and the desert dwellers. We could accurately say it was a divine miracle rock designed to extend the lives of His people.

Positively, the rock in the desert and our life symbolize God, and living waters flow from Him, not from any other person. His perfect word, superior to all other Words, coincides with the strength of solid rock, and He's the miracle worker from above.

Even during droughts, He's still the spring that never dries up, and no other waters are as satisfying as the waters flowing from His throne. The excellent word of God is similar to living waters that sustain and extend every creation's life.

Conclusively, there wouldn't be life on this Earth without water or eternal life without God and His excellent life-saving word designed to prepare us for His kingdom. I want you to realize that man's whole duty entwines with every word of His gospel.

Therefore, I want you to know that the perfect word of God and life-sustaining waters are elements to nourish our body and heart, and thanks to our excellent provider, God, both increase our inner strength to a greater degree.

Furthermore, just as we seek to find water every day of our lives, we should seek the excellent word of God the same way every day. If we seek God's word daily, our efforts will become pleasurable and fill us with great faith.

I assure you that we cannot do without the perfect word of God, no more than we can do without water and live a long life. However, men will seek after and drink water daily, defy logic, and not care about learning the required word of God.

Indeed, most men and women care more about their lives in the flesh than the formula for eternal life. However, men will spend their entire lives drinking water and forget about the life-saving word of God until it's time to leave this Earth behind.

Then they'll think about God and the afterlife and wish they would've been wise and desired the word of God as much as they wanted a cold glass of water. I assure you, even the lukewarm and the Cold Person will bow their knees before God someday, and if you wait too long, it'll be too late.

I guarantee you that the consequences for avoiding the needed word of God are the same as dying of thirst from a lack of water. It's easy to conclude that death is the lingering result in both cases; only the end of the flesh isn't nearly as terrible as death to the soul.

God gave us life-saving water, and His required written word, and one is equally as important to us as the other. I want you to know that we are fools to believe His word isn't as crucial as water because of its life-saving benefits. However, when the flesh dies, loyalty to His word will become more important than water.

This enlightenment story, which I call the spring that never runs dry, illuminates a reference to the perfect word of God more than water. Indeed, drinking from the spring that never runs dry reveals a God enthusiast of the highest degree.

After reading this metaphorical story about the importance of the gospel of God, The Spring That Never Runs Dry, we should think about God's beautiful word and the importance attached to it every time we drink water.

Beyond the shadow of a doubt, most educated and uneducated people are wise enough to know that water is the building block of life. Water is the building block of life if we only consider the flesh and blood body and its everyday need for water.

However, if we desire a second life, we want to live forever in the kingdom of God. Then we better drink from the rock of life and stay connected to His beautiful word every day, and this isn't a problem if we are hot and on fire believers in Christ.

Conclusively, this declaration story, paralleling water to the beautiful word of God, has a specific intention and a severe point to declare before all men and women. Because the grand prize of immortality needs to be secured, this story intends to illustrate the importance of seeking after the word of God as much as we do water.

Furthermore, I hope and pray that you'll drink water from God's literal well and the excellent living waters. If you do, you'll be doing God's will and fulfilling His plan. Then, on Judgement Day, you will be happy that you put His will first.

While visiting the land of Samaria, a woman came to pull water from the literal well, and the Son of God asked her for a drink, which surprised the Samarian woman mainly because she didn't expect a Jew to speak to her since the Jews would avoid the Samarians.

However, the Son of God cares about everyone and their salvation, and the caring Son of God didn't avoid her, nor will He avoid you and me. Truly, it's correct to say we parallel to the Samaritan woman; her being a Samaritan didn't matter to Him, and He said unto her.

John 4:10 If thou knewest the <u>gift</u> of <u>God</u> (which is eternal salvation), and who it is that saith to thee, Give Me to drink: thou wouldest ask of Him, and He would have given thee living water.

Positively, the above scripture proves that Jesus is everyone's Savior, and He proved this fact true because He willingly offered living water to the Samaritan woman. This interpretation means that the wonderful gift of salvation is for everyone willing to believe in Him.

I assure you that this story is all about the living waters of God, and the living waters of God are entwined and parallel to eternal salvation. Truly, when we think about the spring that never runs dry, we should think about our Creator God and His living waters.

I guarantee you: He's the Tree of Life, and the beasts of the field and every living thing will find their needs under His branches. His bounties are the oceans, the farms, and much animal life, and thanks to the generosity of God, we all eat and drink from His bounty.

Indeed, His life-saving word entwines His bountiful promises, and if we try to live by His required word, we'll preserve a grand treasure in our afterlife. Regardless of the value men attach to the word of God, His word holds the keys to immortality.

Furthermore, I want you to realize His enormous bounty, exceedingly tremendous; everywhere men stand on this Earth. It combines water, food, oxygen, and thought to formulate life's essential building blocks.

In this story, we must understand that it is important for everyone who looks for the right way: *The Spring That Never Runs Dry* is intended to be a thankful story, and it gladly thanks our wonderful God for His essence of life spring.

Conclusively, I want you to know that there wouldn't be any great purpose in life if we didn't have the promise of God and an expectation for a better future void of wickedness and hurtful things. Indeed, I know a Great Future waits somewhere ahead of this moment if we drink from the spring that never runs dry.

However, the wonderful word of God tells us there is a specific requirement for a better future, and I am sure we have to drink from the spring that never runs dry before we can expect to secure a better future.

Conclusively, to entwine you and me with the Samaritan woman at the well, Yeshua said I would give you living waters to drink if you ask me. Therefore, conversion to Christianity means we've decided to drink from *His Spring That Never Runs Dry*.

Positively, God wants us to know; all we have to do is ask and believe in God's Son and the words He said to the Samaritan women. Then, we can drink the living waters of life, like the fountain of youth, bubbling up from the spring that never runs dry.

CHAPTER THIRTY-EIGHT
EVALUATING FEAR

Fear has an extended definition, and it means much more than being afraid of a snake, a bear, or a vicious dog. The expanded definition of fear has many examples and includes anything that can make men tremble and afraid.

I assure you that a good scare shakes our real tree, and men do have respect for scary things; that's scary enough to make them tremble with fear. It sounds bold and courageous to say I am not afraid of anything, but there are certain things all men and women need to fear.

Fear is one of those personal things, an unsettling emotion we've all felt; it's a tailored feeling that will fit each individual differently. Because of the things one person fears, another man doesn't fear, and it's easy to conclude that personal fears cannot be stereotyped.

Indeed, there are little fears, there are great fears, there are warranted fears, and there are unwarranted fears. Furthermore, there are even things we should fear but don't fear, and there are things we shouldn't fear but do fear.

Beyond the shadow of a doubt, I am pretty sure the emotion of fear can be triggered by the presence of danger, especially a life-threatening risk. Truly, when danger threatens our lives, I am sure our heart rate will increase, and we will experience the emotion of fear.

Furthermore, the emotion of fear will be triggered by foreseen dangers yet to come, such as dangerous territories lying ahead. Some fears are justifiable, some aren't, some men fear easily, and some men haven't any fear.

Fear is one of those unpredictable emotions, and it can cause men and women to bring their priorities to the forefront and give them a severe evaluation. I agree; we should evaluate our fears and consider their reason.

Some men are realists and only fear what they see with their eyes, and the dangerous situation they're in the midst of is causing them to fear, while other men have a fear complex and worry about the unseen and what might happen to them shortly or somewhere in the future.

I guarantee you that it's easier to fear the dangers we see than unseen dangers yet to happen. However, some men and women are wise enough to look ahead and avoid dangerous things by devising an alternate plan to avoid potential risks.

Meanwhile, the unwise and the unfearful man never looks far enough ahead to avoid potential dangers and life-threatening situations. Truly, I want you to know that living for the moment leaves us vulnerable, and being weak in mind and spirit will not help us avoid potential risks.

Positively, we can be nonchalant and walk unthinkingly, like men and women in the dark, not having enough light to see a potential danger. However, walking mindlessly and being unconcerned concerning unseen hazards cannot be considered a sign of wisdom.

Superior wisdom is proven because we look ahead, evaluate potential dangers, and avoid them before it's too late. For example, we must consider this statement of truth since the following fact affects all of us.

Salvation and damnation are two important subjects of concern; all men must look ahead and into the future to achieve or avoid. I guarantee you that this type of foresight is excellent, and if we believe in Christ, it means we are looking ahead.

I assure you, and you should know without being told, that the wonderful gift of salvation should be the top priority on every person's mind. However, I want you to know that it'll take a look ahead to accomplish and secure the grand prize of salvation.

However, having hindsight and being nonchalant about the danger of damnation secures a person nothing eternal in the heavens above because damnation awaits men and women when they forget to reverence God and keep His commandments.

Indeed, this short story proves that we can evaluate fear in many ways, but living a cautious lifestyle illustrates the best way to live. This truth means we better not forget to fear God because He does have the power and the authority to cast men into the pits of Hell.

Furthermore, the God-inspired Bible warns us to avoid doing rebellious things; He'll send us to Hell for doing them. Precariously, some of us walk the razor's edge, invisible and ever-present, between the gift of salvation and the severe judgment of damnation.

Therefore, I want you to realize that everyone on this Earth needs to know about our Creator God's Highly Important Judgment Scales, and if we know about the Judgment Scales of God, it'll be easier to avoid the judgment of damnation.

The severe judgment Scales of God consist of only three essential words, and the righteousness of our lives is judged from these three words. The three Important judgment words written on the Judgment Scales of God are hot, cold, and lukewarm.

Conclusively, we all fit the definition of one of those three important words, and our ending in the flesh will either be hot, cold, or lukewarm. Truly, this temperature evaluation is an unavoidable identification we'll all have attached to us as we stand before the Judgment Throne of God.

Indeed, this concerning story I call *Evaluating Fear* gives us something to fear, other than snakes, bears, and vicious dogs. The deciding Judgment Scales of God will provide the lukewarm and the cold person plenty to worry about at some point and time in their future.

This truth means that wisdom or ignorance is entwined with choices, and I want you to know that fearing God and the judgment of damnation is a good thing to worry about if we live unsaved. Truly, this type of fear illustrates something the nonchalant and spiritually blind people do not have to do yet.

Therefore, the cold and the lukewarm can bask in the pleasures of life and walk proudly on this Earth. However, being carefree and spiritually blind is the formula for a rude awakening, and the destiny of the rude awakening every unbeliever has attached to their account will be during the resurrection time on Judgement Day.

However, I want you to know that being spiritually wise about the required word of God illuminates the formula for winning the prize of salvation and a life of immortality. I conclude that pursuing this formula will purify our hearts and get us through the pearl gates in Heaven.

Indeed, I hope you fear our wonderful Creator God and are afraid of being sinful. But if you do not fear committing evil acts, then Hell is reserved and waiting for you. This true statement reveals that no fear of God illuminates a bad character quality and a negative potential for spiritual improvement.

Conclusively, as we walk through this life, the main thing for you and me to achieve is a hot and on-fire desire for the commanded word of God and love being strong in Him. If we are strong in Him, and you and I choose to walk in His ways, a new world awaits us.

Within this meaningful story, *Evaluating Fear*, I've tried extremely hard to emphasize entwining fear with eternal salvation. This analogy is because the gift of salvation isn't ours to claim so easily unless we are willing to walk on the narrow road of life.

Positively, we need to know the words of a great Apostle, and because it's fitting, the loyal Apostle Peter should get the last word in this enlightenment story. Knowing the next scripture makes it easier to understand our need to fear God for the practical benefit of perfect clarity.

The following awareness scripture concerning the seriousness of living right reveals that righteous believers in Christ are Scarcely Saved. Truly, if the believer in God is Scarcely Saved, salvation isn't entirely free for the length of our lives. The Bible clearly warns us that we are fools to believe that eternal life is easy to win or a gift from God given to us on a silver platter.

1 Peter 4:18 And if the righteous scarcely be saved, where shall the ungodly and the sinner appear?

The second half of the above scripture asks us where the ungodly and the sinner appear. This truth means that beyond the shadow of a doubt, the ungodly person and the unrepented sinner have a different destiny than the saved believer in Christ.

The Apostle Peter doesn't say that the ungodly person is delivered to the pits of Hell. However, Hell is the only other place if the blood of the Lamb isn't accepted and doesn't save the ungodly person.

As we live and breathe in the flesh, I want you to know that it's incredibly foolish to gamble on our salvation. Conclusively, I call this important short story concerning the emotions of our hearts *Evaluating Fear*. This story is saying regardless of our degree of (fear) concerning dangerous, life-threatening things, we better not forget to fear God and the judgment of damnation.

Positively, I am warning you: if we do forget to fear God, we'll be the ones getting hurt, and we will regret not having fear for Him. Salvation isn't an automatic gift everyone receives, and not respecting the word of God indicates the Son of God will not be their Savior.

CHAPTER THIRTY-NINE
HOW MANY WORDS DOES IT TAKE?

The name of this concerning story, *How Many Words Does It Take*, reveals a tremendous spiritual dilemma—the dilemma between humanity and God. I want you to know that humankind is God's creation suffering from this terrible dilemma, and it's not my wonderful God.

This critical teaching story emphasizes the most crucial question the unsaved person needs to ask themselves. But being unconcerned about this Important question probably means the uninterested person will go to their grave unsaved.

The excellent King James Bible, filled with God-inspired wisdom, consists of approximately seven hundred and eighty thousand story example words. However, the great Ten Commandments of God and their warning words consist of roughly two hundred and ninety-five words.

The conclusion to the whole matter and its teaching words consists of only six essential words. The meaningful Judgment

Scales of God consist of only three profound words, but these three judgment words have great significance to eternal life or permanent death.

I assure you, and you must realize the beautiful God-designed Ten Commandments and the conclusion to the whole matter. Knowing about the three temperature words written upon the Judgment Scales of God is needed to learn subjects, and they are the pinnacle of need-to-know issues.

Positively, the Judgment Scale words are the most important subjects for us to know and understand, more so than all the other story examples within the Bible. However, all the other Bible stories are essential; we should try to understand as many of them as possible.

All story examples within the Bible are critically important, regardless of the events or the people being portrayed, because stories illustrate to us through examples the things men do right and the things men do wrong.

Indeed, it should be apparent to believers in Christ that all Bible stories illustrate good and bad examples, and I guarantee we can learn something from them. I assure you, Bible examples are God-inspired and were designed to teach us the expectations of God.

Furthermore, we can apply these story examples to our lifestyle with the expectation of becoming a godlier person. Especially if they are good examples, we can avoid doing them if they are wrong. My wonderful God expects us to adopt this view concerning Bible stories.

However, the critical question we all need to answer is relevant to our gift of salvation. For this reason, I am asking you *How Many*

Words It Will Take before we can walk on the right path designed by our extraordinary God. *Truly, How Many Words Will It Take* before our faith is strong and our hearts fully accept Him?

Therefore, I am asking you, how many story examples must we learn before we know to do right and abhor doing wrong? I am one hundred percent sure if we read enough story examples, we'll learn the expectations of God.

However, three hundred and one words should be all it takes to win the grand prize of immortality. As wonderful and helpful as it is to learn a lot of Bible stories, three hundred and one words are all it takes to win the grand prize of salvation.

My analogy amounts to the two hundred and ninety-five words designed to make up the Ten Commandments of God, including the six essential words, explaining the conclusion to the whole matter and their connection to the Ten Commandments.

However, since we are inferior flesh and blood, hard-headed and rebellious non-conformers, we people need all the story examples we can get from a divine source. Yet, sometimes, meaningful learning eludes us, so God gave us many illustrations of right and wrong.

We need story examples to know for sure about the reward of salvation and the judgment of damnation, mainly because life on this Earth is a severe test, and to live forever; we must win the grand prize of immortality. Otherwise, an angel will carry us to the abyss, and we'll wait for the second resurrection.

I assure you, and you better know that losing the prize of immortality amounts to losing everything. Sadly, losing the wonderful gift of salvation means we'll become nonexistent in the future, like a puff of smoke, here and gone and never seen again.

Therefore, for this reason, I will tell you about the Judgment Scales of God, how they work, and their primary purpose, mainly because all men and women should know that three words from within the entire Bible will judge and decide their eternal fate.

Indeed, knowing this fact alone should be a good enough reason to respect God's perfect word immensely, mainly because these three judgment words given to us by the God of Heaven and Earth are a primary reason for all the story examples written in the Bible.

I assure you that all people will be treated fairly and judged by these three important words, which I call hot, cold, and lukewarm. Sadly, these three pinnacles of judgment words do not affect the majority of the people in this world today since most of them are lukewarm or cold to the word of God.

I guarantee each person greatly differs; some people take life seriously, and others do not. This truth means it'll take some men and women more words and story examples than others before they walk on the right path in life.

God must've realized this, and He decided to give us thousands of different story examples. However, I am sure the excellent Ten Commandments are the right path in this life, and the hot temperature of the heart is achieved because we keep the Ten Commandments of God.

The Bible assures us that the words lukewarm and ice-cold coincide with the not-very-serious person who lacks deep thought and concern for their soul. The lukewarm and cold person illustrates the image of men and women who do not concern themselves enough with God's wonderful and required Ten Commandments.

Positively, I conclude that the brilliant Ten Commandments

of God put identification to the cold and the lukewarm person. I am correct to say that the great Ten Commandments of my great Creator God is and always will be the definition expert, and they identify all acts of sin.

My great God says lukewarm and cold people have a temperature problem and miss out on the most important character quality. This truth means that the ice-cold and the lukewarm person do not receive the keys to His kingdom, but all hot and on-fire Christians do.

I want you to know that I am basing this statement on a logical point of view parallel to God's word. Above all other things, the Lord's kingdom is also worth being serious about achieving citizenship. I guarantee you, it's a foolish miscalculation if we do not try to secure a home in His kingdom.

Indeed, suppose we care about doing right and achieving citizenship in His kingdom. In that case, we will love God's great and perfect Ten Commandments more than any other words. Simply for the holy things they stand for and the ungodly things they oppose.

Furthermore, if our hearts haven't turned to stone, and we aren't bound to the wickedness in this world, we should desire to be righteous people. We should want to live in a moral world, and His perfect Ten Commandments are the formula for achieving both goals.

I assure you that the excellent Ten Commandments are our answer to a hopeful and, so far, unachieved dream world. However, within the kingdom of God, a Utopian society will be more than a hope and a dream, and the unachieved will be achieved.

Within the peaceful kingdom of God, the truth will shine like a bright light, and all men and women will finally know that the excellent Ten Commandments of God were the light shining the way to a new home and a new and better life.

Although all men and women fail to be prepared and do not have enough oil in their lamps, they cannot see which way to go, and darkness surrounds them on every side. Sadly, they'll stumble and fall until they end up in Hell, and they'll not know they need the light until it's too late.

Indeed, it may seem as though I am dramatic with words concerning the oil in our lamps and the pathway to Heaven and Hell. However, I get straight to the point of revealing the formula for winning the prize of immortality, and it's a shame; too many preachers dance around the bush with the required word of my Creator God and aren't straightforward teachers.

I am seriously concerned and teach straight to the point, mainly because passive words will not help anyone find the right way. I believe straightforward talk is usually the best way to present the commanded word of God, and bending it helps no one.

For an example to consider, I'll give you an illustration. I am sure this illustration illuminates the lukewarm and cold person, and this illustration coincides with the first commandment, the second commandment, and the third commandment.

For example, worship directed to Allah, Dagon, Satan, and all the other imitation gods in this world, other than Yehovah, register cold because the kingdom of God wasn't created for other gods or people determined to worship other gods.

Yehovah, the great King of kings, is the God of Heaven, Earth, and Israel; hot and on fire, Christians worship Him. However, all persons guilty of worshipping other gods register ice cold on God's serious and accurate Judgment Scales.

Mainly because my wonderful Creator God tells us not to consider worshipping any other gods before Him, and our great Creator God says, do not bow down to them. This truth means He expects all believers in Him to reject other gods.

Indeed, my Supreme God tells us to keep His required commandments, not take them in vain, and not trade them for the traditions of men. I want you to know that men's traditions aren't a good trade for God's exact word and a trade for His word is a compromise.

Therefore, men and women not interested in living by His righteous ways cannot call themselves His special children mainly because they are too cold on the Judgment Scales to be called His children. Positively, the ice-cold person, God will reject and say, I knew you not.

Furthermore, if we are curious and concerned about our salvation, you and I can ask ourselves and ponder the unanswerable question. *How Many Words Will It Take* before some men figure out how to achieve eternal life?

The Son of God told us a straightforward way of life when He proclaimed; I am the way, the truth, and everlasting life; no man cometh unto the Father, but by Me. Indeed, this simple statement makes it clear that other gods haven't a connection with our wonderful Creator God.

Conclusively, this story concerning how many words it will take reveals the right question we must ask ourselves. However, if we decide to be hardheaded and reject the wonderful word of God, then we'll be hardheaded on our trip to the pits of Hell.

Beyond the shadow of a doubt, this heartfelt story proves we have a powerful adversary called Lucifer, and Satan hates all hot and on-fire Christians. The devil wants us to be lukewarm, or as cold as ice, rather than be hot and on fire for the righteous word of God.

I assure you that most people living in this world have a temperature malfunction or a burnt-out heating element gone wrong within the center of their hearts. Sadly, I must say, their belief in Him is weak, and they cannot build up their heat and be hot enough for the required word of God.

However, I wonder How many words it takes to restore the heat they need before they can be hot and on fire for the word of God. Truly, wood, coal, and gas will not provide the correct heat for their journey back home to God. However, I am sure His commandments and Bible stories will crank up the heat, and we cannot overheat by studying too much.

CHAPTER FORTY
ADDED REQUIREMENT TO GRACE

Within this informative story, *Added Requirements To Grace.* It portrays initial grace and the things we must do after receiving the wonderful gift of grace. However, before this story about the grace of God is started, I want you to know that God wants something back from us after giving us the gracious gift of grace.

The following few scriptures I've taken from the New Testament are the words of Jesus Christ, and He's our Authority figure expert. I want you to realize His superior gospel adds requirements to the gift of eternal life and the prize of immortality.

Therefore, if you think the words of the Apostle Paul clash with the words of Jesus, written within the following few scriptures. Then please remember that the words of Jesus are the ultimate words of authority, and His superior and excellent words supersede the words of any man.

Please closely notice the answer Jesus gives to a man who

desires to inherit eternal life and live in His kingdom within this following scripture. I guarantee after reading the following two scriptures, you'll realize the importance of commandment-keeping.

Mark 10:17 And when <u>He</u> (Jesus) was gone forth into the <u>way</u> (from Judaea), then came <u>one</u> (person) running, and kneeled to Him, and ask Him, Good Master, what shall I do that I may inherit eternal life?

Then, the excellent Son of God said back to the concerned man, and He would say the exact words to us if He were alive and here today in the flesh simply because the corridors of time do not change His requirements for gaining eternal life.

Mark 10:19 Thou knowest the commandments, Do not commit adultery, Do not kill, do not steal, Do not bear <u>false</u> <u>witness</u> (means do not lie on someone), defraud not, honor thy father and mother.

Even though the words of the Apostle Paul and the gospel of Jesus seem to clash concerning the requirements for eternal salvation, please keep in mind that the Apostle Paul is describing to us the initial beginning of salvation and the first day of conversion to Christianity.

However, the perfect Son of God describes the long-term fulfillment of salvation and our day-to-day requirements as Christians. Truly, just because the Apostle Paul says we obtain the gift of salvation through grace, Paul only explains half the picture.

Indeed, the gift of salvation doesn't mean we're living in some erased commandment grace age. Nor are we living within a new time frame where the commandments and laws have become less critical or abolished.

Positively, I want you to realize that eternal life through grace doesn't mean we can be sinful and lawless before the eyes of our Creator God and still have a Savior. The once-saved, always-saved philosophy isn't an accurate analogy, and I wouldn't give up the ghost or go to my grave believing that eternal life can't be lost.

Therefore, I want you to know because we've obtained the gift of grace, God forbid we use it as an excuse to sin and then wrongly believe that we'll not be held accountable for our sins. The expanded definition of foolish means we are foolish to think we'll not be held responsible for our sins.

However, the wonderful gift of grace is our calling to salvation, and we do not have to work for our calling to receive the gift of grace. However, every converted believer in Christ must do good works to please God and keep their salvation.

Therefore, I advise all professing Christians to try to be model Christians. I am telling you that all model Christians are glad to do good works for the glory of God, and He will help when the need arises. Truly, being a commandment-keeping believer in Christ exemplifies the best effort we can put forth.

Especially if we Christians want to set an excellent example to the unsaved sinner, doing good works for the glory of God will always be a shining light before the eyes of sinners. Positively, doing His righteous works will benefit our image in the eyes of God, and please realize that every tree that doesn't bear good fruit will be plucked up and destroyed.

Because our concerned Creator God is watching us from above, I assure you that our decisions and actions have a say concerning our closeness to Him. Furthermore, our actions will affect our blessings and long-term plan for salvation, and wise men and women will live by His Ten Commandments.

Furthermore, even though good works are not a requirement for salvation, we shouldn't avoid being helpful Christians. Truly, when the need arises, we shouldn't refuse the opportunity to improve our image before the eyes of our beautiful Creator God.

Indeed, even if we have received the gift of grace and been saved by the blood of the Lamb, it's still the whole duty of man to reverence God, serve God, and keep His required Ten Commandments. Remember and never forget living by His word will always be his greatest expectation of us.

I assure you that within this informative story, *Added Requirements To Grace*, the beautiful Son of God commands us to keep His perfect commandments. As sure as the moon shines at night, this truth means that the wonderful Yeshua desires you and me to try and be as perfect as possible.

This truth means that the beautiful Son of God doesn't want us to be excuse-makers and say, I cannot keep His commanded word. However, He wants us to be devout commandment keepers who try to be as perfect as His righteous commandments.

Indeed, I want you to know that we should follow Yeshua's advice and live holy, and we do need to keep His perfect commandments if we expect to inherit eternal life. Remember, we can repent and correct ourselves whenever we fall short or make mistakes.

Beyond the shadow of a doubt, I am sure all professing Christians want to inherit eternal life, and if they revere His commandments, they'll inherit the gift of eternal life. For this reason, all Christians should purposely put a great deal of emphasis on keeping the commandments.

Furthermore, commandment-keeping is a glory to our conversion to Christianity, and keeping His righteous commandments proves intense sincerity. Truly, commandment-keeping separates the hot from the cold and the hot from the lukewarm.

Positively, commandment-keeping is a perfect indication, proving our character change. Commandment-keeping illuminates the new us in Christ and illustrates an excellent character quality. I want you to realize that commandment-keeping entwines doing good works for the glory of God and the creation of a white robe we'll wear in His kingdom.

This truth means that regardless of our interpretation of the beautiful gift of grace, we should love to keep God's great commandments. Surely, to prove our heart is right with God, we should love doing good works because He wants us to do both.

Therefore, ending this educational story, *Added Requirements To Grace*, is fitting. Simply by repeating the words of the Son of God, He says; thou knowest the commandments. Truly, as easy as they are to learn, we are fools to reject their soul-saving advice.

CHAPTER FORTY-ONE
COUNSEL FROM ABOVE

I call this declaration story, *Counsel From Above*. It intends to edify God and lift Him higher than the stars in the sky, mainly because His honest words and excellent works illustrate the formula we need to know to return home to Him.

Positively, above all other things, He wants us to be honest and honorable like Him and utilize His incredible formula for winning a Christ-like body. His astonishing formula illuminates the right way to live, the right way to end our lives, and the right way to achieve happiness forever.

Furthermore, I hope you'll agree that everyone's goal should be to improve the shape of the clay and return home to Him. However, I want you to realize that we'll need to be coached by the *Counsel From Above* before returning home to our Supreme God.

I assure you: we, flesh and blood, men and women living on this Earth, are far from our original home in Heaven, and it's a long journey back home. Indeed, the counsel of God is our Earth-based instructions, road map, and guide to getting us back to our original home.

It's for sure; the loyal immortal angels of Yehovah are ascending and descending up and down the ladder between Heaven and Earth daily, and someday, after the death of our flesh, and when the spirit of life departs from our flesh and blood body.

Then, if we've accepted His righteous counsel as the gospel truth, the helpful angels of God will come to us and carry us back to our wonderful God. Truly, being picked up in their arms and carried by the immortal angels is an excellent way to return home to God.

In many ways, most of us symbolize the Laodiceans, and we are happy if we are prosperous and need nothing. However, being successful and well-to-do doesn't have any bearing on you and me finding our way back home to God. Sadly, the lukewarm person will not walk on the narrow road and find their way back home because of an indifferent lifestyle.

Furthermore, for this reason and other secondary causes, the wise seek the excellent counsel of God. Sadly, it's easy to conclude that His righteous counsel isn't essential to ungodly, lukewarm men and women snared in the sin traps of this Satan-influenced world.

However, before the death of our flesh, some concerned men and women will discover their way back home to their heavenly residence. However, sadly, some men and women will not figure out the formula for eternal life, and they will not return home to God.

In many ways, God's excellent and righteous counsel is symbolic of a lamp full of oil, and I hope you realize that not enough oil in our lamp means we didn't receive enough counsel from above. Furthermore, all our terrible compromises are probably caused by a lack of counsel from above.

I guarantee that everyone Satan catches in this world's sin traps and snares, regardless of race, color, or gender, is symbolic of an empty lamp and someone stumbling around in the dark. Surely, a lack of lamp oil means we weren't thinking ahead far enough.

Therefore, I want to give you an example to consider as we journey through this obstacle course of life and make critical decisions concerning our oil needs: the five foolish virgins didn't have enough oil in their lamps, and because of the darkness of mind, they couldn't find the marriage feast.

Indeed, I want you to know that having plenty of oil is a metaphor; God's counsel is our lamp, illuminating our way back home to our Creator God. I want you to realize that the value of lamp oil and the value of the word of God are the same.

Oil in our lamp means we are living by God's counsel and looking and waiting for His return. However, the empty lamps void of light and insufficient oil means God's righteous counsel given to us on Mount Sinai is rejected for the other things in this sinful world.

Empty lamps without enough oil mean that the beautiful word of God was neglected and not taken seriously enough. Indeed, I want you to know that ascending into the land of Utopia requires a lot of lamp oil, and if I were you, I would stock up on lamp oil.

Empty lamps not having enough oil reveals a troubling sign and a terrible gamble. The worrisome sign indicates that lukewarm or relaxed men thought they could receive their lamp oil at the last minute, and this high-stake gamble means that the dice toss wasn't in the gambler's favor.

Positively, the empty lamps sitting around too long, gathering too much dust, and not having enough oil means that some people wait until it's too late before they find their way back home to the God of creation. However, I do not want to discourage deathbed salvation, but deathbed salvation is a half lamp of oil and not a good gamble.

I assure you, a lamp full of oil is much better than a useless empty lamp. However, we do have to look ahead and fill our lamp reservoir with oil before darkness falls. This truth means that submitting ourselves early in life to the counsel of God is the only thing making our lamp full of helpful oil.

Indeed, this is a metaphor story, and it's mixed with the literal truth, but understanding the message is the main thing. Indeed, to put it bluntly, the excellent counsel of God is the only workable formula available for finding our way back home to the place where our spirit began.

Indeed, we loyal believers in the Son of God should keep an abundant oil supply in our lamps and never let the flame go out. Furthermore, because we believe entirely in our Creator God and love His righteous word, we should burn hot daily.

Positively, our above message is that five foolish virgins played around doing foolish things too long and let their flame go out. They were too late for the wedding prophesized to happen between the bridegroom and the living church of God, and when our flame goes out, neither will we find the wedding feast.

Positively, my God was the doorkeeper at the wedding, and the marriage feast was for His Son, and the cold and the lukewarm tarried too long. Lingering too long, lamps not having enough oil, the door closed, and not letting certain persons inside.

It means the kingdom of God closes its doors on foolish persons guilty of rejecting God while being alive in the flesh. This truth means we must secure our invitation to the wedding feast before the death of the flesh body while lamp oil is still available.

Therefore, because I care about your soul, I want you to know for sure so you'll be prepared for Judgment Day. A lamp not having enough oil means the same as going to the grave without obtaining the grand prize promise of the first resurrection.

CHAPTER FORTY-TWO
SAVED

I want you to realize that being saved from the judgment fire and converted into a new person should be everyone's priority in this life, and attending a church building or a meeting place isn't one of the necessities to getting saved and staying saved.

Furthermore, we can spend day after day meticulously searching the scriptures, and there's no place in our informative Bible where our Creator God requires us to attend a specific type of building to be saved and stay saved.

For this reason, I want you to know that if the Holy Ghost lives within our hearts, our heart is God's living church. Furthermore, I guarantee that no church or temple building can replace the living church of God.

This one hundred percent accurate story, I am calling Saved, isn't a good subject story with most preachers and priests. It's because they insist we gather at a building on Sun-day morning, and I conclude that it's a tradition for men to come together at a building on Sunday morning.

However, I am sure too much priority is placed on a church building and the Sun-day morning Sabbath Day when the primary focus should be on the required word of God and the way we conform to His rules and His authentic Sabbath Day.

I guarantee you that the meaningful word of God isn't contained in a building, nor is the Holy Ghost held inside the doors of a manufactured building. However, the perfect gospel of God and the ever-available Holy Ghost can be found anywhere in this world if we seek to find them.

Therefore, a failure to find them lies on the shoulders of each individual, void of their presence and understanding. Truly, seeking and finding responsibility will always be our obligation. Whenever we decide we want a new life, we must discuss it with the Lord, and if we are sincere, He will integrate us into His flock of happy believers.

Before this story starts, I want to say that much knowledge of God is available and found inside the Sun-day churches. This truth means the good news is everywhere: devout men and women of God gather together. Truly, it's good whenever men assemble and teach each other the gospel of God.

Furthermore, I believe much good is accomplished in many Sun-day churches, even if they have flaws in some doctrines. As much as we wish all churches preached perfect authenticity, sadly, they do not, and false teaching is a problem.

However, I want you to know that the Sun-day churches and all stationary gathering places are one option among other great choices, especially since we believers in Christ do not have to attend a manufactured church building to be saved and stay saved.

Sometimes, church groups think they provide the only way to find and understand God, and this point of view isn't valid at all. I am sure we'll discover Christians who never walk through a church door, much more Bible-savvy than members inside a church building.

For example, this example can portray the imagination of a holy prophet of God. Elijah thought he was the only prophet in Israel, determined to fight against the wicked Ahab, Jezebel, and the false god Baal.

Therefore, God said to His servant Elijah I have seven thousand other servants who haven't bowed down to Baal. I am willing to believe that the living church of God does exist outside the walls of stationary buildings, and it's probably the largest church of God.

Within the churches and the temples, appearances seem to matter a lot to most professing Sun-day Christians. However, when we belong to God's redefined living church, our appearance only matters to God, and being a believer in God qualifies us as a member of the living church of God.

Mainly because He sees the real you and me, not veiled by fake smiles, deceiving words, and expensive clothing. Indeed, when we are alone at home worshipping our wonderful God, the sincere you and I are one hundred percent authentic.

I assure you, my great Supernatural Creator, God cannot be deceived, and false appearances do not work within the living church of God. However, because its members are loyal and love the God of Heaven and Earth, they follow the teaching of the living Holy Ghost.

Positively, I want you to know that my wonderful Creator God is the preacher man behind the pulpit, teaching within the living church of God. Counterfeit appearances or insincere words cannot deceive my great God; my sincere God is straightforward and honest and does not fool anyone with deceiving talk.

Therefore, as shocking as it sounds to many Christians, going to a Sun-day church made from wood, stone, and metal is not essential. However, it's vitally important and an absolute requirement for every professing Christian to belong to the living church of God.

People belonging to the living church of God will eat mana from Heaven and drink pure water flowing from His throne. Compliments of God: living church of God members will receive the keys to His peaceful kingdom and walk, talk, and live among the saved in Heaven.

Indeed, we cannot say that everyone who belongs to the Sunday churches and temples is saved and will receive a home in His special kingdom. However, we can say that everyone who belongs to the living church of God has a Savior, and His name is Yeshua, and they will live in His kingdom.

This truth means everyone belonging to God's living church will be blessed and rewarded with the grand prize of immortality. The reward of immortality connects with my great Creator God and not with a manufactured building, even with a cross over the door.

Therefore, the only way to be one hundred percent sure and know for certain you and I are a child of God and will receive the gift of eternal life. It's to belong to the living church of God, a Special church, invisible and as tangible as the stars in the sky, where the Holy Ghost is our teacher.

I assure you the beautiful Holy Ghost is the Greatest Preacher on this Earth, and He lives within every hot and on-fire believer if they have a clean temple suitable for the righteous and special Holy Ghost to live inside their heart.

Because the scriptures say so, I am sure the great preacher man from the book of Ecclesiastes gave us the conclusion to the whole matter. However, I am sure the beautiful Holy Ghost was responsible for giving him the answer to the Conclusion of the entire subject of worship.

Furthermore, it's easy for me to conclude that the great preacher in the Old Testament illustrated his exceptional wisdom when he summed up the whole word of God and said it's the entire duty of man to reverence God and keep His commandments.

Indeed, I believe that the beautiful Holy Ghost of God was responsible for giving the great preacher man his brilliant words of wisdom to preach and teach to all men. I know the excellent Holy Ghost shares knowledge with you and me.

Beyond the shadow of a doubt, the ultimate message called the conclusion to the whole matter has an urgent mission in life to accomplish. It's the greatest and the most important news in our entire bible, and it should be shared and preached to all men, women, and children everywhere.

Every divine gift God gives us hinges on the conclusion of the whole matter because it's the beautiful message of salvation and the formula for immortality. The conclusion message reveals all our requirements, and the Ten Commandments of God illustrate what He expects every Christian to fulfill daily.

I assure you that nearly every message and every story example between Genesis and Revelation point to the beautiful message I call the conclusion to the whole matter. Furthermore, everything God, the Son of God, and the prophets taught all point to the

Conclusion to the Entire Matter.

However, I want you to know if we fall short of living by the whole word of God, make a mistake, and desire to correct ourselves and get right with God. Then, the amazing grace of my Creator God allows us the privilege to repent and change.

Positively, God's caring Son voluntarily suffered death upon the cross and gave His life, so we'll have the privilege to amend mistakes. He knows we'll make mistakes and Knows whether we are remorseful for making them or not sorrowful.

Indeed, conversion, repentance, and change mean we desire to live our lives according to the conclusion of the whole matter. I am confident that if we live according to the Conclusion to the Whole Matter, we fulfill our obligation to God, and we can be sure a Savior saves us from the pits of Hell.

Furthermore, regardless of the church or the home we worship within, abiding by the conclusion to the whole matter is the main thing. Truly, living by the Conclusion to the Whole Matter has a parallel, and living by the ways of God is parallel to the conclusion.

The conclusion to the whole matter is unchangeable and summed up in six words, and the six essential words are to reverence God and keep His commandments. This truth means that reverence for God and keeping His commandments is the whole duty of men and angels.

Furthermore, regardless of whether we live on this Earth or dwell in the heavens above, I am correct to say that reverence to God and commandment keeping will always be a requirement in both places. I want you to know that God's beautiful commandments will be as crucial in the next life as they are in this life.

Conclusively, the grand prize of immortality is obtainable, and we can depart this life as a winner, and it's because we try to keep the commandments of God. I want you to know that keeping His commandments highlights His greatest expectation of us.

Beyond the shadow of a doubt, we illustrate reverence to Him because we are determined to live according to His righteous word. I want you to know that the gift of grace doesn't mean we aren't bound to His required word because living by His word is the pinnacle of doing right.

This explanation story concerning our standing with God is called Saved, and it reveals the weightier word of God as essential information. I assure you, His perfect Ten Commandments are the Weightier word of God.

Furthermore, knowing we are saved people is comforting, and it's much better than not knowing where we stand with our Savior God. Indeed, whoever loves God's original word and keeps His commandments is saved.

The bread of life is God's beautiful word and saved people love the word of God the same way bees love honey. This truth means that the excellent word of God is the ultimate thing, and it's, by far, purer and sweeter than the best honey.

CHAPTER FORTY-THREE
STEREOTYPED

This revealing story, meant to entwine everyone together in this world, which I call *Stereotyped*, has one specific purpose and intends to illustrate common characteristics all people share. Shared characteristics are between everyone, regardless of religion, color, gender, or nationality.

Therefore, we can call this story the truth analogy if we choose to because there's nothing debatable in this one-of-a-kind personal story, and all of us living on this Earth are entwined with this story to some degree.

I want you to know that within this unusual story called *Stereotyped*, I'll do my best to illustrate a similarity and sum up everyone living in this world, regardless of whether the person is a believer in Christ or an unbeliever, not having faith in my great God.

This impartial story, meant to illuminate a link between us all, called *Stereotyped*, doesn't exclude anyone, regardless of our stance in this world, whether rich or poor, race, gender, or nationality. Or the God, the goddess we worship, or whether or not we have a God.

I assure you, beyond a doubt, I'll leave no one out of my analogy. Everyone will be stereotyped in this declaration story because men and women worldwide share some characteristics, but no one has precisely the same character qualities.

I'll evaluate everyone within this fair-to-everyone story, which I call Stereotyped, and not individualize anyone. Positively, my analogy will include everyone from all four corners of this Earth, and similarities must entwine for the benefit of being stereotyped.

Furthermore, after considering the spectrum of achieving success in writing this unusual story, I conclude that evaluating everyone the same way illustrates an exceptional accomplishment. Truly, it's possible; since the beginning of time, no other person has succeeded in doing this accomplishment properly.

Therefore, please take your time and read this equally fair story called Stereotyped slowly; it'll be easier to understand the full effects of its meaning. After reading this story, you'll be forced to realize all of us are running in the same race.

The world is symbolic of a wilderness, and we humans are symbolic of wild and unclean beasts; even at our best, we are none good, and all of us trapped in the flesh are helplessly flawed, and no person is perfect.

It's for sure; we humans are the victims of frailty, and death is the only thing able to set us free and loosen our chains of bondage to hurtful things. The flaws of the flesh are like horrible demons or sharp, painful thorns that penetrate and pierce our souls.

I want you to know that our scars of abominations will never heal because they are pictures reflecting our sinful past, and the things done cannot be undone; no more than a bullet can stop in mid-air after leaving the gun.

Life is like a clock, only turning clockwise, and time cannot be turned back. Whatever we do today, we'll live with it until we die because there isn't a mistake eraser able to erase our past, and all the foolish things we've done and the regrets in our life cannot be taken back.

Therefore, I conclude that the only hope we mistake-makers have to inspire us as we go forward in this world of flaws is that our past abominations will not be repeated. However, because we learn from our mistakes, we can be remorseful and use hindsight to shape us into better people.

Indeed, regardless of what we are, life goes on as our future extends, and it doesn't stop until the unknown ends. As one life dies out and ends, another one begins. This pattern coincides with the natural order of things, and there's nothing we can do to change our predetermined life cycle.

I assure you that God set the life cycle in motion, and we cannot change anything concerning the natural order of things. As sure as the rivers flow in one direction, the flesh will fail us someday, and no man can choose the hour and the day; no more than we can grow wings and fly away.

Our autobiography, written in the Book of Life, accurately records deeds we like and dislike. We can do nothing to change the events recorded in the Book of Life. Assuredly, no secrets will go untold because everything said and done will be brought into the light.

I assure you that fair judgment on anyone cannot be accurate until the heart reveals its secrets. However, before the Judgment throne, all the secrets hidden within the heart will gain a voice and speak from the rooftop, and the unknown will become known within the realms of Heaven.

I want you to realize that our abominations are the sins of our past, the terrible things we did, unapproved by our Creator God. As much as we do not want to, we'll all fall short of perfection. However, sadly, I must say, we humans are fallible and will need forgiveness.

Furthermore, I am sure if another hand wrote on the sand or scribed on the wall. The great message would say, do not cast the first stone to see another man's house fall.

This truth is said because everyone lives in a glasshouse; all men and women are laden with abominations and sins. None of us was created so perfect that we can cast the first stone at another person's house because they've done something wrong.

Right or wrong are our choices, and a doer of abominations is wrong. However, our compassionate and revealing Bible assures us that life can be Right through repentance and change, with the beautiful gift of salvation to gain.

Therefore, the hardheaded and the stubborn, laden with sin, will not pass through the gates where eternity begins. For this reason, flee abominations and seek purity, and do not be a wasted soul condemned to leave this Earth sorrowful and unhappily.

Indeed, I advise you to girt up your loins, face life with a grin, and not be afraid to call God your friend. He will be your special friend and be fair to you if you reverence Him and keep His commandments.

This revelation story, which I call *Stereotyped*, entwines the facts of life with our frailty, past failures, and the ability to start a new life. Because of these common characteristics, I call this story *Stereotyped*.

I assure you that God's mercy is excellent, and Bible stories declare that being able to start a new life is one of the reasons Yeshua died on the cross. Truly, if He was willing to sacrifice His life for us, we should be ready to carry His cross everywhere we go.

It's correct to say His pure, undefiled blood allows us to repent, change, and start a new life. I want you to know that if we can be stereotyped a certain way, then being similar to Christ is the right way to emulate.

I assure you that picking up His cross and walking in the footsteps of His commandments means we aren't taking His blood sacrifice in vain. However, we are wrong if we think we can blaze our trail through this life, do right on our own, and be exempt from the judgment of damnation without having a Savior.

Therefore, for this reason, and clarification, I am telling you that picking up His cross means we've decided to entwine our life with His gospel. I want you to realize that His gospel is a Savior from the claws of demons and the fires of Hell, and we haven't got much hope without having it to study.

I firmly believe that if it's possible to repay Christ for His human sacrifice? He would say, be a hot and on fire Christian, care about salvation for the unsaved, walk in My ways, and keep My covenant. I assure you, it's a terrific feeling to be hot and on fire for the beautiful word of God and to know we have a future in His kingdom.

CHAPTER FORTY-FOUR
THE HOOK IN LUCIFER'S JAW

This exposure story, meant to look behind the scenes, has a dual meaning and amounts to literal and metaphoric stories. For your protection, I warn you: the hook in Lucifer's Jaw could quickly become the same kind of hook in our jaw.

Therefore, and for our benefit, we better desire to live godly and avoid doing the wicked things that became a hook in Lucifer's jaw. The hook is real; he baits and casts the hook at us every day. The symbolic hook in his jaw means that he couldn't resist overwhelming temptations, and they pulled him in the wrong direction.

I firmly believe that if we can avoid doing similar things identified with destroying his righteousness and closeness with our great Creator God. Then, I am telling you that we'll be blessed to learn a valuable lesson from his rebellious mistakes.

This informative story entwining the evil prince of this world explains the hook in Lucifer's jaw, the reason for his lust, and the things he wanted the most. I conclude that Lucifer was a thief and wanted to possess a valuable item he shouldn't have wanted.

Indeed, clarity must be explained and established before this informative story goes any further. The definition of the Hook In Lucifer's Jaw needs to be explained for better understanding. The phrase hook in his jaw means sinful thoughts overtook him, and evil thoughts are a hook in anyone's jaw.

Positively, I want you to realize that things become much worse whenever we act on sinful thoughts because sinful thoughts are the beginning of evil, and I firmly assure you that every act of wickedness begins with a wicked thought.

I am sure that the blindness of the heart overcame the wicked Lucifer, and his mind became corrupted, and he wanted more power than my great Creator God possessed. Sadly, I must say, his sinful thoughts were more influencing than his resistance to doing evil.

Indeed, his conscience was destroyed and burned as if a hot iron had seared his desire to be a righteous and loyal angel to God. The hook in his jaw and his seared conscience illustrate the only way we can explain the evil he did against his Creator God.

Furthermore, the hook in Lucifer's jaw expanded, and after recruit time, it included one-third of the vain and rebellious angels. Because their thoughts were wicked, they formed together in Heaven, and Lucifer put together an army of rebel angels, all of whom had sinful thoughts.

Indeed, they weren't satisfied with their angel status and verbally and physically opposed God and His obedient, good angels. Undoubtedly, they wanted much more than a noble position in Heaven, eternal life, and a beautiful city to call their home.

Indeed, they had so much of everything in Heaven; they were

spoiled angelic brats. The only thing they could want more than they already had would be to be gods themselves and not have anyone in authority ruling over them and making the rules to live by forever.

Positively, Yehovah is the ruling authority in Heaven, and He always was, and always will be, until the end of time. His rules are absolute and cannot be successfully challenged or redesigned, especially not by created creatures of His making.

Without a doubt, and I firmly believe, the rebellious and evil Lucifer was Hitler's example in Heaven, and just like the wicked Hitler, Lucifer was willing to take whatever he wanted by force. I am sure securing great power was the desire of his heart.

Lucifer was the unthankful person the corrupt and defiant angels chose to lead them in their rebellion against God. Because of their overwhelming, vain, and foolish imagination, they sought to take by force the most significant spoils and treasures in Heaven as a reward for their rebellion against God.

Indeed, you might be inclined to think that precious metals, jewels, gold, rubies, and diamonds are the most significant spoils in heaven, but they aren't. And I guarantee you, the supernatural Lucifer wanted more than precious metals and valuable stones.

Mainly because the Living Coals of Fire continually living upon the altar of God, inside the temple of God, and upon the mountain of God are the greatest treasure in Heaven, and no other material treasure as alive as anyone will compare to them.

Furthermore, what I call the Living Coals of Fire is most likely the God element, the spark of life, and the essence of pure energy. It's entirely possible; the unique and special Living Coals of Fire is the beautiful Holy Ghost.

These Living Coals of Fire that live upon the altar of God are the most remarkable substance throughout the universe. I am sure they are animated and alive, possess immortality, and have greater power than any known substance anywhere within the realms of Heaven.

Although as informative as the Bible is about most things, a full explanation of the Living Coals of Fire is elusive. For some unknown reason, a complete description of them cannot be located anywhere in the Bible. For example, if someone is formed entirely from the Living Coals of Fire, they'll live forever.

Furthermore, our Bible doesn't reveal the substance and creation of the Father, the Son, and the Holy Ghost. Nor does it tell us where the Spark of Life originated, a great mystery; only our great Creator, God, knows the answer.

The Bible also does not reveal the material and the temple's creation in Heaven, but we can be sure it's an exceptional substance. As for myself, this is an assumption on my part, but the beautiful temple in Heaven may also be animated and alive.

Furthermore, I think the Father, the Son, and the Holy Ghost were created from the incredible Living Coals of Fire. The Living Coals of Fire consistently and continually live upon God's sacred altar and inside God's holy and sacred temple.

Beyond the shadow of a doubt, the Living Coals of Fire is God's element and the spark of life. I believe the Coals of Fire can give life to other material objects, and their supernatural abilities make them highly valuable and sought after by some heavenly creations.

Lucifer was the thief in heaven, and I believe he was stealing something of great value—not precious metals and jewels. However, the scriptures indicate Lucifer was merchandising something of enormous importance. Without a doubt, the valuable substance he was stealing belonged to God.

There's no logical reason for us to believe the wicked Lucifer would want to steal gold, rubies, diamonds, and pearls in Heaven. Besides that, the value of precious metals and jewels will not compare to the value of the Superior Living Coals of Fire.

Without a doubt, the wicked Lucifer was using his stolen merchandise to gain popularity and rebel support for his upcoming rebellion. The takeover he had planned in Heaven proves his conscience was seared with a hot iron, and it's easy to conclude that his terrible imagination controlled his heart.

Positively, the wicked and devious Lucifer needed help from the other rebellious angels, who admired him too much. Bribery was most likely the hook in their jaw, and they were blind with greed and wanted the same kind of superpower Lucifer wanted.

Therefore, it's logical to believe the valuable and wonderful animated Living Coals of Fire was his most significant motivation for rebellion. The extremely valuable Living Coals of Fire was the greatest motivation the other rebellious angels desired to enhance their strength.

The Special Living Coals of Fire is a mighty power source, and whoever controls the Living Coals of Fire controls life. The God element is the spark of life and the great elixir of strength for every living thing, and it belongs to God, even though the rebellious angels wanted it for themselves.

Beyond the shadow of a doubt, God's precious and mighty

throne belongs to whoever controls life, and I am sure that the wicked Lucifer was a power-hungry angel who wanted to be the God in Heaven and on Earth and control life and death in both places.

I believe the jealous and evil Lucifer was stealing and merchandising small amounts of the Living Coals of Fire who live upon the altar of God. Surely, he was doing it to build his army of rebellious angels stronger than they usually were at the beginning of their lives.

Beyond a shadow of a doubt, the supernatural Living Coals of Fire have multiple advantages. They give life to material substance, enhance our lives, and give us greater strength, energy, and longevity.

Lucifer wasn't a dumb angel or an average thinker. He was fully aware that he and the other rebellious angels would need a lot of strength to overcome God, especially if they were going to be successful and forcefully take His throne, His holy temple, and His beautiful city away from Him.

I am sure Lucifer was well acquainted with the Coals of Fire and knew there was only one substance in the universe to give them the strength to succeed. However, they would have to steal it from God first, and being the guardian cherub was handy. Sadly, the wicked Lucifer was one of the guardian cherubs.

Most likely, the wicked and devious Lucifer started stealing small amounts of the powerful Living Coals of Fire while guarding the throne of God inside the temple in Heaven. However, I believe his lust for power and stealing increased as time passed.

The golden altar in Heaven probably isn't small, and it's much more significant and different than we are accustomed to seeing inside a church building. I believe the great altar of God is much longer than it is wide, and I am pretty sure it has many Coals of Fire living upon it.

The wicked and traitorous Lucifer was overwhelmed by lust for power and determined to take the throne away from God. He probably began distributing the Living Coals of Fire among his rebellious angel friends, or at the least, Lucifer was touching them with the Coals of Fire and increasing their strength.

Otherwise, he may have secretly devised a different plan, disobeyed God, and let his angel friends slip inside the temple of God. Then, he may have allowed them to walk up and down amid the Living Coals of Fire. Positively, when war finally started in Heaven, their strength was greater than that of the average angel.

Indeed, the rebellious angels were overconfident, and after they were caught stealing from God's altar, the war started in Heaven. They thought they were strong enough to forcefully take the throne, the temple, and the Living Coals of Fire away from God. I believe the Living Coals of Fire became a hook in Lucifer's jaw, and his lust for power was too strong to resist.

Lucifer was a cruel, rebellious angel, guilty of having a seared conscience, and he thought he could take control of Heaven away from our wonderful Most High God simply because he and the other rebellious angels took some of the Living Coals of Fire.

I assure you that Lucifer and the other rebellious angels were brilliant. Before they decided to war against God in Heaven, they knew they needed to enhance their strength to a higher degree and make themselves mightier than the average angel.

Indeed, Lucifer and the other rebellious angels were impressed with themselves because they had multiplied their strength. Thinking of themselves as wise, they became fools. They unthinkingly followed their hearts, and their lust for power and foolish imagination were the hooks in their jaws.

I can accurately say that the beautiful and wicked Lucifer was the biggest fool of all the fools in Heaven. Furthermore, we shouldn't forget to mention his rebel partners in crime because the other rebellious angels who followed him were equally foolish.

The other rebellious angels, ungrateful and uncaring, were fools for listening to Lucifer's great swelling words and for partnering with him, even though Lucifer promised them a great reward of great power. All their troubles started with a sinful thought, the same way trouble knocks on our door.

Beyond the shadow of a doubt, all our troubles begin with sinful thoughts, and evil thoughts are a hook in our jaw as much as theirs. For our benefit, we better suppress our sinful thoughts before they cause us to do something the Lord considers ungodly.

Lucifer's lust for power and control overwhelmed his sense of righteousness, and the desire in his heart turned out to be a hook in his jaw and the beginning of his troubles with God. Positively, his unrealistic promises to the other angels who supported him turned out to be lies, conjured up from a rose-colored and foolish imagination.

Furthermore, it's easy to conclude that he didn't have a good heart; sadly, his imagination was evil. Hindsight proves that sinful thoughts are enemies of our well-being and are responsible for provoking Lucifer, and after having sinful thoughts, the charming Lucifer lusted in vain for the throne of God.

I am sure that sinful thoughts were the hook in his jaw, and evil thoughts caused him to lust for the Living Coals of Fire, who live upon the holy altar of God. Sadly, I must say, the evil Lucifer wanted the Living Coals of Fire more than friendship with God, and he made a bad choice.

Hindsight proves an undeniable fact; the lustful and vain Lucifer became the fool in this awareness story and a victim of his runaway imagination. This statement is true because Lucifer was willing to do wicked things to acquire the valuable things he wanted in Heaven.

Indeed, this illustrated story illustrating the rebellious angels, their apostasy in the Kingdom of God, and the incredible power source in Heaven proves a fact. I am saying that angels, men, or women can sear their conscience, and through free will, they can reject God to pursue a foolish imagination.

Positively, a foolish imagination is nearly the same as sinful thoughts. Sadly, ungodly evil thoughts are similar to magnetic abilities, and they are a hook in our jaw and will pull us away from our perfect God.

Lucifer claimed himself to be unique, and he declared himself wise among his angelic followers, and they must've admired him tremendously. Initially, it probably seemed like his plan to conquer and divide was working. However, evil plans usually have short-term success, and Lucifer's plan to overthrow God was short-term. Truly, hindsight and Bible scriptures prove that the wicked Lucifer was wrong.

Bible history proves that the rebellious angels made the wrong choice to follow Lucifer, and bible scriptures prove it was unreasonable to campaign among the other angels and promise them the things belonging to God only. I conclude that his foolish imagination was his downfall, and sadly, I must say, he spiraled downward into the image of a shameful angel.

Positively, Bible scriptures and evidence reveal there was an uprising in Heaven, and the evil Lucifer and the rebellious angels foolishly decided to war against our wonderful Creator God. Positively, it's easy for us to conclude that Lucifer and the rebellious angels made a terrible error.

The foolish rebellious angels became blind fools and foolishly followed a blind guide. Sadly, they couldn't see the big picture and calculate their blessings for being loyal to God. They purposely covered their eyes with rose-colored glasses created and developed by their foolish imagination.

Their problem occurred when the foolish rebellious angels became blind after letting their hearts be deceived and captured by the beautiful, smooth-talking Lucifer. For this reason, we better be cautious of charming talkers offering us advantages in opposition to the word of God.

The lies and false promises the wicked and deceiving Lucifer made became the hook in their jaw. I assure you, false promises and lies pulled them away from our marvelous Creator God, the same way the forbidden fruit pulled at Eve until she sinned.

In conclusion, I want you to realize that concerning you and me, the purpose of this explanation story also benefits us. This story goes beyond explaining the hook in Lucifer and the rebellious angel's jaw and why sinful temptations separated them from their Creator God.

Indeed, this awareness story reveals what they thought was important enough to separate them from our great Creator God. However, considering all their firsthand wisdom, greater than Solomon's, they should've realized that it's foolish to let anything come between our wonderful God and us.

Therefore, it's appropriate to create a metaphor and say, in many ways, we are symbolic of a fish. The hook is baited with foolish imaginations, sin, lust, and rebellion, and when the bait is cast before us, we can bite what's on the hook or refuse to swallow the bait.

Positively, I want you to know that the hook in anyone's jaw is symbolic of anything able to pull us away from our marvelous Creator God. However, please remember that the wicked Lucifer only throws out the baited hook, and it's our choice to swallow it or refuse the temptation.

Anyway, sin is a hook in our jaw, and sin separates us from our great God. Bible scriptures reveal that sinners are similar to rebellious children running away from doing the right thing. Positively, we are running away from doing the right thing whenever we act on a sinful thought.

Therefore, please remember, and never forget, that our thoughts will work against us sometimes, and doing the wrong thing always begins with a Sinful Thought. It's easy to conclude that sinful thoughts are created in our minds within a foolish rose-colored imagination. I want you to know whenever Pandora's box is opened, which symbolizes you and me, evil thoughts transform into commandment-breaking.

Positively, I conclude that a hook in our jaw isn't different from being reeled in at the end of the fishing line. Truly, the analogy of this story reveals that the ungodly people in this world have a hook in their jaw. However, always remember that it's the wicked Lucifer using the sin bait.

I call this revealing story *The Hook In Lucifer's* Jaw, designed to be about the wicked and corrupt Lucifer and the other fallen angels. However, this story purposely expands to include you, me, and everyone else because the baited hook is cast into more places than one.

CHAPTER FORTY-FIVE
SERVE OR REJECT

This critical story concerning you and me, *Serve Or Reject*, has a Parallel Meaning and cannot be valid by one party. This accurate truth means it'll take an agreement from both parties before our covenant with God can be valid because *Serve Or Reject* has to be mutually agreed to by two individuals.

Before this story starts, I want you to know what the subject serves or rejects refers to has a definition. This story relates to the world of God, and Serving or Rejecting is every person's choice. This truth means that everyone is a free thinker, and no one is forced to be a God supporter or an opposer of His word.

Beyond the shadow of a doubt, serve or reject began in Heaven with the angels, and they had free will to Serve or Reject God. The history of the angels proves that they had a thinking mind, and not all thought the same way or honored God with the same respect.

Positively, we flesh, and blood people living on this Earth have the same free will and the choices the rebellious angels had in

Heaven. The same options mean that we can serve or reject God with the same free will, and the population on this Earth illustrates a split in what men and women do.

I assure you, the word serve doesn't mean that we are slaves to a Master or a tyrant God who doesn't allow freedom to a weaker race. Indeed, I want you to know that we would be foolish to believe we are enslaved people who are forced to follow His commandments.

The word serves in this story means that we are servants to a righteous way of life; only our great God provides. For this reason, the servants of righteousness worship our Creator God, and you should too, and we should gladly be servants of righteousness.

Anyway, I assure you that our Creator God isn't a tyrant Ruler of Heaven and Earth and doesn't want to make servant-enslaved people out of everyone. However, for the benefit of everyone living in His kingdom, we'll be expected to live righteous.

However, in His perfect and peaceful kingdom, we won't have the freedom to be sinners, rebellious residents, or lie and steal. He's looking for men and women in love with righteousness, willing to serve righteousness for eternity.

The word rejects in this awareness story refers to men and women who purposely reject being servants of righteousness. Truly, I want you to know that living an ungodly lifestyle is the same as not loving our Creator God, and I ask you how we can love Him and be rebellious to His commandments.

Furthermore, the wonderful gift of free will allows every person living in the flesh the exclusive privilege to accept Him or deny Him. However, our choice to serve or reject Him must be decided while we are alive and live on this Earth.

I want you to realize that after the death of our flesh, our choices disappear, and our ability to serve or reject Him is set in solid, concrete decisions. This accurate statement truly means we cannot choose a different option or direction in life after the death of our flesh.

However, I am one hundred percent sure that whenever men and women realize that the Son of God is our Mediator between God and us, the ungodly dead will change the thoughts of their hearts and wish they hadn't rejected the Lamb of God while being alive.

Especially after ungodly people discover rejection of our Creator God means damnation and eventually a swim in the lake of fire. For this reason, I warn you so you'll know that the beautiful gift of salvation isn't automatic to everyone, and terrible sinners will not receive the same privileges as lovers of righteousness.

However, our Creator God is portrayed as merciful because of His extraordinary compassion toward us. But being a merciful God means He'll gladly forgive sinners if they repent and sincerely change into servants of righteousness.

However, we must sincerely seek the option to repent and change, and change must be achieved while alive. Truly, it would be considered extremely wise if all sinners submitted themselves to the ways of the Lord before their option to change disappeared.

I also assure you that we do not know what's around the corner, and death can come unexpectedly and suddenly. Even when men gamble and believe they have a long life ahead. Since we cannot foresee the future, we better repent and change today and quit gambling on our souls.

Our excellent God-inspired Bible reveals many important

things for our benefit, but it's up to us to discover the wisdom of God and utilize His advice. If we do not, we may not be invited to the wedding feast prepared for the bride and groom.

Indeed, our excellent teaching Bible reveals Heaven and Hell as one of our future destinations after our death. Therefore, every day, anyone puts off giving themselves to our Savior Lord; it's a gamble with the gift of salvation and immortality.

Positively, I am one hundred percent sure; the only logical and wise decision to make in this life before it's too late to correct ourselves. It's for us not to wait another day to be a child of God and a scripture warrior, and we should tremble with fear whenever we think about dying unsaved.

Indeed, being a child of the God of creation illustrates a wise decision no one will regret if they desire a better way of life. I am compelled to tell you that the change from a sinner person to the conversion of a Christian is an improvement in anyone's life.

Furthermore, I am one hundred percent accurate in saying that the change from a sinner to a sincere God-lover illustrates the formula for a better person in every way, not perfect, and not void of mistakes. However, still yet, a much better person.

Indeed, regardless of our previous lifestyle and mistakes, we can start a beautiful new life through prayer. Our forgiving God will allow us to pick up the cross and follow Him if our hearts are sincere about change.

I assure you that obedience to the righteous word of God illustrates our most significant proof of change and evidence of sincerity. However, on the other hand, rebellion against the moral word of God demonstrates proof of rejection and our failure to change.

Furthermore, any person not interested in picking up the cross and carrying the gospel of God wherever they go. Then they are not worthy of being called the sons and daughters of God, nor are they worthy to live in His kingdom after the death of their flesh.

I want you to know that the uninterested person will never know about God's beautiful things in store for everyone who loves Him. However, choosing to serve Yehovah or reject Him is our decision, and He will not interfere with our right to choose.

I assure you that because of the possibility of urgency, the wise decision to choose is clear: do not wait too long to choose to serve the ways of God. This truth is because sometimes unexpected tragedies happen, and we'll suddenly leave this world.

Sometimes, beyond our control, we'll leave this world swiftly, and we haven't enough time for death-bed repentance or conversion to Christianity. I assure you, this unexpected tragedy happens to many unsaved people and is unnecessary.

This concern story, *To Serve Or Reject*, describes me and the critical option I faced during a crucial time. This personal story reveals me as a sinner who gambled on my life until I chose to serve Him instead of rejecting Him.

I assure you that converting to Christianity is the wisest decision I've ever made. I don't intend to look back or forget to be thankful. I appreciate my opportunity for a new life with Christ, and I thank God for my new life.

Indeed, I am sure that plenty of people stand at the crossroads in life and have to decide to serve or reject Him. I hope and pray that this story about me and plenty more people will inspire men and women to worship Him instead of refusing Him.

CHAPTER FORTY-SIX
INCURABLE, INCURABLE, INCURABLE

This sad story parallels ungodly people to a lost condition of the soul, and the phrases *Incurable, Incurable,* and *Incurable,* will reveal a fatal heart disease. Surely, on a scale of one to ten, this disease exceeds the long-term terribleness of all other diseases. Sadly, I must say, incurable entwines with the sad spiritual condition of unbelief in God.

This sad story illustrates the chief priests and the Pharisees and, sadly, I must say, their incurable unbelief in the beautiful Son of God. Bible scriptures reveal that He openly performed miracle after miracle for needy people, and still, the chief priests hated Him anyway.

However, every generation has unbelieving men and women guilty of emulating the same feelings and thoughts they felt. We could tell them story after story about our Creator God, and they still wouldn't repent, change, and be loyal and happy members of His family.

This story is all about Yeshua and His obstacle course in the flesh. It's full of intellectual depth and pivots on straightforward and absolute truth. However, some men and women will live by the ungodly ways of the world and will not change. These incurable men and women will always be the servants of darkness for one or another illogical reason.

This exposure story, *Incurable, Incurable,* and *Incurable,* illustrates the fatal disease of unbelief. I want you to know that incurable unbelief is not connected to physical ailments, health impediments, or something medicines will not cure.

However, this heartbreaking story does reveal the beautiful Son of God and Him curing and healing a blind man. Bible history tells us He spent His entire life advancing the wonderful gospel of God, doing good works, and teaching the word of God wherever He traveled on this cruel and violent Earth.

Indeed, I am one hundred percent sure; no one knows how many other unrecorded miracles the compassionate Son of God accomplished while being alive in the flesh. However, as much as He did, I am willing to believe that it was much more than the Bible history writers have told us.

Indeed, many blind men were cured and received sight when Yeshua appeared and performed miracles. However, the corrupt Pharisees and the chief priests wouldn't change and continued being incurably blind. It's the same with many people today, mainly because they like the corrupt lifestyle and reject the Spirit of God.

Indeed, after all the divine accomplishments they had seen the compassionate Son of God do to heal the impaired, they were still living submissively to the powers of darkness. After observing Him heal many times, they were still loyal servants to Lucifer, alias the God hater from Heaven.

It's easy to conclude that their conscience was flawed and seared with a hot iron, and no number of miracles and healings could soften their wicked, incurable hearts or open their blind eyes to the truth. Indeed, when the eyes refuse to see, the truth becomes invisible, as if they were wearing blinders.

Furthermore, I hate to say that incurable blindness still exists today, and there doesn't seem to be a cure for a flawed heart when it's suffering from incurable unbelief. But the truth is the truth, and we can lead a horse to water, but we cannot make the horse drink, nor can we cure the incurable feelings of unbelief in God.

The above analogy means that nothing could compel the Pharisees and the chief priests to love and accept the beautiful Son of God as their Savior from the judgment fires of damnation. Truly, we must realize the flaw of incurable unbelief will result in damnation.

Not anywhere within the scriptures have I found one word saying; the chief priests and the scribes cried out and said, Hosanna, Hosanna to the Son of God. Nor did they say, *save us, we pray*. It's still the same today, and this illogical behavior illustrates incurable unbelief.

Still yet, someday in the near or the distant future, after the death of the flesh. Every person suffering from incurable unbelief will find that no man sees the Father without first seeing His Son. For this reason, I must warn you after temptations cease to exist, it's too late to see with perfect clarity.

The following scripture proves that the chief priests and the scribes were privileged to witness the miracles performed by Jesus, and being an eyewitness proves the truth. However, we've seen it too many times; the spirit of unbelief is incurable, especially if supernatural accomplishments cannot compel a person to believe in the beautiful Son of God.

Matthew 21:15 The chief priests and the scribes saw the wonderful things (meaning miracles) that Jesus did, and the children were crying in the temple and saying <u>Hosanna</u> (and the word Hosanna means, save us we pray, Son of God).

This truth means that the word Hosanna is an exclamation or a shout of praise to the honorable Son of God. This exclamation of faith in Hosanna expresses concrete belief in Yeshua. Truly, some people believe in Him with all their hearts, and nothing can convince others to believe in Him.

Matthew 21:15 and they (the believers inside the temple) cried saying, Hosanna to the son of David; and they (the chief priests and the scribes) were sore (meaning outraged and bitterly) displeased.

Indeed, at the temple in Jerusalem, where the excellent Son of God chose to teach the crowd of hungry believers in God, the priests were still incurable blind even after watching Him do incredible miracles. Sadly, the chief priests and the scribes hated hearing the group calling Jesus Hosanna.

Therefore, it seems conclusive to believe that it must be factual when the eyes see and the ears hear. However, because of unbelief, the perception of sight and sound isn't always enough for some people. Sadly, I must say, accuracy is dismissed because of spiritual blindness and an uncaring attitude.

Beyond the shadow of a doubt, unbelief is an incurable worldwide problem, seemingly insolvable; it negatively affects the heart and soul. I believe that unbelief causes blindness to the truth and deafness to righteousness and holiness.

Although I am sure that the extraordinary and Supernatural Son of God could've healed His enemies of their unbelief and spiritual blindness, I know He could've cured them of spiritual deafness.

However, if He did cure them of their spiritual blindness, deafness, and unbelief, He would've forced His will on the loyal servants of Satan and taken away their free will. I want you to know that my great God doesn't force anyone to live godly, and whoever chooses to be His friend must do it by choice.

Therefore, when ungodly men defy logic, the more excellent light will not enter them. Whoever purposely opposes Him and His good works, who cannot force themselves to believe His words, are the wicked tares, and an unseen force from the demonic spirit world controls their nature.

I guarantee you that the unseen force is the wicked guiding spirit of Lucifer, or it's one of his many demon angel friends. Truly, whenever we meet a person suffering from incurable unbelief, we can be sure we've crossed paths with a servant of a wicked guiding spirit.

Although, for the first time since they became men, the chief priests and the scribes saw holy things they had never seen before happen. However, seeing miracles didn't matter to them because they were incurable of unbelief, and seeing Miracles will not cure the incurable.

Positively, the chief priests and the scribes should've been pleased to witness the great miracles accomplished by the honorable Son of God after seeing the Son of God perform miracles. I assure you every day; He was breaking the odds of being lucky when He healed many people afflicted by various diseases.

The chief priests and the scribes should've repented and joined themselves to Him and should've gladly started carrying the wonderful gospel of God wherever they went. Carrying the cross is what all people do after the light enters their hearts and we become believers in Christ.

Positively, if their sight was good, and their ears could hear, without hate and unbelief causing blindness of the heart. Then they, without suffering from spiritual impairments, would've loved the beautiful Son of God and the incredible gospel of God.

Without a doubt, they would've cried out to the honorable Son of God and said, Hosanna, Hosanna, save us, we pray. Furthermore, I want you to know there will come a time and a day when the scales will fall from their eyes, and every interested person will say, Hosanna, Hosanna, save us, we pray.

However, the chief priests and scribes didn't cry out and didn't say Hosanna, Hosanna, save us, we pray. It was mainly because of their incurable blindness, deafness, and incurable unbelief, including an Incurable wicked heart, a guiding demon spirit, and no sincere desire to repent and change.

I am sure this kind of terrible condition I've just described means ungodly people are incurable and uninterested in being cured of spiritual blindness and the curse of unbelief. Sadly, I must say, incurable unbelief is a terrible heart condition, hardened over time, and too hard to understand the truth.

I know seeing is believing, and if an accomplishment could soften a hardened heart, open blind eyes, and deaf ears, and cure spiritual blindness. Then, it would've been the genuine miracles and worship they witnessed in the temple of Jerusalem whenever

Jesus was present.

However, had they been wise temple priests and scribes, they would've asked Jesus to forgive them for their unbelief. However, they were incurable, and Bible history proves that the chief priests and the scribes wouldn't ask the supernatural Son of God to forgive them for their unbelief.

Suppose they had been wise temple priests and scribes; they would've asked the Son of God to forgive them for their hypocrisy. Hypocrisy means they were acting like men of the cloth, purposely deceiving and insincere in the house of God.

However, it's easy to conclude they wouldn't change their corrupt walk with the wicked and rebellious Lucifer, and I am unaware of any scripture within the Bible saying they saw the light, converted to a loyal believer in Christ, and decided to walk with God.

Therefore, I believe the chief priests and the scribes preferred to remain incurably blind, deaf, and numb to the truth. The story about them in the New Testament indicates that they chose to keep their hardened hearts and hate for the Son of God and remain incurable.

Sadly, I must say, regardless of the evidence contrary to their unbelief, they couldn't see a Great Savior standing among them. This truth means the wicked Lucifer had them encased in an invisible barrier, blocking the truth from rescuing them from Satan.

Indeed, their hearts wouldn't soften, regardless of the miracles and the healings they saw the Son of God do for all the people around them. I firmly believe that if the loving Son of God cannot inspire a person to repent and change, they are incurable and will suffer from the judgment of damnation.

The grand prize of salvation through repentance was within their grasp, and all they had to do was open their eyes and believe in the beautiful Son of God. Unfortunately, I must say, their hearts suffered from hardness, and they couldn't or wouldn't believe in Him.

This truth means that they were so spiritually blind by unbelief that they let conversion to authentic Christianity, entwined with salvation, pass by their grasp. It was mainly because of their misplaced loyalty to the Roman authority and the wicked prince of this world called Lucifer.

It was evil, uncaring, and uncompassionate for the chief priests and the scribes to hate the Son of God so much. Sadly, they hated Jesus so much that they didn't want to see the crippled walk, the blind see, or the ungodly converted to Christians.

I assure you that no one can hate the Son of God, reject God's miracles, claim salvation, or have faith and love for God. This truth means that we all either believe, do not believe, hate, or love the beautiful Son of God.

It's absolutely for sure; belief or unbelief between God and us is what it all boils down to while we live in the flesh. I conclude that being an incurable believer in Christ is highly acceptable, but incurable unbelief in the Father, the Son, and the Holy Ghost is unacceptable.

Indeed, I want you to understand that all of us living in the flesh are confronted with either rejecting the Son of God or accepting the Son of God. This truth means you and me and everyone else will end our lives as believers or unbelievers. However, the spiritually blind person will not realize it until their time has expired and it's too late.

Positively, the chief priests, scribes, Pharisees, and many others who suffered from the curse of unbelief had the same choice as us. However, a hardened heart is without compassion for others, and haters of the gospel of God have an unbelieving heart.

However, it's pretty easy for me to conclude that a hardened heart lacks compassion for others, and without believing in the validity of the Son of God, a hardened heart may be incurable. Truly, when I say it might be Incurable, I am too gentle with the truth.

Therefore, I want you to be ready whenever the Spirit of God calls on your heart to save your soul. When He does, you better be sure your heart is soft enough to see, hear, and believe in Him.

This revealing story concerning the unbelievers in this world, which I call incurable, includes the chief priests, the scribes, and the Son of God. It's an awareness story and a warning story that entwines with another story from the New Testament.

The New Testament story proves that unbelief is incurable if we are willing servants of Satan, enjoy the pleasures of sin, and suffer from the terrible curse of unbelief. I want you to know that the common denominator among Lucifer's servants is unbelief, or they wouldn't be his servants.

This unnecessary, sad story, Incurable, entwines with the illogical stance of unbelief. It should stir up our curiosity concerning why some men believe in God and why some do not.

Indeed, in our corrupt world today, many people suffer from supernatural curses, some of whom are born a certain way. For this reason, we should ask ourselves, why does it seem like some people are born with an ungodly disadvantage?

Furthermore, to increase our understanding, we should seek to know the reason; some men and women easily believe in our Creator God. We should want to understand the cause; some men refuse to believe in the validity of God, regardless of any reason.

Indeed, I want you to know that the answer might have originated in our past, from a previous Earth age, before the excellent cleansing flood, or even further back to a heavenly period when we knew God from before. Surely, if we analyze the reason, as of here and now, then the answer will elude us.

I assure you this existence we are living in isn't our first time in life, and you and I have an unknown history our minds cannot recall. Not knowing the moral direction of our previous life is a blank to us, but not to God because our wonderful Creator God knew us from the foundation of this Earth.

Furthermore, I want you to know that this Earth's foundation is old, and it had its beginnings during the Ancient of Days and possibly billions of years ago. Unknown to us was the age of the dinosaurs, and afterward came the rebellious angels from Heaven and then the flesh and blood race.

This truth means, unbeknownst to us, our belief or unbelief in God has a long history, and we may be older than the dinosaurs. Our beliefs or unbelief, loyalty, or disobedience could be inherited from another time in history.

Indeed, it's entirely possible; the incurable unbelievers suffer from the Recompense of a supernatural God-imposed curse. It's pretty likely; *because they received not the love of the truth*, they will receive a strong delusion to believe a lie and be damned.

Bible scriptures reveal, and I firmly believe, that we aren't totally in control of all our circumstances. Not any more than

King Nebuchadnezzar was after our great God and other heavenly creations imposed a seven-year curse on him.

I assure you that the supernatural curse imposed on King Nebuchadnezzar caused him to suffer personal hardships for seven years. The curse proves that mighty creations from the kingdom of Heaven can and do sometimes control our minds and hearts but to an unknown degree.

Therefore, I assure you that God and the holy ones in Heaven have power over our minds, and for perfect fairness, they will accomplish whatever their hearts desire. This truth means, to a great extent, our calling into the family of God and our belief in Him without proof may have a supernatural origin.

Furthermore, whoever suffers from the incurable unbelief curse may also have a supernatural problem from the heavens. I want you to know that the great gift of free will and the price tag for sin may entwine together until all sin debts are accounted for and paid in full.

Indeed, our incurable unbelief may also have a supernatural origin from the heavens. A new beginning means our old memories have faded, and as we proceed through life, we may never know the extent of our free will and the degree of spiritual control controlling us.

Therefore, if we receive a calling into the family of God, we better accept it immediately and be glad for our calling. I advise you that taking our calling is the only wise decision if we want to live forever, and turning our calling down illustrates a sign of incurable stupidity.

Furthermore, throughout the portals of time, we may not receive another opportunity to claim salvation and be a confirmed

child of God, and it's because options will disappear sometimes. This truth means that if we do not believe in God before we die, then we'll have to face Him on Judgment Day while suffering from incurable unbelief.

CHAPTER FORTY-SEVEN
BEAUTY AND THE FLESH CONTEST

This enlightenment story concerns most people worldwide and revolves around beauty and the flesh. Even though our lives shouldn't, it portrays an ongoing contest between our physical appearance and the flesh and the value some people attach to beauty.

I have to admit, and you'll have to agree, that because of the progression of age, flesh has the advantage of beauty. A quick look in the mirror, day after day, proves that the flesh body usually has a longer lifespan than the appearance of beauty.

As we grow old, we'll watch time destroy beauty much quicker than time destroys flesh, and then I am sure other qualities will become greater in value than beauty. I am sure the image change is the natural order of things and God's intentions for the human race.

Indeed, I conclude that youth's contest between flesh and beauty is strongest. Even though the flesh body has a limited lifespan and is as frail as glass, it'll still outlast the lifespan of beauty if we live more than a few years.

Almost everything created under the sun looks more beautiful when young and new. However, the corridors of time move fast, and age quickly deteriorates beauty faster than the flesh. Indeed, the wise person looks beyond the flesh, evaluates the heart, and values inner beauty more than outer beauty.

The main reason is that the Father, the Son, and the Holy Ghost didn't allow us pictures of them. They want us to realize that our image on the outside of our bones isn't as important as the image of our inner character.

I assure you, it's vain to believe the image of our flesh will always be beautiful, even if we are beautiful in our youth. The beauty of youth disappears with age, and no one can defeat the progression of age or drink from the fountain of youth.

This truth means the body clock never stops ticking away, and beauty doesn't last long before old age replaces it with wrinkles and scars. Our lifespan is compared to a vapor, lingering a moment and gone.

Although I wish all men were handsome and never grew old, I wish all women were beautiful forever. However, the fact remains true, and reality is our mirror. God designed our life cycle to deteriorate with age.

This truth means nothing known to man can stop the body clock from ticking away, and we can see ourselves growing older daily. Truly, we all know the clock ticks away, and with each passing day, our beauty fades away.

I want you to know it's not debatable, so I do have to tell you a fact. However, fret not; the beauty standards don't judge us, and in the end, after much wear and tear, we'd have hell to pay if beauty were our eternal life judge.

Indeed, it's good for us men and women; our heart's beauty is the barometer God reads, not the smile or frown of the flesh. I am confident that our heart will indicate that we have partial power to decide where the soul ends.

Positively and too often, the conclusion concerning beauty illustrates that it is a contest between our character and the beauty of our flesh. For this reason, I warn you that we shouldn't prefer outward beauty over a godly character.

Furthermore, I want you to know that our appearance is often the reason for our decisions or how we dress today. However, the beauty of our appearance shouldn't be our decision-maker or a reason for doing anything.

I guarantee that reading romance novels and looking at ourselves in the mirror isn't the formula for a beautiful heart. However, reading romance novels and constantly looking into the mirror illustrates a terrible, vain character.

Indeed, I want to warn you that getting a lot of attention isn't always beneficial to our souls. Beyond the shadow of a doubt, a vanity character is a formula for ungodliness, adultery, and all sorts of immoral and carnal sins, and sometimes, beautiful flesh falls into the traps of all of them.

As you've learned through examples, old age has the last say, and popularity decreases as beauty fades away. This fact indicates that the advantages of beautiful flesh are temporary, and the fallout from making wrong decisions will last longer than the beauty of the flesh.

Therefore, I am sure it's correct to say that youth and beautiful looks symbolize the flowers blooming in the spring. But still yet, as pretty as the flowers look, they'll fade away and die in the fall.

It's for sure; too much emphasis is put on beauty rather than godliness, even though it will not compare to godliness. Surely, if we make an accurate analogy, we'll have to conclude that godliness wins all contests between beauty and the flesh.

Therefore, I assure you that godliness will increase our longevity in the next life and much more than the advantages of beauty. The final results at the end of our life will prove good character is worth much more in the long run than beautiful flesh.

Therefore, God bless all beautiful people with beautiful hearts and character qualities, but never forget to cherish your beautiful heart because a beautiful soul is an everlasting treasure, much more valuable than gorgeous flesh.

Conclusively, if we could pattern a characteristic, then without a doubt, a beautiful heart will cause a person less trouble than gorgeous flesh. For example, please consider that Lucifer was lifted because of his attractive appearance, and beauty is why he's had a troubled life from the beginning.

For the above reason, and it's entirely possible, his beautiful appearance was his most significant obstacle in life; it gave him a false image of himself. This truth means an attractive appearance has too much influence on carnal, corrupt, and immoral opportunities and how we proceed through life.

This beauty and flesh contest story entwines you, me, and others living among us. It has a declaration to declare: Do not let beauty influence our decisions or get in the way of putting godliness first.

Indeed, the beauty of nature is our illustration, proving a beautiful landscape is tranquil to look upon if we do not get bitten by a copperhead or a rattlesnake living on the same landscape.

CHAPTER FORTY-EIGHT
EQUAL LOVE

This fair-to-everyone story, *Equal Love*, revolves around the Father, the Son, the Holy Ghost, and their inner emotions. Because we need to know, this story describes how our Creator God feels about all people, and I am glad to say it's regardless of the nation we live in or our skin color.

Equal love means we can be loved equally by God, but it's up to us to accept His love. Surely, we must give to receive, and believing in the righteous word of God illustrates the right formula for creating equal love.

I assure you that if we do not believe in the infallible word of God, then we'll not be loved by God, and this analogy illustrates equal love. Many people will say God loves us but doesn't love what we do, and I say He will not love us if we do not believe in Him.

Love flows two ways, or love doesn't flow at all, and this accurate analogy means two-way love is the pinnacle of equal love. I conclude that one-way love doesn't amount to anything worthy, nor does one-way love possess anything fitting the definition of equal love.

However, the following revealing scripture purposely portrays equal love, but it takes both of us to create equal love. Truly, being baptized into Christ, regardless of race, nationality, or gender, illustrates equal love from above.

It might be accurate to say that the loyal Apostle Paul was the first apostle chosen to preach salvation to heathen nations. However, if he was, I am sure he based his teaching on the words of Jesus. Written in Galatians 1:16, the Apostle Paul says that I might <u>preach</u> (means reveal) the Son of God among the Gentiles.

The following few scriptures reveal the teaching of the Apostle Paul to everyone concerned about preserving their soul. The following enlightenment scripture explains equal love in the highest degree and reveals from Whom it matters the most.

Galatians 3:27 For as many of you as having been baptized <u>into</u> <u>Christ</u> (means have given your heart to Him) have put on Christ.

Galatians 3:28 There is neither Jew nor Greek, neither bond nor free, nor male nor female: For ye is one in Christ Jesus.

Galatians 3:29 And if ye be <u>Christ</u> (means one of His believers), then are ye Abraham's <u>seed</u> (means offspring, or heir), and <u>heirs</u> (means children) according to the <u>promise</u> (made to Abraham, Isaac, and Jacob).

I assure you that the above equal love scripture is emphasized as non-exclusive, and no one is left out of his analogy. This truth means that anyone having enough faith to believe in the Son of God also has the right to claim God's promises.

Therefore, this incredible and equal opportunity promise

would be exclusive if made to the Jewish people only. However, I am happy to say that this promise of equal opportunity is non-exclusive. Indeed, this promise includes all Christians faithful enough to believe in Christ.

Please understand and know that we can only be considered Abraham's seed if we believe in the honorable Son of God, even if we are grafted into seeds from a strange nation other than the land of Israel.

For a reason only He knows, the great promise of salvation was given to the Jews first and the Gentiles last. However, the last is loved as much as the first, and the scriptures say neither Jew nor Greek, bond, free, male nor female is more privileged to claim His promises, and this truth illuminates Equal Love.

Indeed, the above need-to-know and sincere words the Apostle Paul speaks say the promise to Abraham's seed is non-exclusive, except for the requirement to believe in the Son of God as our Savior and our divine Deliverer from permanent death.

This truth means that if we have enough faith to believe in the honorable Son of God and are in love with His infallible word, we accept Him as our only Savior and are willing to put on Christ by wearing His righteous gospel. The best suit to wear daily is His covenant-designed commandments.

Then we faithful Gentiles, or whatsoever is our nationality, who live in other lands all over this Earth are His children. The scriptures reveal that we believers in God are Abraham's grafted seed, regardless of race, color, or gender.

Therefore, I want you to know that all the blessings and favors accompanying the promise to Abraham are ours to claim, especially if we put on the gospel of Christ and are proud of His perfect word. I am sure devout believers in God are pleased with the Son of God and will follow His ways forever.

I want you to realize that regardless of who we are, we can claim the gift of eternal salvation and live the life of an immortal if we have enough faith and determination to follow and believe in the excellent gospel of God.

However, I assure you, a severe warning comes from this declaration story called *Equal Love*. The strict warning is written in the beautiful book of Revelation, chapter three, verses fifteen and sixteen. For this reason, we cannot straddle the fence and be almost convinced.

I want you to know that true believers in Christ have a monumental requirement. This truth means our Father in Heaven expects all of us believers in Christ to be hot and on-fire Christians, loyal to His perfect word.

Definitely, not cold or lukewarm like the Laodiceans and not make-believe like the Nicolaitans. However, being committed to God's beautiful word and believing that nothing else is acceptable secures us a home in His kingdom. Because Knowledge of God increases our faith, I want to share an important fact: God's gospel is *The Image Of God!*

Surely, knowing this truth will inspire those who love God to study more often, and a lack of study reveals weak love.

CHAPTER FORTY-NINE
BRAIN POWER

This revealing story, which I call *Brainpower*, is one hundred percent correct. It looks deep at the subject and points out an absolute and unchangeable fact. Observation proves brainpower doesn't influence every decision we make or guarantee we'll make a correct decision.

I want you to realize that superior brainpower has nothing to do with choosing our God. Many gods are claimed and scattered around this world. Observation proves that knowledgeable men and women have different opinions and worship various gods.

Furthermore, I want you to know that different nations and foreign people believe in their god as much as we believe in our Creator God. It's as baffling as a complicated puzzle; the way so many gods and goddesses became acceptable to people is beyond my comprehension.

Because of years of observation, I conclude all of us loyal Christians believe we worship the right God, regardless of how unrealistic it may seem to someone, not a Christian or someone determined to worship a different god or a manufactured god.

From the Ancient of Days, when nothing else existed, our Father, His Son, and the Holy Ghost were created from the Living Coals of Fire. They became the pure and holy righteous trinity, and they cannot taste the sting of death. However, wise men and women often reject them, not because of ignorance but because of unbelief.

The Father, Son, and Holy Ghost are the creators of life, the takers of life, and the orchestrators of every living thing we see, whether on the land, in the sea, or flying through the air. Truly, it would be silly to believe that anyone other than our supernatural Creator can be our Supreme God.

Furthermore, the three judges between righteousness and unrighteousness throughout every generation, past, present, and future, is our Father in Heaven, the Author of the great and perfect Ten Commandments. He builds up kings, tears down kings, and molds the clay differently.

The Father, Son, and the Holy Ghost bless some men and women and some angels and curse some men and women and some angels. Truly, being blessed or cursed depends on our relationship with the excellent word of God. If I could give good advice, I would say to love God and keep His commandments.

Positively, their judgments are perfect, and every man and every angel can expect a fair Judgment from them. For the benefit of fairness, the sword of the Lord cuts whoever falls under its blade, regardless of the composition of our body formation.

Furthermore, I want you to know that there's an intangible world beyond our reach, and spirit creations in the heavens above inhabit it. I conclude that flesh-and-blood men and women do not live in the supernatural world. However, we are influenced by spirit creations, some good and some evil, regardless of our degree of brainpower.

Indeed, Bible scriptures reveal spirit creations move freely through the air we breathe, and being invisible and void of physical form doesn't mean they aren't brilliant ghost spirits. They are among us regardless of whether we are aware of them or not aware of them.

The Intangible world surrounding us is permanent, and this tangible material world is a stepping stone into the intangible spirit world. I hope you realize that after our flesh dies, you and I will change into a spirit creation for an unknown time.

Furthermore, it's easy to conclude that most all things have a circuit, similar to the rivers flowing into the sea and back again. The course of nature includes the four seasons rotating the same way, year after year, or the Earth revolving around the sun or the moon millions of miles away, affecting tidal waves.

Therefore, it's easy to believe that flesh and blood creations also have a circuit that began in Heaven. Furthermore, after our death, some of us will return to Heaven again, and you and I, and every sincere believer in Christ, will end our journey in the same place we began.

Positively, as unrealistic as it sounds to humans, who have limited understanding and knowledge about the heavens above. Three supernatural creations are more phenomenal than angels and have unlimited powers because of their body formation.

I assure you that the Father, the Son, and the beautiful Holy Ghost have unlimited power, and their abilities are beyond our comprehension. We are living proof; they give life to material substance, and I know that our Potter Man in Heaven works with more things than clay.

Positively, because of the creation of everything we see, regardless of the material substance, such as the flesh and blood man, created from the dust of the Earth, or the woman made from the rib of Adam, or an angel formed from gold, silver, diamonds, and precious jewels. Our wonderful Creator God created everything that breathes, regardless of our material construction.

Indeed, humankind has limited knowledge and understanding, and man only knows the simplest of things when compared to heavenly creations. Bible evidence proves God created other life forms with excellent knowledge and great insight, and their abilities exceed our wildest dreams.

I assure you that humankind lives in a daze when we compare ourselves to heavenly creations, and our intellect will not equal their intellect. Positively, the angels understand reality, godliness, and ungodliness, similar to living in a clear blue sky, not hindered by heavy fog.

However, I want you to realize regardless of our limitations or how little brainpower we have when, our wisdom is compared to the angel's knowledge. Compared to the angels, we are similar to lost children stumbling around in the dark, and we haven't enough oil in our lamps to shine bright. But undeniably, loving God doesn't require a higher degree of intelligence, just faith.

Lucifer and the other rebellious angels illustrate an example of extraordinary brainpower, but they don't care enough to be helpful angels. This truth means Lucifer and the rebellious angels prove that superior brainpower isn't always the formula for making the right decisions.

Therefore, we frail Earth creations, formed from the dirt of the Earth, who have limited brainpower, prove a fact. This truth means we can become godlier and make better decisions based on righteousness than many of the brilliant angels have done in Heaven.

This truth means godliness and righteousness do not coincide with a certain amount of intelligence and haven't any bearing on superior or limited brainpower. Bible history proves that brilliant, rebellious angels and intelligent men and women will fail God and be cast into Hell.

While other creations with limited brainpower will receive the gift of eternal salvation, this analogy means that the value of brainpower will not compare to the value of our hearts. Surely, this accurate fact proves brainpower is secondary to the feelings of our hearts.

Simply because we follow our heart, more so than our brain, the godliness we exhibit, and our love for God isn't based on our I.Q. I conclude that our faith in God isn't measured by brainpower.

CHAPTER FIFTY
DRAGON TRANSFORMATION

This need-to-understand story, *The Dragon Transformation*, reveals an interesting fact. For higher learning and a greater understanding of the Bible, I am telling you the rebellious and wicked Lucifer has many different identification names, and the dragon transformation describes him well.

Furthermore, I guarantee that the evil dragon in this teaching story isn't a monstrous animal-like creature living in a cave, surrounded by the remains of humans he devours. I want you to know that the cruel dragon in this exposure story doesn't breathe fire from his mouth or have clawed feet.

Nor does the fierce dragon swoop down from the mountain tops in this story. Nor does he snatch up people during a dive from the sky, and he isn't carried through the air by strong winds, and an accurate observation proves that he doesn't burn people to a crisp with flames of fire.

However, I want you to know that the wicked dragon in this

informative story has a long and colorful history, and during better days, he walked on two feet in Heaven. Sadly, he walked upon this Earth before the excellent cleansing flood removed his physical appearance, and like a rattlesnake, his poison was strong.

The fierce dragon's body was extraordinary, unique, rare, and not ordinary among the angels in Heaven since he was formed from precious stones, gold, and silver and made animated and alive by the supernatural power of my excellent Creator God.

Somehow, the supernatural Living Coals of Fire fused the materials of his body, and the dragon became flexible after it became alive. The dragon was a beautiful creation; the other angels admired it greatly and wished they were strong and beautiful like him.

This truth illustrates the wicked and charming Lucifer wasn't considered a hideous evil dragon at the beginning of his creation. Furthermore, I assume the evil Lucifer might've been a good angel for many years before he became rebellious, corrupt, and wicked.

Indeed, cruel and heartless, the charming Lucifer was said to be an angel of light among all the inhabitants of Heaven, and it's entirely possible he was for an unknown time. However, it's for sure he did turn rebellious, wicked, evil, and untrustworthy.

However, we must consider the facts and be wise enough to realize that appearances are deceiving. After an unknown amount of time, Lucifer's character changed, and he wasn't an angel of light underneath the exterior of his beautiful outward appearance.

I do not know, and the Bible scriptures do not reveal if my great God could read the heart of the supernatural Lucifer. Truly, if He couldn't read his heart, Lucifer had the advantage of deception, and he managed to deceive God for an unknown time.

Even with all His wisdom, the God of all creation didn't know that the beautiful Lucifer would turn out to be His great adversary or arch-enemy from within the inner circle. Until undeniable evidence surfaced, and the veil of his insincerity was exposed.

I guarantee you it's the same with humans since we cannot read another person's mind, and we cannot know the real them until they expose their true character. However, after a while, the veil will lift, and everyone will reveal the true nature of their heart.

The wicked Lucifer appeared to the naive Eve as an angel of light instead of a hideous snake and deceived her with his charm and beauty, and she disobeyed God. Indeed, inside the beautiful Garden of God and within the realms of Eden, Lucifer revealed his true character and the ugly lying underneath his beautiful image. Now we know within the midst of all his evil accomplishments, even from the beginning, deception is at the heart of his plots.

I assure you, the beautiful Eve was unaware and taken by surprise, or she wouldn't have been deceived, tricked, and seduced by a hideous talking snake. I want you to know that we are a little silly in the head if we believe a garden snake tricked the beautiful Eve into eating from the profile of his tree.

The example of Eve being tricked proves beyond the shadow of a doubt that appearances can be deceiving, and the Dragon Transformation proves extreme evil hides behind the image of light. As the old saying goes, the sweetness of honey will catch more flies than vinegar, and a silver tongue laced with insincerity and dripping with smooth lies is the Dragon's bait.

The following enlightenment scripture proves that the wicked and deceiving Lucifer has the power of transformation. This ability means he becomes what benefits him the most at the time, and we could correctly say the wicked Lucifer is a human flytrap. Temptations of profit and immorality are his honey, and like Eve, most people eat the honey dripping from his tree.

Beyond the shadow of a doubt, the wicked Lucifer is a sly old fox who can present himself as an angel of light or a fierce dragon. I believe the demonic Lucifer played the same game in Heaven as he does on this Earth, generation after generation, and the silver tongue never quits deceiving.

I assure you that the Apostle Paul shares a good understanding of how a dragon can present an appearance as an angel of light. Truly, this evil dragon transformation analogy entwines with deception and honey-baited traps.

2 Corinthians 11:14 And no man marvel; Satan himself is transformed (means changes) into an angel of light.

I am sure the insincere deceiving dragon, evil, uncompassionate, and quite experienced at game-playing, says to himself, I cannot let people know the real me. Lucifer knows he cannot project his true image since he's played this game many times, called the angel of light deception.

The experienced Lucifer positively realizes that more flies are caught with sweet honey by an angel of light than a dragon could subdue with an aggressive appearance. For this reason, I believe the wicked Lucifer tries to wear a halo to deceive the naïve.

However, the dragon transformation has a dual meaning, meaning many dragon men living on this Earth emulate the dragon transformation. This truth means many people on this Earth present themselves as a person of light when they are fierce deceivers.

The sincere and wise Apostle Paul reveals a distinction for the benefit of you and me when he likens fierce deceivers to the dragon. Paul wants you and me to know deceivers present themselves as a person of light; in reality, they are powerful liars and evil men and women practicing the dragon transformation.

Beyond the shadow of a doubt, the following exposure scripture reveals appearances aren't always what they seem to be. Furthermore, judgment calls are a serious issue, and judging a man, woman, or angel by appearance would be foolish.

Undoubtedly, most people living on this Earth are probably more like actors than sincere, especially people in business and many self-proclaimed prophets behind the pulpit who are willing to deceive for the love of money. I am sure the love of money creates fierce preacher men who practice the *Dragon Transformation.*

2 Corinthians 11:13 For such are false apostles, deceitful workers, transforming themselves into the Apostles of Christ.

I firmly believe the power of transformation is within all of us if we aren't bothered by being insincere hypocrites like the wicked Lucifer. I want you to realize that everyone playing the actor game is a phony hypocrite and a fierce dragon disguised as an angel of light.

The wise Apostle Paul gives us an example of the *Dragon Transformation,* and we could be deceived like the innocent Eve if we aren't careful. Because an angel of light deceives much better than a fierce dragon, the Apostle Paul says so in the next scripture.

2 Corinthians 11:3 But I fear, lest by any means as the serpent *beguiled* (means tricked, or seduced, or both) Eve through his *subtlety* (means crafty way).

2 Corinthians 11:3, so your minds should be corrupted from the simplicity that is in Christ.

The above warning scripture is meant for you and me. It indicates a person of light if it's a dragon in sheep's clothing. If we let our guard down and do not look past the appearance, it'll charm, trick, and seduce even the very elect through the appearance of light.

I assure you that God's perfect and excellent word and the power of discernment are our only armor against the wicked dragon because the fierce dragon will purposely disguise himself as an angel of light.

In this exposure story requiring our full attention, I call the *Dragon Transformation*. It illustrates that everyone's character doesn't always align with the exactness of their appearance. This truth means that if money is involved, a deal is in the works, or seduction of some sort is contemplated, then the transformation of the Dragon is highly probable.

Therefore, I want you to know pretty words aren't always valid, but fierce dragons hide behind lovely words. Sadly, I must say, a person of light may not be what they appear to be, and actions are the true discerner between fierce dragons and the authentic person of light.

CHAPTER FIFTY-ONE
HE LOOKED LIKE OTHER MEN

This dedication story, *He Looked Like Other Men*, portrays the perfect Son of God, disguised in the flesh, not presently here on Earth in His supernatural form. Because He wanted to blend in with us and be like everyone else, His physical appearance was the same as yours and mine.

Even though the excellent Son of God was humble and caring, He experienced many things we experience daily. His flesh was frail, the same as ours, but Yeshua was still the supernatural Son of God, and He walked on water and accomplished many miracles.

Furthermore, I assure you that our life in the flesh will not compare to His life in the flesh; living inside a flesh body is the only thing we have in common. The Special and perfect Son of God was the most special flesh and blood man to walk upon this Earth, and none of us are as Special as Him.

Indeed, the perfect and excellent Son of God, wiser than all other men, had divine power He didn't use. I want you to know that

He was a great warrior, unafraid of anyone, but He refused to fight with His enemies or physically harm anyone, and He was called the gentle Lamb of God.

Indeed, the Son of God didn't come from the kingdom of Heaven to express great physical power. However, because of stories about Him, it's easy to conclude that He didn't come here to prove Himself as a great warrior among men and didn't kill His enemies.

Positively, the beautiful Son of God came here as a Teacher and a Savior. He desired to shine His light into this sinful world, enveloped by overwhelming darkness caused by His wicked arch-enemy from Heaven, and the light He shined was pure truth.

By the time the beautiful Son of God arrived on the world scene, the needed quality of godliness had eluded almost all men and women. Sadly, the nation of Israel was a terrible mess and the cruel Roman invaders occupied Israel, and snakes and vipers controlled the temple of Herod.

Beyond the shadow of a doubt, Christianity had to be revived by the gospel of God, and men needed to learn more about Him. For this reason, His goal was to remove myths and establish authenticity, and He accomplished this goal while looking like other men.

Furthermore, He was the only person able to revive Christianity, and while doing so, He intended to save lost men from the grips of Lucifer. It's apparent He diverted multitudes of people from traveling on the wrong path in life, and because of Him, masses of people are still being saved by His blood.

His name was Yeshua, the excellent Son of God, manifest in the flesh, and, like everyone else, He looked like other men. Good people loved and believed in Him with all their hearts and were glad for His arrival upon this Earth, and I am patiently waiting for His second return.

Indeed, Bible scriptures reveal evil, wicked, and corrupt men, including the cruel prince of this world and all the demon spirits of the air. Who was having their way with most men and women and were entering into unguarded and unclean individuals?

They weren't happy to see the Son of God here in the flesh, and they didn't want Him walking on their turf; they were controlling quite well. Lucifer knew the honorable Son of God would interfere with his establishment of domination and control.

Positively, I am sure we could correctly say the evil Lucifer was happy with how things were going before the excellent Son of God was born as other men in the flesh. I am also certain that Lucifer knew Yeshua would oppose him and set men free from his bondage.

Beyond the shadow of a doubt, the wicked Lucifer desperately wants to keep most people from winning the grand prize of immortality and a permanent home in the kingdom of God. I want you to know we are his victims of prey; he purposely desires to destroy us, and he doesn't quit.

I assure you that the evil Lucifer didn't want the Son of God living here in his controlled area or for Him to authenticate and teach the life-saving word of God. Lucifer knew that, given enough time, the Son of God would free men from a life of sin and retrieve lost souls from him.

The excellent Son of God was a wanderer and had a noble purpose on this Earth to accomplish, and He chose to travel the highways and the bi-ways to fulfill His purpose. However, He looked like other men as He taught at the temple in Jerusalem or walked down the road.

However, after meeting Him and hearing Him teach the great gospel of God, blind eyes would open, and deaf ears would listen to the gospel they hadn't heard before. It became apparent to everyone that He was different from other men and never ceased doing His Father's good and righteous works.

Indeed, the outstanding Son of God and some of His Disciples traveled toward Jerusalem. They were on their way to the temple of Herod, and as they journeyed through the village of Jericho, which must've been a poor city, having people with many needs.

Many village people at Jericho gathered by the highway, and an unknown number of poor people were begging travelers for food and money. This ritual was probably a common practice among the disabled as the Passover of the lamb drew near.

However, joy and hope started filling their hearts when they saw the well-known Son of God approaching them. Unhealthy men and women knew that Yeshua was the right person to help them, especially everyone in the crowd who needed a divine miracle.

For example, two blind men, disabled by their lack of sight, heard Jesus coming their way and cried out and asked Him for mercy. The Son of God listened to them cry for Him, and He stopped among the crowd, asking the blind men, What wilt thou, I should do unto thee?

It's for sure; the disabled men believed in the Son of God and asked Him for their sight, and the compassionate Son of God gladly healed them. Immediately after the two blind men received their ability to see, they happily followed Jesus toward Jerusalem.

The extraordinary Son of God and His loyal disciples were

going toward the temple of Herod, and people everywhere along the way were glad to see Yeshua among them. For various reasons, He was the person the people needed and is the same person we need.

Many Bible stories reveal the goodness and mercy of the Son of God was well known ahead of Him wherever He traveled on this Earth. The history of humankind proves that many people believed in Him with all their hearts, and I gladly testify I do, too.

Beyond the shadow of a doubt, His excellent reputation went before Him like an intense wildfire spreading through dry grass in fast winds. This truth means that the name of the beautiful Son of God was known far and wide, and He's still known far and wide today.

Indeed, He looked like other men and ate, drank, and slept the same way. However, His supreme intelligence, supernatural abilities, and unlimited mercy separated Him from them.

Furthermore, because He's the supernatural Son of God, the corridors of time don't have any restrictions concerning His ability to walk among men undetected. The unknown author responsible for giving us the excellent book of Hebrews said not to forget to entertain strangers.

Hebrew 13:2 For there-by <u>some</u> (means flesh and blood men and women) have entertained angels unaware.

This truth means we could also entertain the Son of God unaware and not even realize it's Him we are talking to at the time because He can look like other men. I am sure He steps from His throne, walks through the gates of Pearl, and visits every generation of people living on this Earth.

Indeed, because you love His righteous ways, I hope you'll meet God's Honorable Son someday and become a noble son or daughter to Him. Truly, because men and women love righteousness, I believe all hot and on-fire Christians share this same hope.

Undoubtedly, the odds are against us meeting Him in person on this Earth, but thanks to God, He did leave us something extraordinary behind to remember Him. It's the God-inspired New Testament, which is all about Him and the foundation of Christianity.

Yeshua came to do His Father's work, and the New Testament is an extension of the Old Testament. They bind perfectly well, similar to a clear blue sky and the sunshine on a lovely day. Because we have faith and believe the words He spoke many hundreds of years ago, many today study the New Testament and call themselves believers in Christ.

Furthermore, I want you to realize that God's Honorable Son is an extension of His incredible Father. Even though He looked the same as other men, I must say, He'll look quite differently within the realms of Heaven than He did as Yeshua in the flesh.

CHAPTER FIFTY-TWO
TWO FATHERS

This story entwines a terrible worldwide practice, and all Christians need to understand this story called *Two Fathers*. It's a parallel story revolving around respect, love, thankfulness, and reverence, and these are the considerate things both our fathers deserve.

Furthermore, when we consider ourselves and how we believe our children should treat us fathers. Then please remember, our Father in Heaven feels emotions, and He desires the same respect as we expect from our children.

I have two Fathers I love and respect to an extreme degree, but when I pray, I do so to my excellent Father in Heaven. I pray to my heavenly Father because He's my Creator God, and I thank Him for the wonderful earthly father He gave me to love on this Earth.

My earthly father is gone to be with the Lord in Heaven, and I miss him tremendously and think about him every day of my life. However, I assure you, he parallels with my Creator Father in many ways because I think about Him every day I live and breathe.

Indeed, my heavenly Father gave me and everyone else the fifth commandment, which is important to Him. Even though the fifth commandment requires me and everyone else to honor our earthly father, it also has dual meaning to include Him.

I am sure that my righteous God also expects me to honor my mother, and if I do, my days on this Earth will be honorable and long. We'll all feel better about ourselves if we are respectful to our parents and help them as they grow old.

I assure you that there are many uncaring children in this world, and they refuse to honor, love, or respect their father and mother. However, unthinkingly, they pray many prayers to their heavenly Father and ask Him for divine blessings and favor.

They are hard-hearted, haven't any respect for their earthly father, and unquestioningly expect their heavenly Father to respect them. However, a close fellowship with their heavenly Father will be much harder for these hard-hearted children to obtain.

Indeed, these kinds of disobedient and hard-hearted children I am describing have double standards, mainly because they want to receive blessings from their heavenly Father. Still, they bless not their father or mother upon this Earth who raised them from birth.

I assure you that children must be blind or shortsighted if they are foolish enough to believe their heavenly Father doesn't recognize mental cruelty to parents and a seared conscience sort of disrespect.

Therefore, children of disobedience, beware; our heavenly Father is watching and listening to you and observing how we treat our parents. If we reap what we sow, then disrespecting our father and mother may result in discipline from our heavenly Father.

Therefore, children of parents practice forgiveness, do not hate the speck or flaw in their character, and do not hold it against them if they aren't perfect. This analogy includes you and me because our character will have specks and flaws. After all, no one's perfect.

Furthermore, I want you to know that the wicked devil sifts us like wheat, and he'll sift the children of parents, too, and no one escapes his demonic spirit torture. Indeed, if possible, he will destroy relationships between children and parents if we allow him the privilege to influence bad behavior.

CHAPTER FIFTY-THREE
GIVING AWAY HOPE

This real story, *Giving Away Hope*, describes the honorable Son of God entwined with everyone determined to believe in Him, and defining Him is accomplished with three accurate and robust descriptive words. These three words are the pinnacle of His character from when He was born the Son of Mary.

I am one hundred percent sure; the common ground between all the people who knew the incredible and merciful Son of God in the flesh and all of us believers in Yeshua throughout every generation since then. It's the same hope that started with Him in the land of Israel approximately two thousand years ago.

After many generations have passed by, thanks to my Father in Heaven for sending us His Son, the same hope has expanded worldwide. Furthermore, the expansion of Christianity is built on the title of this story, *Giving Away Hope.*

Positively, I know we can offer excellent compliments about God's incredible Son. However, I firmly believe giving us hope for a better tomorrow is one of the best gifts we can receive from Him. Truly, I think all Christians are hoping for a house seat in the kingdom of God, and it takes hope to have this dream.

Indeed, I would hate to believe I'll live and die without having hope for the gift of eternal life. Still, because of Bible illiteracy and unbelief, some men and women die without having a Savior. It is sad to leave this world and not have a Savior before we die, and the ungodly do not have any hope.

Indeed, this story, *Giving Away Hope,* is an enlightenment story, and it's written because it identifies with the Son of God. Fittingly enough, the Son of God is called our Savior, mainly because He gives us hope to escape sin and damnation. I want you to realize our only hope to live in the next world depends on us finding Him in this world.

Indeed, as He lived upon this Earth in the flesh, the people having authority in the temple of Herod weren't His friends, and they didn't support Him. It was mostly the poor and oppressed people who looked forward to seeing Him and listening to Him teach the authentic word of God.

The excellent and caring Son of God genuinely had compassion for the poor, and He healed them and taught them the righteous ways of His Father. They loved Him and gathered everywhere He was present to hear Him teach His Father's authentic gospel.

Because of His love and compassion and His sincere desire to save lost souls from the judgment of damnation, He gave them hope to live in a better world, have a better body, and have a life of immortality in the kingdom of God.

I assure you that there's never been any other person living on this Earth responsible for giving so much hope to everyone with a good heart. Thanks to His birth in the flesh, the same hope the loving Son of God gave the people during His time of life, we have the right to claim, too.

I call this past, present, and future story about the Son of God *Giving Away Hope* and a wish for a better life, a man's dream for a new world. This story illustrates two blind men receiving their sight and leapers cleansed by God—a sinner woman caught in adultery and not stoned to death after meeting Yeshua.

This dedication story illustrates Lazarus being raised from the dead and a woman having blood leakage for twelve years healed. I believe all their hopes had vanished, and they didn't have hope until they met the wonderful Yeshua.

Indeed, this is an accurate story for every generation, including every one since Yeshua's time, *Yeshua Gives Away Hope*. It identifies with every person touched by God's wonderful and caring Son, washed clean of sin and given a new heart. For the glory of God, this analogy includes you and me.

The common link between the blind men, the unhealthy leapers, Lazarus, and the woman who leaked blood was faith in the caring Son of God. Furthermore, every Christian must have faith in their heart before having hope.

I want you to know that without having faith and hope in the Father, the Son, and the Holy Ghost, I guarantee that none of us would be invited to live in their Special kingdom. It's entirely possible; the faithless and the hopeless are different types of people, not the children of God, and hope wasn't placed in their hearts.

If we didn't have hope, then we wouldn't want to live by the commandments of God, and we wouldn't gladly carry His cross; we wouldn't care about perfecting our lifestyle and being presentable before God. Sadly, I must say, we would lean toward an imaginary understanding and probably believe that our life ends at the grave.

Positively, I believe the hope God gives inspires us to be better Christians, and we wouldn't be loyal Christians if we didn't have the gift of hope. I want you to know a new world waits for the arrival of us Christians, and life doesn't end at the grave for a hot and on-fire Christian.

Without having hope in our hearts, we wouldn't believe in His miracles, and we wouldn't trust the story examples told to us by the prophets to be true. If we do not believe His story, examples, and miracles are the gospel truth, we lack hope to be a child of God.

Positively, Noah and his sons wouldn't have built a boat on dry land, anticipated a great flood, and stocked their boat with food, water, and animals without hope for a better life. However, they did build Noah's Ark, all because they believed in the beautiful word of God.

Beyond the shadow of a doubt, *faith and hope* share a close bond; they cannot be separated. We carry Faith and hope in our hearts, which go together like bees and honey, steak and eggs, or ice cream and apple pie. Surely, we should rejoice in the Lord because we have faith and hope.

I assure you that without having hope for better land and a life of freedom after four hundred and thirty years of slavery to the cruel Egyptians. Then Moses wouldn't have crossed the Red Sea and walked between two great walls of water to live in a barren desert where hardly anything could live.

I assure you that without having faith in God and hope for victory over death, the young David couldn't have slain the giant the Bible calls Goliath. Nor could he have hoped to escape the clutches of the jealous king of Israel, Saul, the first chosen king of Israel before King David.

Indeed, without faith in God and hope for a better tomorrow, Job would've weakened and submitted himself to Lucifer's wishes. Undoubtedly, he would've cursed the Lord and died a diseased person, but Job didn't forsake the Lord and didn't pass away by the death of a diseased person.

However, Job endured terrible pain and tribulations because of his strong faith, entwined with hope for a better tomorrow. He refused to curse the Lord and die because he loved God and believed in Him with all his heart, and because of his enduring faith and hope, he received great rewards.

Indeed, the Bible tells us that after his tribulation and testing were over, Job was healed and rewarded twice as much as before his sickness, and he lived to be one hundred and forty years old. Truly, Job was honored because his belief in God didn't weaken as Lucifer predicted.

Without faith and hope in the Supernatural Son of God, His mother wouldn't have asked Him to turn water into wine. However, He did; it was the best-tasting wine at the wedding feast. Indeed, it's pretty apparent; His mother knew He was a miracle worker.

Beyond the shadow of a doubt, without having faith and hope, a ruler of the synagogue named Jairus wouldn't have fallen on his knees before the Son of God and asked Him to save his twelve-year-old daughter. Being a synagogue ruler means he's probably seen the Son of God do many miracles and had faith to believe in His power.

I assure you the honorable Son of God was compassionate, and He proved it again in the city of Nain. A place where a widow's only son was being carried out in a coffin, and when the Son of God touched the wooden coffin, the widow's dead son sat up.

Furthermore, without having faith to believe in Yeshua's death, burial, and resurrection and hope for resurrection ourselves, we cannot fulfill the requirements for receiving the gift of salvation because our requirements must include faith and hope in a supernatural Savior.

Conclusively, whether it's faith-inspiring hope or whether it's hope-inspiring faith. One enhances the other, the same way the Left-hand helps the right hand, or the Right-hand will help the left hand. I want you to know that faith grows more robust as our interest in the word of God increases.

Therefore, I want you to know that hope and faith are the correct formulae for making us great teammates in God's ball game of life. I pray that your faith and hope will increase after reading this story about the beautiful Son of God giving away hope.

Indeed, our wonderful heavenly Father is watching you, me, and everyone else in this world, and whenever He sees a good heart, He gladly gives it hope and faith. For this reason, we see multitudes of Christians living everywhere on this Earth, hoping to live in the kingdom of God forever.

Therefore, I conclude that the gifts of hope and faith belong to Him, and we probably cannot experience the feelings of either one unless He instills those Special feelings within our hearts. I believe many believers in Christ aren't aware that God has given them the gift of faith and hope, and I hope to enlighten them through stories like this one.

This truth means that if we have strong faith and hope, we should thank the beautiful Son of God for our strong emotions, and I do every day because I strongly believe in Him and hope for a better tomorrow.

Gory to the Lord, Halleluja!

CHAPTER FIFTY-FOUR
CHRISTIANITY BY DEGREE

This declaration story, truthful and direct, I call Christianity by degree is personal and evaluates the strength of our Christianity by degrees. In the same way, Christians on milk aren't on the same level as Christians on solid meat.

This truth means some Christians are stronger, and some are more devout than others. Devoted Christians walk a straighter line and put more effort into being Christ-like Christians, and they try to live by the infallible word of God.

I guarantee you that Christians exhibit a wide range of Christ-like characteristics, even though it's an obvious observation. This statement means that the spectrum of their servitude to the loving Son of God varies greatly from Christian to Christian.

Positively, we would be foolish to believe that all Christians serve God to the same degree, have the same amount of faith, or practice the same amount of righteousness. I assure you, this analogy goes for all preachers and teachers, regardless of the name of their church.

I assure you that some Christians study the word of God much more than others, and some Christians are much more Bible-savvy than others. I conclude that some Christians have a hotter fire burning inside them than others, and they work harder to spread the gospel of God to the unsaved.

It's easy to conclude that some Christians are misguided about the gospel truth and lean on the gift of grace as if it's a free ride to Heaven. Meanwhile, other Christians put the word of God to use, walk in it, and depend on it for everyday guidance.

Furthermore, I hope you realize there are many blind guides in this world today and many wolves in sheep's clothing, and they call themselves Christians, too, even if they serve God to a lower degree of Christianity and do not walk the Christ-like walk.

I am sure not all Christians believe precisely the same concerning Bible-related subjects, and sometimes, some devout Christians are set in their ways and as blind as a bat to scripture authenticity. Sadly, the traditions of men have crept into many churches, and Christians observe them.

I guarantee you that clear eyesight proves there are a lot of different denominations in the world of Christianity, and they all claim to be Christian. However, they have various doctrines that separate them to some degree because they interpret scriptures differently.

However, I am happy to tell you that there's only one doctrine of God, and the authenticity of His Bible is the pinnacle of Him. Everything else we encounter is counterfeit, artificial, or a figment of someone's imagination, and it would help if you remembered these alterations to the truth whenever you hear different versions of the same subject.

Definitely, and it's for sure, regardless of the Bible-related subject, all opposition to His unchangeable and perfect word isn't authentic Christianity. The outstanding Son of God assures us that the traditions of men aren't authentic Christianity.

However, this problem is constantly happening, with Christians suffering from a lower degree of Christianity, and Christians suffering from a lower degree of Christianity will ignorantly oppose His word sometimes. Sometimes, they realize they are fighting His authenticity, and passive is the best way to describe them.

Furthermore, not practicing Bible authenticity reveals a compromiser within the church of God. A compromiser claims to be a Christian and is a Christian, but for some illogical reason, they aren't bothered by compromising the perfect word of God.

Positively, this awareness story, I call *Christianity By Degree*, says there are different degrees of Christianity. I want you to know that Christians are in a category, and whenever they look at each other, they are observing a high or low degree of Christianity.

I guarantee that some Christians aren't making a difference between the holy and the unholy, clean and the unclean. Sadly, I must say, many of them are so Bible illiterate they aren't aware of the compromises; they are guilty of committing against the word of God.

For example, as common as salt and pepper on the dinner table, there's only one authentic, holy, sacred, and hallowed Lord's Day. If we exchange it for another day, we aren't putting a difference between the holy and the unholy, and God expects all Christians to flee from anything counterfeit or unholy.

For another example, as easy to see as a full moon on a clear night, the definition of unclean means the same thing God tells us in Leviticus, chapter eleven, verse eight. Still, many Christians oppose His truthful word all the time and eat pig meat.

Furthermore, I know that many Christians are so polluted by the unclean that they'll never know how it feels to think with a clean heart. However, they'll falsely believe their heart is pure as light and their thinking abilities aren't affected by the unclean meats they eat.

I believe, and I may be wrong, but eating the unclean and compromising the authentic Lord's Day as long as we do it ignorantly and not on purpose or because everyone else is doing it. Maybe it'll not affect our relationship with God, and I do say maybe, but the chances are slim.

However, I am one hundred percent sure that the moment we learn the truth concerning whatever we are doing wrong. God expects us to quit compromising His word unless our ox is in the ditch, and it needs to be rescued from disaster on the seventh day of the week, the Sabbath of the Lord.

I want you to know that God's excellent word is absolute, and we are foolish if we do not take His righteous word seriously. It's for sure; the pits of Hell are full of foolish people who didn't take His required word seriously.

The common denominator in Hell among all its residents is compromisers, who found out the hard way; they couldn't depend on the gift of grace to absolve all their sins. Truly, if we are extreme sinners, not trying to change, the excellent assistance of grace will not help us escape judgment.

Indeed, we are foolish to believe the gift of grace means the same as unlimited leniency. This truth means the excellent gift of grace allows us the privilege to repent and change whenever we do wrong. However, the superb assistance of grace doesn't relax the restrictions on sin

This awareness story requires our thoughts and full attention; I call *Degrees Of Christianity*. It doesn't intend to elaborate or debate some Christians' unclean and unholy actions. Still, it wants to illuminate that nearly all Christians practice a different degree of Christianity.

Even if different degrees of Christianity shouldn't exist and shouldn't set the standards for other Christians, seeing is believing. Truly, we would have to be blind and deaf and unconcerned not to see the different degrees of Christianity most Christians exhibit.

Anyway, I want you to know that there's a cure for the different degrees of Christianity, and the conclusion to the whole matter sums up the highest degree of Christianity. For our benefit, the conclusion to the whole matter fulfills the definition of perfect authenticity.

I guarantee you that perfect Bible authenticity is revealed to all of us through the conclusion of the whole matter. However, I want you to know that the excellent gift of grace doesn't entwine with the Conclusion to the Whole Matter. The gift of grace is perfect, but it doesn't challenge our need to be Christ-like.

However, the conclusion to the whole matter illuminates the expectations of God, and the Conclusion To The Whole Matter will challenge our need to be Christ-like. The excellent gift of grace will clean up our honest mistakes if we repent for them and change to conform to His Ten Commandments.

The conclusion to the whole matter is to reverence God and

keep His perfect commandments, which is man's full duty. I assure you, we are a compromiser if we live in opposition to our duty to God. For this reason, the challenge to be Christ-like is the pinnacle of our total commitment to God.

Therefore, an analogy needs revealing, and I am saying that if God expects us to keep His perfect commandments. Then He desires us to grow into perfection and become more Christ-like, day after day, until our degree of Christianity reaches one hundred percent.

Positively, I want you to realize that every important decision we make will probably hinge on commandment keeping. I am sure God's excellent and perfect commandments are the ultimate thing. I want you to know that the works of our hands don't hinge on the gift of grace, which has no connection with our decision-making.

Conclusively, putting a difference between the holy and the unholy, clean and unclean illuminates our greatest challenge, and we can rise to the occasion or forfeit our challenge. Otherwise, we can wrongly believe that the challenge to practice authenticity isn't essential.

Before this awareness story ends, I have a prayer for you. I hope and pray that you'll try to achieve the highest degree of Christianity and use authenticity to subtract compromises. I hope you'll take the challenge to be a commandment keeper and not say the gift of grace has me covered.

Conclusively, a scale of one to ten is a metaphor for the mountain you and I climb daily, and the closer we get to number ten means, we are conquering the metaphor mountain through the adherence to authenticity. I assure you, the highest degree of Christianity waits for us on the highest peak of the metaphor mountain.

CHAPTER FIFTY-FIVE
THE BARRIER

I've been writing Bible stories for approximately twelve to fifteen years, and I would read approximately five million words yearly for many years. I am proud to say that I've written about fifteen hundred individual Bible stories throughout the years, and my love and respect for Him and His word hasn't faded with time.

After many years of study, I've discovered that God's excellent and perfect word is the pinnacle of wisdom, and He wrote mostly in simplicity. His word isn't complicated to figure out, and He wants you and me to know our requirements to Him and know the whole duty of man.

The excellent and outstanding King James Bible consists of approximately seven hundred and eighty thousand crucial words. It seems we have to know many story examples before comprehending the whole matter's conclusion, and every time we learn something new about Him, our closeness to Him increases.

My great God wants us to know that the conclusion to the

entire matter is summed up in six words, and the six important words are to reverence God and keep His Ten Commandments and infallible decrees. However, mainly everything revolves around His perfect Ten Commandments.

I want you to know that I call this story *The Barrier* because humanity has a perception problem. A close observation proves that an invisible demonic barrier of unknown power is holding us prisoner and keeping us from absorbing and committing to the whole matter of man, and the power hindering our vision is the pinnacle of Lucifer's accomplishments.

The prohibiting barrier we cannot see or feel and aren't aware of surrounding us seems similar to an enclosed reflector shield designed and used daily by the demonic Lucifer. The reflector shield appears to encase us and prohibits the clarity of reality from getting through to us.

This truth means there's a powerful supernatural force in this world, invisible and undetectable, and it's a cruel source of power, encasing us within a barrier. Sadly, everyone trapped within the Dome-Shaped Barrier does not realize they are a victim caught inside an Encased Barrier. Otherwise, our eyes would focus on God, and we would be perfect, ladies and gentlemen, and live honestly.

The cruel dome barrier blinds the mind and heart; we drive through this life in a thick fog, and the invisible barrier keeps us from seeing not far past our hand. Sadly, our ability to be perfect in godliness is hindered, similar to a thick fog impeding a driver's ability to keep between the lines on the road.

The enclosed barrier encasing us has walls we cannot see, and only a few men and women in every generation will escape it. Sadly, the rest of the world will live their entire lives and not realize they've been trapped inside an enclosed barrier, and we will have to be Bible-savvy before we can escape.

I want you to realize that the strong encased barrier, invisible and undetectable, traps us within variations by degrees. It can get thicker or thinner, and its thickness depends on our determination to learn and abide by the beautiful word of God.

This truth means that the more Bible-illiterate we are, the thicker our barrier becomes, and the more Bible-savvy we are, the thinner our Barrier. However, after we fall hopelessly in love with the authentic word of God, our eyes will open, and the barrier may disappear altogether.

Indeed, the objective of the beautiful word of God has a specific goal: to release us from our encased barrier and deliver us to a place where we can see further than our hands, like driving under clear skies and bright sunshine on a beautiful day.

Furthermore, everyone fortunate enough to escape from their encased barrier will consider the wonderful word of God every time they make a decision. After escaping the slavery of the Encased Barrier, they will try and do as God wants them to do.

Indeed, it's easy to conclude that most people live within an encased barrier, and it's easy to see that most people are driving through life in a thick fog and having difficulty keeping out of the ruts and between the ditches.

Positively, the encased barrier we live within has ditches on all four sides, and we'll have to make the right moves to keep between the trenches. The right moves mean we will live according to God's word. However, falling into the ditches means the fog impairs our vision and decisions, and the barrier will not lift.

Conclusively, the invisible barrier is a heavyweight held down by strong gravity, and it'll take exceptional strength of the heart to escape from an Encased Barrier. Our failures in life illuminate trials, tribulations, and past experiences, proofing we'll have to overcome the air's demonic spirits before fleeing an Encased Barrier.

Beyond the shadow of a doubt, I am sure that most people in this Satan-controlled world will live all their lives and never escape from their encased barrier. Sadly, it's because they are weak in the Lord and let an evil demonic power blind them and hold them down.

Positively, the written word of God is our most significant source of wisdom, and the word of God tells us that men and women perish for lack of Bible knowledge. A lack of Bible knowledge identifies with an invisible encased barrier, and whoever lacks Bible knowledge is usually a permanent Encased Barrier resident.

The exceedingly strong encased barrier some men and women live within has no restraining walls or bars on the doors and windows. However, because the fallen angels have incredible mind control abilities, invisible demonic spirits are weaving webs of deception outside the encased barrier.

I want you to know that we are at war with the demonic spirits of the air, and it'll take the whole word of God to destroy our encased barrier. Indeed, it's a strong barrier the passive and indifferent person will not escape from during their entire lifetime.

Therefore, it's fitting to end this story with me saying, get on fire for God's perfect and excellent word, be a passionate believer in Christ, and escape from your encased barrier. Whoever lacks biblical knowledge will be trapped in the fog all their life.

I call this unique and expressive metaphor story *The Barrier.* Because of its importance, it has an extraordinary and revealing message for you and entwines the beautiful bread of life. I want you to know that God's wonderful gospel is the image of God, and keeping our eyes on Him illuminates the path leading out of the encased barrier.

Therefore, I conclude that my wonderful God holds the key to the barrier, holding us prisoners trapped within its dome. The wonderful gospel of God may not look like a key, but it opens and closes many doors and dissipates invisible barriers. Therefore, please be wise, out-fox the fox, and be a thorn in the serpent's side that builds walls between God and us.

The Spirit of God has taught me privately, and I've been publicly taught in many prayer houses for sixty years. For many years, I would read approximately fifteen thousand words every day.

I've written approximately seventeen Bible-related books with more than one thousand individual stories, maybe more than anyone worldwide. I've written one love story.

Owner of a construction company. Master electrician and certified by the state in low, medium, and high voltage. Skilled welder. Skilled mechanic.

I owned and operated a mine equipment rebuild shop. I competed in archery tournaments and placed in the state's top ten two times.

Delegate at the forty-eighth constitutional convention of the UMWA.

I've accomplished many other occupations, but the one I love the most is writing Bible stories for everyone to read and increase their knowledge of God. My unique works speak for me and prove I am an accomplished theologian. I do not conform to the philosophies or traditions of men, and these characteristics set me apart from many other men of God. I conform to Bible-quoted practices and doctrines only and expose everything false.

Bible story writer,

Paul Douglas Castle

www.ingramcontent.com/pod-product-compliance
Lightning Source LLC
Chambersburg PA
CBHW041110120626

46547CB00019B/2646